July 22, 1994

New Leaves

MICHIGAN MONOGRAPH SERIES
IN JAPANESE STUDIES
NUMBER 11

CENTER FOR JAPANESE STUDIES
THE UNIVERSITY OF MICHIGAN

New Leaves

Studies and Translations
of Japanese Literature
in Honor of Edward Seidensticker

EDITED BY AILEEN GATTEN
AND ANTHONY HOOD CHAMBERS

Ann Arbor
Center for Japanese Studies
The University of Michigan
1993

Library of Congress Cataloging in Publication Data

New leaves : studies and translations of Japanese literature in honor of Edward
    Seidensticker / edited by Aileen Gatten and Anthony Hood Chambers.
        p. cm. — (Michigan monograph series in Japanese studies : no. 11)
    "Bibliography of Edward Seidensticker's writings in English, compiled and
edited by Aileen Gatten and Frank Joseph Shulman": p. 253
    Includes bibliographical references and index.
    ISBN 0-939512-56-4
    1. Japanese literature—History and criticism. 2. Japanese literature—
Translations into English. I. Seidensticker, Edward, 1921– . II. Gatten, Aileen
Patricia, 1947– . III. Chambers. Anthony H. (Anthony Hood) IV. Series.
PL717.N48   1993
895.6'09—dc20   91-48341
                                                                         CIP

A Note on the Type
This book was set in Baskerville, a transitional typeface that bridged the gap between Old Style and Modern typefaces. It was designed by John Baskerville (1706–75), an English printer and typographer who was the printer to Cambridge University from 1758–68, and has been used as a standard book typeface.

Composed by The Composing Room of Michigan, Inc.,
    Grand Rapids, Michigan
Printed and bound by Thomson-Shore, Inc., Dexter, Michigan
Book design by Lisa Jacobs

∞The paper used in this publication meets the requirements of the ANSI Standard Z39.48-1984 (Permanence of Paper).

Printed in the United States of America

Contents

Abbreviations

NBKSS   Nihon Bungaku Kenkyū Shiryō Kankōkai, ed. *Nihon bungaku kenkyū shiryō sōsho*. 100 vols. Tokyo: Yūseidō, 1969–86.

NKB   Yoshida Seiichi. *Nihon kindai bungaku no hikaku bungakuteki kenkyū*. Tokyo: Shimizu Kōbundō Shobō, 1971.

NKBT   Takagi Ichinosuke et al., eds. *Nihon koten bungaku taikei*. 100 vols. Tokyo: Iwanami Shoten, 1957–67.

NKBZ   Akiyama Ken et al., eds. *Nihon koten bungaku zenshū*. 51 vols. Tokyo: Shōgakkan, 1970–76.

NKDBT   Itō Sei et al., eds. *Nihon kindai bungaku taikei*. 61 vols. Tokyo: Kadokawa Shoten, 1969–75.

TYAZ   Kimata Osamu et al., eds. *Teihon Yosano Akiko zenshū*. 20 vols. Tokyo: Kōdansha, 1979–81.

Preface

Edward Seidensticker's contributions to the study of Japanese literature in the West are as diverse as they are substantial. One of the preeminent translators of his time, Seidensticker introduced the Western world to *Kagerō nikki* (The Gossamer Years), the tenth-century journal regarded as the first prose masterpiece written by a Japanese woman; produced a definitive translation of Murasaki Shikibu's eleventh-century classic, *The Tale of Genji*; evoked the twentieth-century nostalgia for the vanished teahouses, courtesans, and entertainers of Edo and Meiji through *Kafū the Scribbler*; and brought great modern novelists to Western attention with his book-length translations of works by Kawabata Yasunari and Tanizaki Jun'ichirō. Seidensticker's love of the modern Japanese short story is evident in his more than fifty published translations in this genre, and his articles on current literary theories in Japan attest to his interest in an evolving tradition. All this, considered with his writings on cultural history—especially that of the Meiji through Shōwa periods (1868–1989)—and his essays and articles on Japanese subjects ranging from political parties, fisheries reform, and baseball to the art of translating, reveal Edward Seidensticker to be a literary and cultural generalist in the best sense of the word, a man whose knowledge of Japan gives breadth and vigor to his most enduring legacy, his studies and translations of Japanese literature.

Seidensticker's work in Japanese literature is especially significant for those who have been his students. His expertise in both classical and modern Japanese literature, his emphasis on questioning established opinion, his high standards of scholarship, and the encouragement he has given his students to strike out into unknown territory have stimulated them to produce a combined body of work remarkable for its wide range of method and subject matter. In requesting that the contributors to his *Festschrift* be limited to former students, Seidensticker has ensured that the content of *New Leaves* will be diverse in period, subject, and style. This volume includes essays and translations focusing on Japanese literature from the eleventh century to the 1980s; the approaches range from scholarly to discursive to whimsical, in keeping with Seidensticker's own various styles; the genres examined or translated include prose fiction ancient and modern, medieval and modern literary criticism, *kanbun* diaries, Edo and modern poetics, Shinnai ballads, modern poetry, and discursive essays.

Not even Edward Seidensticker can claim mastery in all these fields; but it is his example, as of a tree rooted in solid scholarship that stretches new branches into the great forest of Japanese letters, that has inspired the contributors to *New Leaves* in their work as writers and scholars. May the "new leaves" put forth by us seedlings follow the pattern set by our parent in scholarship. These essays and translations are offered in his honor, with gratitude, respect, and affection.

The Editors

Edward Seidensticker: A Biography

AILEEN GATTEN

It has been said that Edward Seidensticker won the 1968 Nobel Prize in Literature for Kawabata Yasunari. This is, of course, an overstatement, but it is useful in drawing our attention to the fact that the best translations come into being through the fruitful contact of two kinds of genius, the author's and the translator's. The extraordinary match of style, language, linguistic rhythm, and other, more intangible elements makes Seidensticker's Kawabata translations more than translations: they are works that Kawabata might have created himself, had he been an English-speaking writer. Seidensticker helped Kawabata win the Nobel Prize by producing excellent translations, thus making Kawabata's masterpieces accessible to a worldwide audience for the first time. This is true as well for such other modern writers as Nagai Kafū and Tanizaki Jun'ichirō. And the same can be said for the anonymous tenth-century noblewoman who wrote *Kagerō nikki*, known to the West through Seidensticker's definitive translation, *The Gossamer Years*.

Then there is Murasaki Shikibu's *The Tale of Genji*. Seidensticker took a classic already known to the English-reading public through Arthur Waley's somewhat abridged translation and produced, over the course of about ten years, a complete version, faithful to the original text, that is also graceful and moving. The "Seidensticker *Genji*," which became the standard English translation upon its publication in 1976, has a spare, restrained style that faithfully communicates Murasaki Shikibu's quiet sensitivity and wit. It is the crowning achievement of a career of inspired translations.

Edward George Seidensticker was born in Castle Rock, Colorado, in 1921, the descendant of a pioneer and prospector who came to what is now Denver in the Pikes Peak gold rush of 1859 and later turned to cattle ranching on land south of Denver. Seidensticker grew up on the family ranch in Douglas County.

1

As with so many of his generation, the Japanese attack on Pearl Harbor on December 7, 1941, changed Seidensticker's life. He was in the middle of his senior year at the University of Colorado, majoring in English, at the time of the attack. The following summer, when the Navy Japanese Language School moved to the university, Seidensticker, up to then wholly uninterested in the Japanese and their language, decided to join the Marines and enter the language school. He spent most of the war in the Hawaiian Islands, translating documents and interrogating prisoners at Pearl Harbor. He saw action only once, but memorably, at the battle of Iwo Jima in February and March of 1945.

What began as an education undertaken out of necessity evolved into an avocation and, later, a calling. During the war, Seidensticker had divided his leisure time between surfing and reading Japanese literature. Following his resignation from the Marine Corps Reserve in 1946, he began a dual education: while continuing to instruct himself in Japanese literature, he worked with Nathaniel Peffer at Columbia University and received a master's degree in international relations, with special reference to Japan, in 1947. This was followed by a year studying Japanese art and civilization at Harvard University.

A concurrent interest in literature and politics manifests itself in Seidensticker's publications: his articles and essays are fairly equally divided between the two fields, with an occasional mixture of them (as in his 1967 "The Japanese Novel and Disengagement"). Although the flow of Seidensticker's published political commentary has slowed somewhat in the last decade, he continues to be interested in politics of all kinds—from American elections and foreign policy to the foibles of Japanese politicians, upheavals in Korea, and the shifting politics of Asia—and in the related subjects of economics and journalism.

Following a brief stint with the United States Foreign Service in Japan, Seidensticker entered the graduate school of Tokyo University in 1950. It was at this time that Japanese literature became his principal concern. He studied under Hisamatsu Sen'ichi and Ikeda Kikan, at that time the foremost scholars of classical Japanese literature and two of the greatest names in Japanese literary studies.

The twelve years between Seidensticker's retirement from the Foreign Service and the beginning of his American teaching career in 1962 were astonishingly productive. Living and working in Tokyo as a free-lance writer, journalist, and translator, he wrote approximately fifty articles for American, British, Japanese, and Japanese English-language magazines and newspapers, translated some three dozen short stories from the Japanese, coedited two anthologies of Japanese short stories in English translation, and introduced Japan to the American reading public in the 1961 Time-Life book *Japan*. Seidensticker was also the author of "This Country," a column that first appeared in the English edition of the *Yomiuri* newspaper from 1958 to 1962 (and recommenced in 1989). In addition to writing, Seidensticker taught from 1955 to 1959 at Sophia University in Tokyo. His intellectual and linguistic versatility is demonstrated by his course load for those years, which included lectures on American literature and American intellectual history to Japanese students, and classes on Japanese cultural history to Western students.

These years are especially memorable in Seidensticker's career because they mark the appearance of five splendid book-length translations: *The Gossamer Years*, first published in 1955 as *The Kagerō Nikki: Journal of a 10th Century Noblewoman*; Tanizaki's *Some Prefer Nettles* (1955) and *The Makioka Sisters* (1957); and Kawabata's *Snow Country* and *Thousand Cranes*, published in 1956 and 1958, respectively. To produce one book a year is normally beyond the abilities of translators of Japanese; one can only marvel that Seidensticker's outstanding translations—respected as English literature in their own right— appeared at such a pace.

In 1962 Seidensticker left Japan to accept a position as visiting associate professor of Japanese literature at Stanford University. In 1964 he was promoted to professor. Despite his teaching commitments, Seidensticker continued to publish widely. *Kafū the Scribbler* (1965), a biography of Nagai Kafū with extensive translations from his writings, appeared during Seidensticker's tenure at Stanford, as did *The Gossamer Years* (1964), a revised version of the 1955 translation. Literary and political commentary and short-story translations also emerged regularly, although the cascades of the Tokyo years diminished somewhat. In 1966 Seidensticker left Stanford, together with the eminent *waka* scholar Robert H. Brower (1923–88), to join the faculty of the University of Michigan.

The years at Michigan (1966–77) were perhaps the most productive of Seidensticker's teaching period, yielding the monumental *The Tale of Genji* (1976), Mishima Yukio's *The Decay of the Angel* (1974)—the final volume of the tetralogy *The Sea of Fertility*—and three works by Kawabata: *House of the Sleeping Beauties* (1969), *The Sound of the Mountain* (1970), and *The Master of Go* (1973). *The Sound of the Mountain* received the National Book Award for Translation in 1970.

Seidensticker taught at Columbia University from 1977 until his retirement in 1985. During this period he published *Low City, High City* (1983), a lively and informative social history of Tokyo from its beginnings as the "Eastern Capital" in 1867 to the Great Earthquake of 1923. The now-retired Edward Seidensticker, who divides his time equally between Tokyo and Honolulu, continues to make his influence known in Japanese and Western scholarly circles with his frequent articles and book reviews. His most recent book is *Tokyo Rising* (1990), a sequel to *Low City, High City* that recounts the history of Tokyo from 1923 to the present.

The varied career and unorthodox scholarly training described above have contributed greatly to Seidensticker's effectiveness as a teacher. His intimate knowledge of Japan, renewed by visits that eventually encompassed half of each year, has been an especially powerful tool in teaching undergraduate students skeptical of professors whose primary data come from books. While always maintaining and requiring the highest scholarly standards, Seidensticker has instinctively given his students a perspective on academic pursuits obtainable only from one who has spent decades in fields beyond the narrowly academic. His broad interests have led his students to specialize in various areas of classical and modern literature, as demonstrated by the breadth of subject matter presented in this book. His prominence as a translator of Japanese literature has also inspired many of his students to distinguish themselves by published book-length translations. Seidensticker's approach to scholarship—to use solid academic training as a basis from which to test and question accepted theories and to pursue the unknown—has encouraged other students to strike out in new directions in their research. Just as great literature enriches our lives by stretching our capacities for thought and feeling, this scholar of great literature has touched the lives of students, colleagues, friends, and readers by expanding their horizons.

Death and Salvation in *Genji Monogatari*

Aileen Gatten

The poet essentially *can't* be concerned with the act of dying. Let him deal with the sickest of the sick, it is still by the act of living that they appeal to him, and appeal the more as the conditions plot against them and prescribe the battle. The process of life gives way fighting, and often may so shine out on the lost ground as in no other connexion.

Henry James, *The Wings of the Dove*

One of the reasons that *Genji monogatari* is a great work of literature, we are told, is the ability it possesses to transcend time and culture to affect readers thoroughly unacquainted with Heian language and customs. Many readers of *Genji* in translation are struck by its modernity, by which they tend to mean its realistic portrayal of the characters' psyches. Murasaki Shikibu is justly famous for presenting in vivid and at times uncomfortable detail the jealousies, possessiveness, and obsessions that characterize the darker, destructive side of romantic love. The depiction of family relationships, particularly those between parent and child, is less renowned but equally admirable.

Given this realistic approach to the emotional lives of her characters, one might expect Murasaki Shikibu to be similarly unflinching in showing the reality of their deaths. Such is not the case, however. Death scenes in *Genji monogatari* are not intended as realistic presentations of dying characters. Like Henry James, Murasaki Shikibu is less interested in the act of dying than in the ebbing life that illumines what has gone before, and what may lie ahead. Death in *Genji* is a symbolic event that can be interpreted on various levels: as a natural process aestheticized, a literary metaphor, or an indication of a character's spirituality and likelihood of rebirth in Paradise.

What follows is an exploration of some of the many death scenes in *Genji,* beginning with their formal and conventional characteristics, and continuing with an analysis of the scenes on the various levels mentioned above. Whichever level is used, the reader will find that the manner in which a character dies, and his or her physical appearance and surroundings, are codes that indicate Murasaki Shikibu's summation of that character, her verdict on the life that has been lived within the pages of *Genji.* The essay concludes with an examination of the role probably played by *ōjōden,* Buddhist "accounts of rebirth" in Paradise, on shaping Murasaki Shikibu's vision of death and salvation in *Genji.*

THE STRUCTURE AND CONVENTIONS OF DEATH SCENES

A death scene in *Genji* is defined here as a passage in which a character is shown dying or dead, or, as in the final two death scenes of the narrative—Murasaki's and Ōigimi's—as a passage describing both the dying and the dead character. Death scenes can be brief and fragmented or long, seamless, detailed descriptions. What all have in common is that they take place *in* the narrative—before our eyes, so to speak—rather than "offstage."[1]

Death scenes in *Genji* follow several unstated conventions—ideas, in other words, that were taken for granted by the author and her contemporary audience and that form the bases on which the scenes are built. One such convention is the view of death as an occurrence in harmony with the natural world; another, that the best death is that foreseen and accepted by the dying person; third, that the presence of light at the time of death signifies salvation; and fourth, that illness and death can enhance human beauty, much as a light frost deepens the color of chrysanthemums. All but the first are also common conventions in *ōjōden,* as will be discussed below.

These conventions are overlaid by a formal structure that is most fully discernable in the death scenes of certain characters. Three scenes, analyzed in detail below, depict what might be called a "good death."[2] The passage describing a good death begins with the character's recognition of approaching death. Later in the passage, the character, who feels pain but has no specific symptoms, speaks calmly of the impending death to close relatives and friends, and makes some last requests. The physical appearance of the dying character ranges from ethereally attractive to alluring.

Both the dying character and close family and friends regret the approaching death, but accept it as inevitable. The moment of the character's death is expressed by a simile or metaphor involving natural imagery. The strikingly lifelike, beautiful aspects of the corpse may be emphasized. Such beauty adds to the intense grief experienced by the survivors. Finally, the narrator presents a eulogy or description of the dead character and a description of the funeral.

THREE GOOD DEATHS

Murasaki Shikibu seems to reserve the good death for her more admirable characters. The death scenes of three such characters—Fujitsubo, Murasaki, and Ōigimi—will illustrate the concepts outlined above.

The scenes occur at widely spaced intervals in the text of *Genji*. The death of Fujitsubo takes place in the nineteenth chapter, "Usugumo" (A Rack of Cloud), in Genji's thirty-second year. Murasaki's death occurs in chapter 40, "Minori" (The Rites), nearly twenty years later. Ōigimi dies in "Agemaki" (Trefoil Knots), the forty-seventh chapter, when Kaoru is twenty-four.[3] It is generally accepted that "Usugumo" was the first of the three chapters to be written, followed by "Minori" and "Agemaki"; thus an analysis of these three passages may also yield conclusions bearing on the author's growing mastery of narrative techniques.

The most immediately perceptible difference among the three scenes is their length. The earliest is the shortest, and the last is the longest. This does not mean, though, that the death of Ōigimi is no more than an elaboration of a formula first seen in the death of Fujitsubo. Murasaki Shikibu shows her skills as a writer, and her imaginative scope, in these three death scenes.

Fujitsubo: The Beautiful Death

Fujitsubo's death scene, beginning with the onset of her final illness and ending with her funeral, encompasses only three and a half pages in a modern printed edition, yet it conforms to the structure described above, and to the conventions on which the structure is based.[4] Fujitsubo foresees that she will not survive her thirty-seventh year, traditionally considered unlucky for women. She prepares for her death with prayers and a last interview with her son, the Reizei emperor. Fujitsubo speaks calmly of her approaching death to the emperor, who is doubly saddened because his mother is still so youthful, a woman in the prime of life (*ito wakaku sakari ni owashimasu sama*; 15: 228). This is the earliest instance of one of the hallmarks of a *Genji* death scene, the beauty of the moribund.

The first stage of Fujitsubo's death scene is divided into two sections: the conversation with her son, followed by Genji's visit to the lady. The Reizei emperor, being a close relative, has the privilege of addressing his mother directly, without the conventional barriers of intermediaries or curtains. Genji, however, is required by protocol to remain outside the curtains and to depend on a lady-in-waiting to relay his final words to Fujitsubo. His only direct contact with Fujitsubo is the faint sound of her voice as she replies to the messenger.

Their conversation is equally public, focusing on the necessity of Genji's continued political support for the young emperor. As Genji is reassuring Fujitsubo, she dies, like a flame flickering and going out: *tomoshibi nado no kieiru yō ni te hatetamainu* (15: 230). The image of light is reminiscent of Fujitsubo's youthful sobriquet, "her highness the radiant consort" (*kagayaku hi no miya*; 14: 47). It is also the first instance of Murasaki Shikibu's use of the imagery of light and darkness in death scenes, a technique discussed in detail below.

The lengthy eulogy presented by the narrator after Fujitsubo's death is as decorous and dignified as the rest of the death scene, in recognition of the empress dowager's exalted station. Her generosity, depth of perception, humility, and piety are eloquently extolled. It is a public eulogy for a public figure.

The progress of Fujitsubo's death scene is paralleled by a natural process, the course of the spring season. Her last illness commences with the beginning of spring, and at the end of the season she is dead. The atmosphere of gloom pervading a court in deepest mourning contrasts sharply with the image of cherry trees in full bloom in Genji's garden on the day of Fujitsubo's funeral.

To return to the idea of the beauty of the moribund: Fujitsubo, a woman in late middle age (by Heian standards) who has suffered increasingly poor health over the years, is described as "very youthful, in her prime." This is not a realistic depiction. Rather, it seeks to ignore the less aesthetically pleasing laws of nature by eliminating the unattractive aspects of terminal illness. Characters in *Genji* who die a good death always become more beautiful as their lives end. As we shall see with Murasaki, death can give a character far more beauty than she ever possessed in life. This deliberate turning away from the realities of death can be interpreted as an attempt to make death a thing of supreme beauty, an aesthetic event.

On another level, the beautiful death may be read as a sign of salvation and the logical result of good karma accumulated over many lifetimes. Characters in *Genji* who die beautiful deaths have already benefited from their good karma during their lives, by possessing beauty, rank, and a superior spiritual nature. Fujitsubo is a pious woman who chooses to become a nun chiefly to lighten the burden of sin acquired through her adulterous relationship with Genji. The manner of her death indicates that her intent proves generally successful.

Fujitsubo's is the first beautiful death, a death that brings together images of preternaturally radiant human beauty and the fragility and glory of nature. The next death scene, that of Kashiwagi in the chapter that bears his name (translated as "The Oak Tree"), begins with a statement intended to disarm more realistically minded readers. "The seriously ill are said to present a repulsive appearance, with dishevelled hair and beard; but Kashiwagi's increasing emaciation only accentuated his fair skin and elegant bearing" (17: 31). The narrator's perceived need to disarm suggests that the convention in *monogatari* of a beautiful dying man or woman may have originated with Murasaki Shikibu.[5]

Murasaki: Death as Apotheosis

The death of Murasaki no Ue most fully conforms to the structure of the "good death." Throughout her long death scene, described in "Minori" (The Rites), Murasaki is the epitome of evanescent human beauty surrounded by an equally evanescent natural world.

She first receives the warning of impending death in late spring, the season with which she is traditionally identified. The realization arrives in a context of natural beauty and grandeur. Having commissioned one thousand copies of the *Lotus Sutra*—an act of devotion often performed before death by Heian aristocrats—Murasaki sponsors a splendid dedicatory ceremony, followed by music and dancing. It is while savoring these festivities and their backdrop of cherry blossoms glimpsed through haze that Murasaki realizes she will soon die.

She grows weaker in the summer heat. We are told that weakness is the principal complaint; she feels no pain or discomfort. Murasaki's deteriorating condition prompts a visit from her adopted daughter, the Akashi empress, and the empress's children. Here Murasaki makes her last requests: that the empress might look after those of Murasaki's servants who have nowhere else to go; and that the child Niou will live in Murasaki's Nijō house when he grows up, and offer blossoms from her beloved cherry and red plum trees in her memory.

These are private matters of concern to a private woman, unlike the dying Fujitsubo's preoccupation with the continuing stability of her son's reign.

Murasaki dies at the height of autumn. The sustained lyricism and fusion of natural and human elements in her death scene make it justifiably the most famous in *Genji*. Murasaki's last hours are carefully described, from dusk, when she, the empress, and later Genji look out upon a wind-tossed garden, until dawn, when Murasaki dies. The central image associated with her death is one of extreme evanescence: dewdrops that form on cloverbush branches only to be shaken off as the branches are whipped by the wind. The composite image is initially expressed in Murasaki's final poem (17: 181):

Oku to miru	You see it settled there
hodo zo hakanaki	for a moment, that is all.
to mo sureba	Soon it shall be
kaze ni midaruru	tossed and scattered by the wind—
hagi no uwatsuyu	dew atop the cloverbush.

Individual elements of this clustered image appear throughout the scene: "autumn" (*aki*), "wind" (*kaze*), "dew" (*tsuyu*), and "cloverbush" (*hagi*) are words repeated in both the *waka* and prose sections, strengthening not only the metaphor of Murasaki's life as dew but also linking the prototypically autumnal setting with the death of a lady who from childhood on has been identified with spring. The metaphor is so complete that by the end of the passage, when at daybreak Murasaki "vanishes" (*kiehatetamainu*; 17: 183), the reader needs no explicit comparison to understand the fusion between this one human death and the evaporation of countless dewdrops in the lady's garden.

The dying Murasaki, though emaciated, is described as possessing unbounded elegance and attraction (*ate ni namamekashiki koto no kagirinasa*; 17: 181) that far surpass the bright, showy beauty of her youth.[6] But the narrator reserves the highest praise for Murasaki until after her death. Her hair, though long left untended, is smooth, thick, and glossy, of unrivalled beauty. Her complexion, in the strong lamplight, is so white as to be radiant (*hikaru yō ni te*; 17: 185); no cosmetic artifice had ever made Murasaki so fair in life. The description concludes with more superlatives. "Needless to say, her appearance was perfection itself. This was not only extraordinary beauty, it was a beauty not of this world" (17: 185). The passage is a eulogy for a private figure, in which peerless, supernatural beauty is substituted for the peerless virtue accorded the public figure Fujitsubo.

As with Fujitsubo, the eulogy is followed by the funeral. Superlatives are again used to describe the grandeur of Murasaki's funeral scene: the *great* field where the cremation takes place is *filled* with mourners, and the funeral rites are conducted with the *utmost* solemnity (*harubaru to hiroki* no no *tokoro mo naku tachikomite kagirinaku ikameshiki sahō*; 17: 186). The imposing setting, like the cherry trees in full bloom on the day of Fujitsubo's funeral, is intended as a backdrop heightening the pathos of the chief mourner. The figure of Genji, blinded by tears and leaning on others for support as he walks behind the cortege, leaves an even stronger impression of desolation by appearing in so magnificent a context.

Ōigimi: The Lifelike Death

The death of Ōigimi has much in common with Murasaki's. Both are of private figures attended by those who love the dying woman; in their last illnesses, both women are praised for their beauty; their loveliness at death is beheld and admired by those who cherish them. Both die in stormy weather. It should be noted, however, that these are formal similarities that reflect the framework of the "good death" as conceived by Murasaki Shikibu. The wide scope of that framework permits the portrayal of what are in fact two very different death scenes.

All the elements of a good death are present in Ōigimi's scene. She is aware that she will die soon; she suffers from a grave but unspecified illness; she warns Nakanokimi and Kaoru of her approaching death; and her last request is that Kaoru look after her sister. Natural imagery is present throughout Ōigimi's death scene, in the shape of a winter storm, and at the moment of her death, when she is compared to a withering plant (*mono no kareyuku yō ni te kiehatetamainu*; 17: 462). She is beautiful at death; this beauty adds to the measure of Kaoru's grief.

The difference between Ōigimi's death and Murasaki's lies not in the conventional framework but in the nature of the characters. One of the most touching aspects of the "Minori" scene is the genuine solicitude Genji and Murasaki have for each other. Genji brightens up at anything suggesting an improvement in Murasaki's health, and Murasaki responds with unspoken concern for how Genji will withstand the shock of her death. By contrast, the death scene in "Agemaki" is lonely and chilling. Ōigimi has not been struck down by disease: she has willed herself to die.[7] Unlike the warm family presence at Murasaki's deathbed, there is no one but Kaoru at Ōigimi's bedside— and Kaoru is the person least welcome to the dying woman in her last moments. In place of the deep communication, especially through poetry, among Murasaki, Genji, and the empress, there is silence, hostility, and reproach at Ōigimi's deathbed.

It is no coincidence that this emotionally frigid death scene takes place beyond the civilizing bounds of the capital, at Uji, and in the depths of winter, when even the days are dark, and the wind and snow have a fury never seen in the city. The appealing, lyrical image of Murasaki's dwindling life as a droplet of dew tossed from an autumn blossom here gives way to a wilder natural simile, of a plant shriveling in the onslaught of a savage winter storm.

Ōigimi's funeral is equally diminished by comparison with Murasaki's. There is no grand ceremony or crowd of mourners; even the smoke from the funeral pyre is disappointingly scant.

Given the severity that characterizes Ōigimi's death scene, it is appropriate that restraint governs the passages describing the dying and dead woman. The author devotes considerably more space to Ōigimi than to Murasaki in showing the transition from life to death, yet there are no superlatives in the descriptions of Ōigimi. Murasaki Shikibu emphasizes quite another attribute in Ōigimi, as is seen by comparing the following passages portraying each woman shortly before her death.

[Murasaki]
Koyo nō yasehosoritamaeredo kakute koso ate ni nama-mekashiki koto no kagirinasa no masarite medetakere. . . . Kagiri mo naku rōtage ni okashige naru onsama ni te (17: 181). [Extreme thinness only enhanced her peerless elegance and attraction. . . . She was surpassingly appealing and lovely.]

[Ōigimi]
Kaina nado mo ito hosō narite kage no yō ni yowage naru mono kara iroai mo kawarazu shirō utsukushige ni (17: 461). [Her arms had become very thin and she seemed as wan as a shadow, but her color was as it had always been, fair and lovely.]

In both cases, the author uses the dying character's emaciation as a paradoxical means of emphasizing her beauty; but note the differ-ent results. Murasaki's beauty transcends that of her prime, while Ōigimi's original beauty remains unaffected by illness. The same methods are employed to describe the two characters after death.

[Murasaki]

Akazu utsukushige ni medetō kiyora ni miyuru onkao
. . . Migushi no tada uchiyararetamaeru hodo kochitaku
keura ni te *tsuyu bakari* midaretaru keshiki *mo nō* tsuyatsuya to
utsukushige naru sama zo *kagiri naki* (17: 185). [Her face
appeared *perfectly* lovely, splendid, striking. . . . Her hair, left
to stream uncombed behind her, was thick and magnificent,
with *not a strand out of place.*]

[Ōigimi]

Kakushitamau kao mo tada *netamaeru yō* ni te *kawari-
tamaeru tokoro mo naku* utsukushige ni te uchifushitamaeru
o. . . . Ima wa no kotodomo suru ni migushi o kakiyaru ni sa
uchinioitaru *tada arishi nagara* no nioi ni natsukashū kōba-
shiki mo arigatō (17: 463). [Ōigimi, her face still covered by
her sleeve, seemed *as if asleep*; she lay there looking *quite
unchanged* in her loveliness. . . . As the women combed her
hair in preparation for the final ceremonies, Kaoru caught its
scent, *exactly the same as it had always been,* alluring, fragrant,
and unusual.]

In each passage, the author first describes the character's face,
then her hair. Murasaki's beauty is dazzling, perfection itself, while
Ōigimi's is familiar and reassuring. Similarly, the extraordinary sheen
and tidiness of Murasaki's long-neglected hair contrasts with the one
modest attribute of Ōigimi's, its retention of the old familiar scent.
The author uses the same conventions to present Murasaki as a creature of supernatural radiance and Ōigimi as a sleeping beauty un-
touched by death.

THE ROLE OF LIGHT AND DARKNESS

The three characters whose death scenes are analyzed above are
the only ones meriting a description of both final illness and death.
Other characters—Genji's mother, the Rokujō lady, and Kashiwagi—
are portrayed as mortally ill but die "offstage," their deaths reported
by another character or the narrator. The deaths of two others—
Yūgao and Aoi—are narrated, but in a different manner from the
scenes examined thus far. Neither character is *seen* to die, because
both die in the dark.

The imagery of light and darkness is employed effectively by
Murasaki Shikibu to depict her characters in their last moments. The

radiance of the dead Murasaki's countenance and the comparison of the dying Fujitsubo with a flickering flame are unambiguous equations of admirable characters to the imagery of light and salvation. What, then, can be said of those whose deaths are closely linked with darkness? Are they less worthy of admiration? Does the presence of darkness denote a character whose life has produced a less enviable death?

Genji characters whose deaths are obscured by darkness die unexpectedly and unprepared. The circumstances surrounding their deaths are also frightening. With Yūgao dying beside him in the dark, Genji fights against his own terror—and calls desperately for light. Aoi's death lacks the melodrama of Yūgao's, but is equally frightening in occurring suddenly, in the middle of the night, with none of Aoi's close relatives at hand.

If a good death is one that gives warning, a time for preparation, these are "bad deaths," unappealing ways to die. Not surprisingly, the mortal remains of those fated to die bad deaths are not described in transcendent or even romantic terms. When Genji finally procures a light in the deserted mansion, he has no difficulty realizing that Yūgao is dead: her body is growing cold and her breathing has stopped (*hie ni hieirite iki wa toku taehatenikeri*; 14: 149). In transferring the body to a carriage, Genji finds it "delicate, appealing, not repellent in the least" (14: 154). The narrator's insistence on the body's lack of repellence reminds the reader that this is indeed a corpse, and that soon it will be truly repellent; the hastily arranged funeral reinforces this message.

Aoi, whose beauty deeply impresses Genji at their final interview —another example of the loveliness of the moribund—is also realistically described after death: "Remembering that the possessing spirits had often robbed her of consciousness, they left Aoi undisturbed for two or three days; but the changes that began to appear in her body finally convinced them that the end had come" (14: 339). It should be noted, however, that even the realism of these deaths is tempered by the explicitly stated beauty of the dying or dead woman. Neither Aoi's nor Yūgao's death resembles Madame Bovary's.

Can a didactic stance be detected in these death scenes? Are good deaths reserved for pious characters with upright natures while bad deaths signify serious flaws in a character? The answer would seem to be an equivocal yes.

Fujitsubo, Murasaki, and Ōigimi die unquestionably good deaths, yet none is a saint. Fujitsubo commits adultery, Murasaki is jealous and sharp-tongued, and Ōigimi is obstinate, proud, and ascerbic. Conversely, neither Yūgao nor Aoi is wicked.[8] Murasaki Shikibu's didacticism is not aimed at rewarding good and chastising evil. The emphasis, rather, seems to be on the character's degree of spiritual and emotional development, and particularly on the dying character's awareness and evaluation of his or her life. Those who die good deaths are spiritually advanced characters whose psyches are well revealed in the course of the narrative. As they near death, they are able to grasp, to some extent, their shortcomings and failures.

Good deaths seem to be reserved for those with an aptitude for reflection, those not overly given to deceiving themselves. Neither Aoi nor Yūgao can boast these virtues. Quite the contrary: both are central figures in episodes emphasizing reckless passion, lack of consideration, and irresponsibility. Yūgao is weak and easily manipulated; Aoi is haughty and inflexible. Neither is interested in self-examination. The manner of their deaths reflects the presence of such negative elements in their lives.

The Rokujō lady, that talented, proud, complex woman made infamous by her wandering spirit, is another character whose death is associated with darkness. Here, surely, is one destined for a bad death; yet hers is mitigated by an ability to see herself for what she really is. On the level of Buddhist morality, the lady's pious acts, including becoming a nun near the end of her life, help to negate her bad karma.

The Rokujō lady dies in "Miotsukushi" (Channel Buoys), not long after returning to the capital from Ise with her daughter, the former high priestess. Genji goes to visit her about a week before her death. His interview with the lady marks her final appearance in *Genji*. The passage is reminiscent of Fujitsubo's death scene, with allowances made for rank. Genji addresses the Rokujō lady directly, though separated by a curtain; and the dying woman's concern is with a private, not a public matter. Yet, like Fujitsubo, the Rokujō lady asks Genji to look after her child. The Rokujō lady thus has the privilege of preparing herself and others for her death.

The lady is so weak that she drifts in and out of consciousness during her interview with Genji (although, as is usual in *Genji* death scenes, her illness is described only in vague terms). Genji, who is sitting in the dark, notices rays of light coming faintly through the curtains of the lady's sickroom. His curiosity is aroused.

"I wonder. . . ." Genji peered through an opening in the curtain. In the dim light, he saw her leaning on an armrest, her hair tastefully cropped. She might have been a figure in a painting, so thoroughly elegant was she. (15: 125)

Here is another woman in late middle age, declining health, and near death, who captivates Genji by her appearance. Like Fujitsubo and Murasaki, the Rokujō lady is beautiful in her last illness. Her shoulder-length hair, a sign that she has renounced worldly ways, seems to be the deciding factor, much as Murasaki's and Ōigimi's emaciation adds to their attraction.

The Rokujō lady, however, lacks the luminosity of other dying heroines. The glorious Fujitsubo's fading life is like a flickering light, and Murasaki is supernaturally radiant even after death; but the Rokujō lady, though elegant to the end, can barely be seen in the near-darkness of her room. Her middling-good death scene may be seen as symbolic of the conflict in her life—and after her death—between self-reflection and heedless passion.

Another question raised by analyzing death scenes in *Genji mono-gatari* concerns the author's reasons for selecting certain characters and not others for inclusion.

This may be safely answered by considering Murasaki Shikibu's instincts and skills as a writer. I for one am relieved not to have had to witness the deaths of Tō no Chūjō (who would probably have been a difficult patient in his last illness), the safflower princess, the Ōmi lady, and several others. Not all characters lend themselves to interesting death scenes. Conversely, no competent storyteller would risk boring the reader with recitals of the deaths of forty-some principal characters.

The only death scene omitted from *Genji* without obvious reason is Genji's itself. The absence of a death scene for Genji has bothered readers since at least the twelfth century, when the title "Kumoga-kure" (Hidden by Clouds, a poetic epithet for death often used with moon imagery) was placed after "Maboroshi" (The Wizard, the last chapter in which Genji appears) in a list of *Genji* chapter titles.[9] At least one attempt was made to supplement the "Kumogakure" title with a text, in the fourteenth or fifteenth century.[10] No one knows why Murasaki Shikibu passed up the opportunity to depict her hero's death.[11]

Whatever her reason, Murasaki Shikibu chooses to prepare the reader for Genji's death by showing him about to enter a monastery. His state of mind in "Maboroshi," as he thinks of leaving behind the secular world, is similar to that of a dying character in a conventional death scene. Genji perceives that his life is ending, puts his affairs in order, and begins to accustom himself to not seeing his family again. At the end of the chapter he is described as being "more radiant than ever" (*mukashi no onhikari ni mo mata ōku soite*; 17: 216), in defiance of reason. Now well into his fifties, an old man in Heian terms, Genji has spent over a year in seclusion mourning Murasaki. His preternatural beauty is the same as that which illumines such dying heroines as Fujitsubo and Murasaki. Our last view of Genji is of a glorious figure shining through the darkness of the waning year. The interplay of light and darkness is continued at the beginning of the next chapter, "Niou miya" (His Perfumed Highness), when Genji's death is announced by the metaphor of light having vanished from the world (*hikari kakuretamainishi nochi*; 17: 219). If reluctance indeed lay behind the intentional omission of Genji's death scene, Murasaki Shikibu may have presented the hero in "Maboroshi" in such a way that readers familiar with the conventions of preceding death scenes would find all the elements necessary to construct their own version of Genji's death.

DEATH SCENES IN PRE-*GENJI* LITERATURE

The beauty of the moribund, it was noted above, may have originated as a fictional convention with *Genji monogatari*. This conclusion is based on two facts: very few surviving works of pre-*Genji* prose fiction contain death scenes, and those that do make no attempt to beautify the dying character.

We will probably never know why authors prior to Murasaki Shikibu avoided death scenes. One may conjecture that the ancient Japanese linkage of death to defilement discouraged writers from approaching this taboo subject in any but the most tangential terms. Murasaki Shikibu's tendency to aestheticize even bad deaths may be partially a response to her culture. Death, in Heian society, was too ugly to be realistically portrayed.

Murasaki Shikibu seems to have had some knowledge of the early Japanese chronicles, including *Kojiki* (ca. 712) and *Nihon shoki* (ca. 720).[12] She would thus probably have known of the legends describing the death of the goddess Izanami and her husband Izanagi's search for her in the land of the dead. Izanami's death scene, the earliest in Japanese literature, is described in strikingly realistic terms.

> Then Izanami gave birth to the deity He-Who-Burns-Fiercely. . . . Because she bore this child, her genitals were burned and she became ill. . . . Having thus given birth to the fire deity, the goddess Izanami passed from this world.
>
> Thereupon Izanagi said, "Oh, my dear wife! Would I exchange you for a single child?" He crawled around the head of her bed, and he crawled around the foot of her bed, weeping. . . . Then he buried the goddess Izanami, who had

passed from this world, on the hill of Hiba, at the border of the lands of Izumo and Hahaki.[13]

The narration is matter-of-fact and strongly sequential. The fecund goddess's childbearing takes a turn for the worse. She sickens and dies; Izanagi mourns and buries her. Interest is focused not on the dying, but on the acts of the living. Izanagi's emotional cry at the death of his wife is the climax of the episode. Izanami is not given any perceptions or emotional response by the narrator, much less attractive physical attributes.

After Izanami's death, Izanagi goes to the underworld to entreat his wife to return. The goddess is willing to speak to her husband in the darkness of the underworld, but begs him not to look at her. When Izanagi impatiently strikes a light so as to see in the darkness, he encounters her decaying corpse, a sight described in vivid if enigmatic detail: "Her body was teeming with maggots that uttered hoarse cries. Great Thunder was in her head, Fire Thunder was in her breast, Black Thunder was in her bowels" and so on for a total of eight thunder deities invading Izanami's body.[14] Just as the narrator makes no attempt to give the dying Izanami an awareness of her approaching death or a response to it, no effort is made to present the dead goddess as beautiful. Death in *Kojiki* is a frightening, repulsive event, and its dead are agents of pollution.

The only surviving death scene from courtly fiction to predate *Genji* appears in its nearest extant *monogatari* predecessor, *Utsuho monogatari* (The Hollow Tree, ca. 983). The "Atemiya" chapter describes the early career of its eponymous heroine, a heartless, extraordinarily beautiful young woman, and the devastating effect she has on her numerous suitors. Her older brother, Nakazumi, is one of those hopelessly in love with her. When he learns that Atemiya will soon leave home to become the crown prince's consort, he "wept and wailed piteously, unable to recognize anyone."[15] Before long he is seriously, though unspecifically, ill. Aware that he will die soon, Nakazumi asks for a final meeting with Atemiya. She goes reluctantly—thinking it inauspicious to have contact with an invalid before entering the palace as a bride—and responds unsympathetically to her brother's prediction of his imminent death. After she leaves the room, Nakazumi "stopped breathing before his attendants' eyes" (11: 94).

This proves to be only a temporary seizure. The unconscious Nakazumi is revived when one of Atemiya's maids traces her mistress's name on his arm and gives him a note from her. Atemiya has meanwhile left for the palace. Nakazumi writes to her again, begging for another meeting. Atemiya, shocked to realize her brother's passion for her, replies with a cool poem noting pointedly that they are "dew from the same field," and expresses her regret that he will predecease her (11: 111). Nakazumi responds to the poem thus: "Folding the note into a tiny ball, he swallowed it with his medicine and, shedding tears of blood, breathed his last" (11: 112).

Utsuho is generally regarded as having influenced *Genji* thematically and structurally.[16] This is certainly the case where death scenes are concerned: Nakazumi's romantic death is a direct precursor of Kashiwagi's, and an indirect model for many of Murasaki Shikibu's death scenes. Nakazumi's awareness of approaching death, his final interview with a close relative, even Atemiya's conventional comparison of their lives to dew, all evolve into necessary elements in the greatest of *Genji* death scenes. Yet Nakazumi's death differs radically in focus and intent from those in *Genji*. As in the *Kojiki* death scene, the reader's attention is ultimately directed away from the dying character toward the acts of those close to him or her.

Nakazumi's death is not presented as an event worthy in itself; it exists as one of a series of episodes intended to underscore the impact of Atemiya's formidable charms. Nakazumi himself is no more than a stock romantic figure with predictable emotions; his appearance is not described.[17] The interest is less in Nakazumi's death, and what it tells us about the character, than in *why* he is dying. Nakazumi's life depends on Atemiya: he sickens, revives, and ultimately dies because of her actions. If Atemiya's acts were removed from the passage, there would be no death scene.

Utsuho monogatari influenced *Genji* death scenes in some formal respects. But the most striking characteristics of death scenes in *Genji*—the beauty of the moribund and dead, the comparison of the act of dying to an event in the world of nature, and the use of radiance and darkness as images underscoring the characters' spiritual states—are absent from the *Utsuho* scene. Was it Murasaki Shikibu's genius alone that inspired her to employ devices unprecedented in *monogatari* narration? Did she use her most admirable characters to transform death into a thing of beauty solely as a reaction to contemporary taboos against death?

Murasaki Shikibu may have been working with a model in mind, though not, strictly speaking, a literary one. Her interest in creating good deaths for such characters as Fujitsubo and Murasaki probably originated from contact with the story collections known as *ōjōden*, "accounts of rebirth" that describe how pious Buddhists from recent history were reborn into the Pure Land Paradise of Amida.

EVIDENCE OF *ŌJŌDEN* IN *GENJI*

Like many members of the aristocracy in the early eleventh century, Murasaki Shikibu was influenced by the increasingly active Amidist movement within Tendai Buddhism. Her interest in Amidism is especially apparent in the Uji chapters of *Genji*, in the personae of the Eighth Prince and the bishop of Yokawa.[18] Murasaki Shikibu records her reliance on Amida in a passage in her *nikki*: "Let people say what they will; I shall devote all my energies to worshipping Amida and to studying the sutras."[19]

Murasaki Shikibu's family was closely connected to the Amidist movement. Her father, Fujiwara Tametoki (d. 1029), was a friend and colleague of the scholar Yoshishige Yasutane (934?–997), one of the founders of two influential Heian Amidist societies that focused on prayer, contemplation, and giving spiritual support to fellow members at the time of death.[20] Yasutane was also the compiler of the first Japanese collection of rebirth accounts, *Nihon ōjō gokurakuki* (Accounts of Japanese Reborn in Paradise, ca. 985).[21] Like its Chinese predecessors, *Nihon ōjō gokurakuki* was intended as a means of communicating Amida's message of salvation to the literate laity, who were generally thought incapable of understanding the abstract contents of such Pure Land sutras as *Muryōjukyō* and *Amidakyō*.[22]

The collection presents forty-two brief biographies of historical figures in Japan, beginning with such illustrious Buddhist personages as Prince Shōtoku and the Nara-period monk Gyōki and ending with the stories of several anonymous women. All follow roughly the same format. The subject is introduced by name and status, and his or her pious virtues are given. The rest of the account is devoted to a description of the subject's death, from its first warning to the indications that the subject will be reborn in the Pure Land. These auspicious signs include the presence of unearthly fragrance, celestial music, a purple cloud, heavenly messengers, and blinding radiance. The subject dies soon after the manifestations. A typical example follows.

Minamoto Ikou was the seventh son of the head of the Bureau of Skilled Artisans. He had turned to the Dharma since childhood. Clever and articulate, he read many books. When he was a little over twenty years old, he became ill for about three weeks and, finding worldly life distasteful, became a monk. His practice had been to contemplate and call upon Amida with all his heart. In his illness, he redoubled his efforts.

As he spoke with his elder brother, the monk Anhō, Ikou said, "I hear music coming from the west. Can you hear it?" Anhō replied that he could not. Ikou said, "A peacock is here, fluttering and dancing before me. Its plumage is radiant and lovely." Placing his hands in the concentration mudra, he turned to the west and died.[23]

The focus of this story is on Ikou's death scene. Everything preceding it serves to prepare us for the manner of his death: the young man's intelligence bolsters his piety, and the onset of mortal illness spurs him to greater devotions. The death scene itself presents a picture of great serenity. The dying man is granted two signs of his approaching death and rebirth in the Pure Land: the celestial music played by Amida's host of bodhisattvas as they come from the Western Paradise to meet Ikou, and the vision of a supernaturally beautiful peacock, one of the birds said to inhabit the Pure Land of Amida. Far from being frightening or polluting, Ikou's death is filled with spiritual beauty.

Some of the accounts in *Ōjō gokurakuki* demonstrate how the protagonist's spiritual glory is manifested in his body at the time of death. The story of Zōmyō (843–927), healer, wonder-worker, and archabbot of Tendai, culminates in the following passage:

The master [Zōmyō] quickly developed a slight illness. He cleaned his cell and told his disciples, "All those born as men must die. The Buddha will be my guide. None of you is to remain near me."

That night a golden light suddenly shone forth, and purple clouds appeared. Music filled the skies and fragrance pervaded the cell. The master bowed to the west in adoration and meditated upon the Buddha Amida. Having burned incense, he leaned upon an armrest and died as if falling asleep. The smoke rising from his funeral pyre was fragrant.[24]

The account of Zōmyō's death is unusual in one respect: mention is made of the effect salvation has on his earthly remains. Most recitals of saintly Buddhist deaths emphasize the serenity and prayerful contemplation leading up to the moment of death, but take no interest in describing the corpse. It is only on rare occasions that the saintliness of the protagonist is given further emphasis by a description of the miraculous properties of his remains. The dead Zōmyō is lifelike, dying "as if falling asleep." Cremation, a rarely described event in either *ōjōden* or courtly literature, is also used to underscore Zōmyō's holiness. His body emits fragrance, reminiscent of the "odor of sanctity" in which saints of many religious traditions die.

Another account in *Ōjō gokurakuki* describes a pious layman who is similarly blessed after death: "Although it was summer and several days passed before the funeral, the body did not decay but remained as it had been in life."[25]

The account of Minamoto Ikou's death, and others like it, may have encouraged Murasaki Shikibu to attempt in *monogatari* what had already been done successfully in *ōjōden*: to present dying and dead characters in such a way as to evoke not repellence or even the simple pathos produced by Nakazumi's death, but a sense of serenity and transcendence. The means were to exalt the character by a good death, as exemplified in the Buddhist accounts of rebirth in the Pure Land; by the use of light as metaphor in death scenes; and, if the character, like the saintly Zōmyō, is worthy enough, by exalting the remains above mere mortal stuff. Thus the dead Ōigimi is presented, against all reason, as warm, familiar, and lifelike. The comparison of the corpse to a sleeper is identical in her and Zōmyō's stories, and the fragrance released by the dead woman's hair evokes that rising from the saint's pyre.[26]

Many religions use the imagery of light and darkness to symbolize the attributes of and the difference between holiness and spiritual confusion.[27] Mahāyāna Buddhism is no exception. Darkness and blindness are used as metaphors of delusion, as in this passage from the *Lotus Sutra*:

> The living beings, ever tormented by pain,
>   Blind and without a guide,
> Do not recognize the Path wherein pain is terminated,
>   Nor do they know enough to seek deliverance.
> Throughout the long night of time they gain in evil destinies
>   And reduce the ranks of the gods.
> From darkness proceeding to darkness,
>   They never hear the Buddha's name.[28]

There is a similar link between light and the Buddha, who symbolizes the awakened (enlightened) consciousness. Amida, one of whose Sanskrit names, Amitābha, means "boundless light," illumines the world of men. His body is golden, his eyes are bright blue; brilliance is emitted from a luminous tuft of white hair between his brows, from his aureole, and from the very pores of his body. He is the embodiment of light.[29]

Brilliant light, the symbol of Amida's saving compassion, often appears in accounts of rebirth. Its usual role is to envelop the dying person and illumine the surroundings. Radiance is occasionally emitted by the dead and dying. This may be considered an afterglow or reflection of Amida's brilliant light. An early example of a saintly person who radiates light appears in *Nihon ryōiki* (Miraculous Stories of Japan, ca. 785–822), a collection of Buddhist legends set in Japan. Some of the stories are biographies of holy people, including one of the eminent monk Dōshō (d. 700). Here is his death scene:

> When he was nearing death he bathed, changed his clothing, and sat upright facing the west. Brilliant light filled the room. He opened his eyes and, summoning his disciple Chichō, asked him, "Do you see the light?" Chichō answered that he did. Dōshō cautioned him not to tell anyone.
>
> Then, near dawn, radiance shone from Dōshō's cell, illuminating the pine trees in the temple garden. Somewhat later, the radiance flew off toward the west. All the disciples were thoroughly astonished. Their master sat upright, facing the west, and died free of worldly distractions. Clearly he had been reborn into the Pure Land Paradise. . . . At his death his body emitted light.[30]

There are two noteworthy elements in this account: part of the radiance emanating from Dōshō's room seems to come from his own body, lingering there after his death; and the holy man dies at dawn. These elements are also found in Murasaki's death scene.

I do not mean to imply that Murasaki Shikibu was directly influenced by these specific accounts of rebirth when I draw attention to the resemblance between them and certain death scenes in *Genji monogatari*. One might conclude instead that Murasaki Shikibu knew of Amidist legends emphasizing the link between beautiful, serene, auspicious deaths and rebirth into the Pure Land, and used her knowledge—shared by her aristocratic, largely female audience—to develop the death scene as a topos of high literary and spiritual value.

Nakazumi's death is meaningful only in the light of Atemiya's actions. By adding aesthetic, symbolic, and religious significance to her death scenes, Murasaki Shikibu ensures that her characters will make powerful statements about themselves when they die. The *Genji* character's response to death illuminates and reflects the life that has been lived, much as Millie Theale's struggle against death "shine[s]

out on the lost ground as in no other connexion." Whatever their
temporal or cultural boundaries, great novelists succeed in portraying
characters capable of deeply affecting us by their lives, and by their
deaths.

NOTES

1. Haruo Shirane estimates that "close to thirty deaths" occur in *Genji*, most in the
   autumn and winter (*The Bridge of Dreams: A Poetics of the Tale of Genji* [Stanford:
   Stanford University Press, 1987], 239). See also Edward Seidensticker, "The
   Japanese and Nature, with Special Reference to *The Tale of Genji*," *This Country,
   Japan* (Tokyo and New York: Kōdansha International, 1979), 5–11. Many of
   these deaths are only mentioned in passing in the narrative. True death scenes,
   in which a character is presented as dying and/or dead, number eight by my
   count: those of the Kiritsubo lady, Yūgao, Aoi, Rokujō no Miyasudokoro,
   Fujitsubo, Kashiwagi, Murasaki, and Ōigimi.
2. "The good death" is a term used by Philippe Ariès in his history of Western
   attitudes toward death, *The Hour of Our Death* (New York: Vintage Books, 1982;
   originally published as *L'Homme devant la mort* [Paris: Editions du Seuil, 1977]),
   to describe "the beautiful and edifying death, . . . the death of the righteous
   man who thinks little about his own physical death when it comes, but who has
   thought about it all his life" (310)—a concept of death that flourished in seven-
   teenth- and eighteenth-century Europe. The "good death" as presented by
   Murasaki Shikibu resembles Ariès's model in its emphasis on beauty and im-
   plied edification, but also includes the individual's awareness of approaching
   death ("the warning") that Ariès believes prevailed in the European Middle
   Ages (7–8).
3. Translations of *Genji* chapter titles are taken from Edward G. Seidensticker, trans.,
   The Tale of Genji, 2 vols. (New York: Knopf, 1976). All translations are my own
   unless otherwise noted.
4. The edition used throughout is Yamagishi Tokuhei, ed., *Genji monogatari*, vols.
   14–18 of *NKBT*. Fujitsubo's death scene is found in 15: 227–30. All parenthetical references to the *Genji* text that appear below are to the *NKBT* edition.
5. Death scenes in antecedent prose fiction are discussed below.
6. In discussing Murasaki's death, Shirane notes that in "Heian aristocratic society a
   roundness in the body and the face was a mark of feminine beauty; but
   Murasaki's extremely frail and slender figure . . . echoes a more poetic aes-
   thetics: the fragile beauty of the cherry blossoms, or, to use the dominant poetic
   image of the chapter ['Minori'], the morning dew on the autumn grass" (*The
   Bridge of Dreams*, 126). Hence the dying Murasaki's attraction—and that of
   other moribund characters in *Genji*—may be due in part to the fragility shared
   by nature and the human body.
7. For a complete discussion of the motives behind Ōigimi's self-willed death, see
   Shirane, 140–48. An alternative reason for Ōigimi's death is offered by Norma
   Field in *The Splendor of Longing in the Tale of Genji* (Princeton: Princeton University Press, 1987), 239–41.
8. Interestingly enough, Murasaki Shikibu does not prepare a death scene for the
   nastiest character in *Genji*, Kokiden. She is last mentioned as among the living
   in "Hatsune" (The First Warbler). The opening passage of "Wakana jō" (New
   Herbs: Part One) refers to her as dead, and a passage in "Wakana ge" (New

Herbs: Part Two) mentions that she died three years earlier. Kokiden's quiet exit from the narrative suggests that Murasaki Shikibu was more interested in exploring the spiritual states of certain principal characters in her death scenes than in showing that bad people come to a bad end.

9. The list, known as "*Genji* no mokuroku," appears in the miscellany *Shirozōshi* (ca. 1199). The convention of inserting the title "Kumogakure" between "Maboroshi" and "Niou miya" is perpetuated in many modern *Genji* editions, commentaries, and chronologies. For a translation and discussion of "*Genji* no mokuroku," see Gatten, "The Secluded Forest: Textual Problems in the *Genji monogatari*" (Ph.D. dissertation, University of Michigan, 1977), 11–15.

10. The medieval "Kumogakure" chapter and its description of Genji's death are discussed and partially translated in Gatten, "Supplementary Narratives to the *Genji monogatari*: 'Yamaji no tsuyu,' *Kumogakure rokujō*, and 'Tamakura,'" a paper presented at "The World of *Genji*: Perspectives on the *Genji monogatari*" (Eighth Conference on Oriental-Western Literary and Cultural Relations: Japan; Indiana University, 1982).

11. Several theories surfaced during the fourteenth and fifteenth centuries: Murasaki Shikibu chose to keep the contents of "Kumogakure" to herself; Genji, a superior being like the Yellow Emperor and other Chinese Taoist sages, leaves the world in a manner too mysterious for human comprehension; the contents of the chapter were destroyed because all who read it were so overwhelmed by a sense of evanescence that they rushed into religious orders, thus threatening the fabric of society. A more down-to-earth possibility is that the author was reluctant to attempt another death scene so soon after crafting Murasaki's, her masterpiece.

12. Murasaki Shikibu records Emperor Ichijō's words of praise for the author of *Genji*: "'This lady seems to know the Chronicles of Japan. She must be learned indeed'" (Ikeda Kikan and Akiyama Ken, eds., *Murasaki Shikibu nikki*, in *Makura no sōshi, Murasaki Shikibu nikki*, NKBT 19 [1958], 500). The emperor's compliment was the source of considerable embarrassment for Murasaki Shikibu, since it was thought unseemly for women of her time to display a knowledge of Chinese (the language in which the *Rikkokushi*, or "Six Chronicles of Japan," were written). *Genji* contains allusions to *Kojiki* and *Nihon shoki* legends, including that of the leech child and the sun goddess Amaterasu's concealment in the rock cave, as well as to other events recorded in the Six Chronicles.

13. Kanda Hideo and Ōta Yoshimaro, eds., *Kojiki*; vols. 101–2 of *Nihon koten zensho* (Tokyo: Asahi Shinbunsha, 1962–63), 101: 184–88. Izanagi and Izanami have already produced countless deities, not to mention the islands of Japan; hence the bereaved husband laments losing his wife from the birth of a single child. The sections deleted from Izanami's death scene deal not with her death but with the birth of yet more deities from the mother's vomit and excreta and the father's tears.

14. *Kojiki*, 101: 191. In his translation of *Kojiki*, Donald L. Philippi cites several scholarly theories regarding the identity of the thunder deities. They may be snakes representing the spirits of the dead or evil spirits, or they may be the maggots transformed into snakes (*Kojiki* [Tokyo: University of Tokyo Press, 1968], 63n). Whatever their shape, the thunder deities are unquestionably agents of decomposition.

15. Kōno Tama, ed., *Utsuho monogatari*, NKBT 10–11 (1961), 11: 93. All subsequent quotations are from this edition; volume and page numbers appear in the text in parentheses.

16. See, for example, Oka Kazuo, *Genji monogatari jiten* (Tokyo: Shunjūsha, 1964), 248–53. Oka draws a number of comparisons between plot conventions and situations in the two works, but does not mention the similarity between Nakazumi's and Kashiwagi's deaths.

17. Nakazumi's character is strongly reminiscent of the poetic persona of the man dying of unrequited love, a persona exploited with great success in *waka*. One of many possible examples from the love books of *Kokinshū* is no. 571:

Koishiki ni	If, distraught by love,
wabite tamashii	my spirit should wander off,
madoinaba	leaving a cold corpse,
munashiki kara no	might people say that I died
na ni ya nokoramu	because I had yearned in vain?

(Helen Craig McCullough, trans., *Kokin Wakashū* [Stanford: Stanford University Press, 1985], 130.) Kashiwagi's death, though the culmination of a far more psychologically complex situation, is similarly based on *waka* precedents. See Shirane, 125–26.

18. The Eighth Prince is a devotee of Amida and a regular participant in the ten-day *nenbutsu* recitation and contemplation sessions that were a focal part of the Amidist societies formed by monks and laymen (see n. 20). The bishop of Yokawa is generally assumed to have been modeled after Murasaki Shikibu's contemporary, Genshin (942–1017), a Tendai monk residing in the Yokawa precinct of Enryakuji. Genshin wrote *Ōjō yōshū* (Essentials for rebirth), probably as a manual for the two Amidist societies he helped found, the Kangakue and the Nijūgo Zanmaie.

19. *Murasaki Shikibu nikki*, 501.

20. Yasutane, who became a monk in 986, was a founder of the Kangakue (964–84) and, with Genshin, of its successor, the Nijūgo Zanmaie in 986 (see n. 18). The purpose of the societies was to meet at stated times to practice the *nenbutsu*. This was done in two ways: by contemplating Amida and by invoking his name with the *Namu Amida Butsu* formula. Members of the societies were also expected to be present at the deathbed of a fellow member to help him compose his mind at the moment of death, thus ensuring birth into Amida's paradise (Inoue Mitsusada and Ōsone Shōsuke, eds., *Ōjōden, Hokke genki* [hereafter *Ōjōden*]; vol. 7 of *Nihon shisō taikei* [Tokyo: Iwanami Shoten, 1985], 712–14; Allan A. Andrews, *The Teachings Essential for Rebirth: A Study of Genshin's Ōjōyōshū* [Tokyo: Sophia University, 1973], 38–39).

21. Yasutane probably based his collection on one or more Chinese models, including the Tang collection *Wangsheng xifang jingtu shuiying chuan* (Accounts of those auspiciously reborn in the Pure Land Paradise of Amida; *Ōjōden*, 714–15).

22. Yasutane states this objective in his preface to the work (*Ōjōden*, 11).

23. Story 35; *Ōjōden*, 38.

24. Story 6; *Ōjōden*, 21.

25. Story 33; *Ōjōden*, 37.

26. *Hamamatsu Chūnagon monogatari* (ca. 1060), one of several late-Heian *monogatari* influenced by *Genji*, takes this method one step further in its depiction of the death of the Yoshino nun. Not only does the nun experience the warning of death, an unspecified illness accompanied by weakness, and the opportunity to entrust her child to the hero; she also dies like a saint, seated upright, contemplating Amida, and hearing heavenly music until she is enveloped by a fragrant

purple cloud. Matsuo Satoshi, ed., *Hamamatsu Chūnagon monogatari,* in *Taka-mura monogatari, Heichū monogatari, Hamamatsu Chūnagon monogatari, NKBT* 77 (1964), 330–33. An English translation of the passage appears in Thomas H. Rohlich, *A Tale of Eleventh-Century Japan: Hamamatsu Chūnagon Monogatari* (Princeton: Princeton University Press, 1983), 172–74. Perhaps in keeping with the general *ōjōden* tradition, little is said of the nun's funeral and nothing of her remains.

27. In the Judeo-Christian tradition, dazzling light and splendor are equated with God and the Son of God, and darkness with sin and the rejection of God. For example: "Arise, shine, for your light has come, / and the glory of the Lord has dawned upon you. / For behold, darkness covers the land; / deep gloom enshrouds the peoples. / But over you the Lord will rise, / and his glory will appear upon you. / Nations will stream to your light, / and kings to the brightness of your dawning" (Isaiah 60: 1–3); also, "In him [Jesus] was life, and the life was the light of men. The light shines in the darkness, and the darkness has not overcome it. . . . The true light that enlightens every man was coming into the world" (John 1: 4–5, 9).

28. Leon Hurvitz, trans., *Scripture of the Lotus Blossom of the Fine Dharma* (New York: Columbia University Press, 1976), 133.

29. These attributes are given in *Kanmuryōjukyō*; see Andrews's discussion, 12–17.

30. Endō Yoshimoto and Kasuga Kazuo, eds., *Nihon ryōiki; NKBT* 70 (1967), 122–25 (book 1, story 22). An English translation also appears in Kyoko Motomochi Nakamura, trans., *Miraculous Stories from the Japanese Buddhist Tradition: The Nihon Ryōiki of the Monk Kyōkai* (Cambridge: Harvard University Press, 1973), 134. The account of Dōshō's death is one of the earliest recorded instances of Amidism in Japan. Dōshō, founder of the Hossō school of Buddhism in Japan and Gyōki's mentor, was cremated, the first recorded case of this practice in Japan (Nakamura, 81).

Genji Gossip

T. J. HARPER

The canonization of *The Tale of Genji* seems to have taken a little less than two centuries. Fujiwara Shunzei's famous dictum, that "for a poet not to have read *Genji* is simply unforgivable," dates from 1193.[1] In that same decade, as if to demonstrate the weight of Shunzei's words in the cultural marketplace, thieves broke into the home of his son Teika and stole his carefully collated text of *Genji*.[2] A process of transformation—from entertainment reading to canonical text—was clearly underway; from the thirteenth century forward nearly every form of attention given to *Genji* was of the sort appropriate to a classic.

These were the years that saw the beginnings of the great flood of scholarship that was to produce the first (and still) "definitive" texts of *Genji*, a sea of commentary (the favored metaphors are of droplets, brooks, rivers, floods, seas) the full extent of which is still unknown, and a myriad of other tokens of veneration, from allusive poems and apocryphal supplements to learned treatises and tomes of reference. In its totality it constitutes the world's richest record of the reception of a work of fiction.

For all of this we can only be grateful; we may owe the very survival of *Genji* to it. Yet, for all its beneficence, the flood also did some damage. It overwhelmed, and probably drowned, a voice of another sort that was beginning to be recorded at about the same time. This was the voice of gossip, which had been the principal form of attention paid to *Genji* in the first two centuries of its existence.

We can only speculate what *Genji* gossip might have grown into had it had a bit more time to establish itself. The larger history of Japanese letters suggests that it might have become something quite splendid. Gossip is a genre for which the Japanese have long—and rightly —thought themselves to possess a special affinity. Catalogues of the classical canon always rank Sei Shōnagon's *Pillow Book* some-where near the top, and will usually include one or two more works of

29

the same genre (under the more polite name of *zuihitsu*) among their Ten Best. In the more specialized realm of criticism, much of what we now call "Japanese poetics" consists of "evening conversations," "nighttime chat," "old men's ramblings," "whispered nothings," and the like, which is to say the written record of gossip about *waka*, very little altered from the condition well described by its titles.

There must have been a vast deal of gossip about *Genji* too. We catch glimpses of tipsy noblemen at it in Murasaki's own journal. The Sarashina diarist tells us what a favored topic it was amongst her relatives. And if literary ladies, such as those at the court of the Kamo Saiin, could chat for hours on end about the likes of *Sumiyoshi*, to what flights must *Genji* have inspired them? We shall never know; there was ample precedent, but apparently too little time, for a genre to develop. The entire corpus of *Genji* gossip would barely equal in volume a single chapter of one of the more substantial learned commentaries. Once the tide of seriousness had begun to flow, no one bothered to write down the gossip any more.

The three texts translated below—*Genji shijūhachi monotatoe no koto* (Forty-eight Exemplars from *Genji*),[3] *Genji kai* (A Key to *Genji*),[4] and *Genji monotatoe* (Exemplars from *Genji*)[5]—constitute the known whole of one small sub-genre of *Genji* gossip: lists of superlatives. Almost nothing is known of their provenance, and none survives in its original form. They are assigned to the Kamakura period mainly because they would seem out of place in the company of later, more tendentious works. There is speculation, based upon traces of feminine insight that some can detect, that one or more may have been written by a woman. Affinities have been noted with Sei Shōnagon, and, more interestingly, with digest versions of *Genji*. But in the end no one has much more to say about them than did the anonymous copyist of *Genji kai* in 1650 (p. 35); and it was he who said the most important thing—that they are a delight to read.

The order in which the three works are arranged is an attempt to represent what may have been a genetic relation between them. *Genji kai* appears to be a riposte to *Genji shijūhachi monotatoe no koto*.[6] They share twenty-nine categories, many of which appear in the same order in both texts; and where *Shijūhachi* states the obvious (Man: Genji; Pretty Face: Fujitsubo), *Kai* tends to offer less conventional choices (Kaoru; Akikonomu). *Genji monotatoe* appears to be even more closely related to *Shijūhachi*.[7] Thirty-six categories are shared, and more than half appear in identical order. We may know nothing of when or by whom these lists were written, but we can at least catch a glimpse of the process by which they grew. And we can certainly wish there were more of them.

Of the usual problems of translation, only one need be mentioned. It soon became apparent that *koto,* repeated in most category headings, could not in every case be translated as "thing" (or any other single word), and I was quick to accept Motoori Norinaga's assurance that it would be wrong to try.[8] An attempt at consistency has been made in translating the adjectives of the headings, though this goal too has, in a few cases, proved unattainable. For quotations from *Genji,* I have wherever possible given the Seidensticker translation, marked as such by quotation marks. In a few instances, however, it has been necessary to give a new or altered rendition in order to relate the quotation to its present context. In every entry, a transliteration of the original heading follows its translation; for specific references to *Genji,* page numbers in the *NKBZ* edition and the Seidensticker translation ("S.") are given in parentheses at the end of the entry.

FORTY-EIGHT EXEMPLARS FROM *GENJI*[9]

Man (*otoko*). It need hardly be said anew that the Shining Genji is the very foundation of this tale. And of course, General Kaoru's very genuine thoughtfulness is without parallel.

Woman (*onna*). Who but the lady Murasaki?

Pretty Face, Good Looks (*mime katachi*). Fujitsubo.

Character (*kokorobase*). The elder of the Uji sisters.

Good Karma (*kahō*). The Akashi lady.

Chapter (*maki*). "Suma."

Poem (*uta*).

> *Furusato o izure no haru ka yukite mimu*
> *urayamashiki wa kaeru karigane.* ("Suma" 2: 206–7; S. 244)
> "In what spring tide will I see again my old village?
> I envy the geese, returning whence they come."

Prose Passage (*kotoba*). *Oraba ochinubeki hagi no tsuyu, hirowaba kienan to suru tamazasa no ue no arare.* ("Hahakigi" 1: 156; S. 32) ["The dew that will fall when the *hagi* branch is bent, the speck of frost that will melt when it is lifted from the bamboo leaf." The dewdrop alludes to *Kokinshū* 223; the source of the hail crystal is uncertain.][10]

Extraordinary Scene (*koto naru tokoro*). [Tō no Chūjō's dance] "Garden of Willows and Flowers," which was thought rare even for the past four illustrious reigns, and which would surely be regarded as a model for ages to come. ("Hana no en" 1: 432; S. 155) [A slightly confused entry. In fact the Minister of the Left praises Genji's arrangement of the festivities as the finest he has seen in four reigns; Genji returns the compliment by insisting that the contribution of the minister's son, rather than his own, would be the one remembered by history.]

Wondrous Event (*medetaki koto*). When the Akashi consort becomes empress. [Perhaps referring to "Wakana ge" 4: 188; S. 592? There is mention here of dissatisfaction in certain quarters that a member of Genji's faction would probably be appointed empress, but the event itself is never described. In "Minori" she is referred to as *kisaki*.]

Moment of Joy (*ureshiki koto*). One can well imagine how Kumoinokari felt when her father the minister relented and accepted Yūgiri as his son-in-law. ("Fuji no uraba" 3: 428f.; S. 525f.)

Sight to be Seen (*miru koto*). The dance "Waves of the Blue Ocean" at the palace rehearsal. ("Momiji no ga" 1: 383f.; S. 132f.)

Heartening Scene (*tanomoshiki koto*). Where the Akashi lady says "today let me hear the song of the first warbler." ("Hatsune" 3: 140; S. 410)

> [*Toshi tsuki o matsu ni hikarete furu hito ni
> kyō uguisu no hatsune kikaseyo.*
> "The old one's gaze rests long on the seedling pine,
> Waiting to hear the song of the first warbler."]

Desolate Place (*wabishiki koto*). The mansion of the Hitachi princess [the safflower lady].

Heartbreaking Scene (*itōshiki koto*). When Kashiwagi, on the verge of death, is visited by Yūgiri and tries to talk to him. ("Kashiwagi" 4: 30f., S. 644f.)

Disgusting Deed (*nikuki koto*). The guards lieutenant, when he learns that Ukifune is not the daughter of the Governor of Hitachi, marries her younger sister instead. ("Azumaya" 6: 16f.; S. 938f.)

Marvelous Moment (*mezurashiki koto*). When Genji first sees the newborn prince, son of the Akashi consort and the emperor. ("Wakana jō" 4: 102–3; S. 572) ["The emperor" at this point is still crown prince and does not succeed to the throne until the following chapter.]

Perfection (*aramahoshiki koto*). When Genji, at the firming of the teeth celebration, "shows Murasaki the mirror." ("Hatsune" 3: 138–39; S. 410) [. . . *ue ni wa ware (mochiikagami o) misetatematsuramu*, i.e., "let me offer my lady New Year's felicitations."]

Ineptitude (*kokoro okuretaru koto*). Tayū gives Genji the garment box. ("Suetsumuhana" 1: 371f.; S. 126–28)

Magnificent Thing (*imijiki koto*). General Kaoru supersedes all the princes to become the emperor's son-in-law. ("Yadorigi" 5: 462–63; S. 926–27)

Unpleasant Moment (*muzukashiki koto*). When the ashes from the censer are dumped upon General Higekuro. ("Makibashira" 3: 357; S. 497–98)

Grief (*kanashiki koto*). Nakanokimi's feelings when her elder sister dies and she is left behind. ("Agemaki" 5: 320f.; S. 867f.)

Devastation (*mune tsubururu koto*). Kojijū's feelings when she realizes that Genji has seen Kashiwagi's letter. ("Wakana ge" 4: 240–41; S. 623–24)

Longing (*koishiki koto*). The lady Murasaki's feelings when Genji leaves for Suma and she must remain behind in the capital. ("Suma"; specifically described as *koishiki* at 2: 182; S. 232)

Heartless Deed (*kokoronaki koto*). The Kokiden consort's evening of music, held just after the Kiritsubo lady has died and the emperor is sunk in grief. ("Kiritsubo" 1: 11–12; S. 12)

Amusing Thing (*okashiki koto*). The Ōmi lady aspires to become wardress of the ladies' apartments and composes a petition requesting that she be appointed to the post. ("Miyuki" 3: 315–16; S. 481)

Affecting Scene (*aware naru koto*). When the emperor dispatches Myōbu to call upon the mother of the Kiritsubo lady, who has survived her daughter. ("Kiritsubo" 1: 102–13; S. 7–12)

Moment of Shame (*hazukashiki koto*). When Genji says to the Third Princess, "What shall it answer, the pine among the rocks?" ("Kashiwagi" 4: 314; S. 650)

> [*Ta ga yo ni ka tane wa makishi to hito towaba*
> *ikaga iwane no matsu wa kotaen.*
> "Should someone ask who sowed the seed,
>   What shall it answer, the pine among the rocks?"]

Thing of Beauty (*omoshiroki koto*). The music played by the ladies of the Rokujō mansion, each on her individual instrument. ("Wakana ge" 4: 177f.; S. 599f.)

Unfortunate Thing (*hoi naki koto*). That the lady Murasaki never had children.

Irritating Thing (*modokashiki koto*). That Ukifune, finding it impossible to choose between the love of General Kaoru and Prince Niou, simply abandons them both and tries to do away with herself. ("Ukifune")

Wretched Situation (*kokoro uki koto*). Oborozukiyo, with Genji secreted within her curtains, is discovered by her father the minister. ("Sakaki" 2: 135–38; S. 210–13)

Deplorable Thing (*urameshiki koto*). That "upright young man" [Yūgiri] spends alternate nights—fifteen days each per month— with Kumoinokari, who had loved him from long past when he wore the green sleeves [of the Sixth Rank], and with Princess Ochiba. ("Niou miya" 5: 14; S. 736)

Astonishing Event (*asamashiki koto*). When Yūgao, at that "certain mansion," is possessed by a spirit. ("Yūgao")

Absolutely Perfect Response (*tsukizukishiki koto*). When Koremitsu asks, "How many Rat-Day sweets am I to provide?" ("Aoi" 2: 66; S. 182)

Surprising Thing (*omowazu naru koto*). Kogimi fails to accompany Genji to Suma. ("Sekiya" 2: 351; S. 304)

Mortification (*kuyashiki koto*). The Rokujō lady, fearful lest she become a laughingstock, departs for Ise. ("Sakaki" 2: 75; S. 185)

Desperation (*kokorozukushi naru koto*). Genji's feelings as he laments [to Fujitsubo], "How few our nights together." ("Wakamurasaki" 1: 306; S. 98)

> [*Mite mo mata au yo mo mare naru yume no naka ni*
> *yagate magiruru waga mi to mo ga na.*
> "So few and scattered the nights, so few the dreams.
> Would that the dream tonight might take me with it."]

Regrettable Thing (*ushirometaki koto*). That Kojijū revealed Kashiwagi's feelings. ("Wakana ge" 4: 208f.; S. 611f.)

Unsettling Event (*kokoromotonaki koto*). When the Third Princess is added to the company at the Rokujō mansion, and Murasaki—so unaccustomed to sleeping alone, and who now so often must—conceals her sleeves, which are soaked from crying the whole night through. ("Wakana jō" 4: 63; S. 556)

Unseemly Behavior (*hitowaroki koto*). When Genji stops to inquire after the safflower princess, her ladies complain of their lot. ("Yomogiu" 2: 336–37; S. 299)

Timorousness (*kokoro yowaki koto*). Captain Kashiwagi calls at the Rokujō mansion, sees that he is held in ill regard, and immediately falls into a decline. ("Wakana ge" 4: 268–71f.; S. 633–34f.)

Rare Event (*arigataki koto*). Ukifune, in Ono, watches and listens while robes are prepared, to be offered in her memory by those she left behind, all of whom think her dead. ("Tenarai" 6: 348; S. 1077–78)

Anguish (*kokorogurushiki koto*). The feelings of the elder sister in Uji, who, in a state of anguish at the thought of what might become of her younger sister, dies. ("Agemaki" 5: 317; S. 866)

Fearsome Thing (*osoroshiki koto*). The amorous designs of Tayū no Gen upon Tamakazura, as in his poem, "Should my feelings ever change; well, before the God of Matsura. . . ." ("Tamakazura" 3: 91; S. 391)

[*Kimi ni moshi kokoro tagawaba Matsura naru*
kagami no kami o kakete chikawamu.
Should my feelings for you ever change—well,
    by the Mirror God of Matsura let me vow. . . .]

Enviable Thing (*urayamashiki koto*). The splendor in which the Akashi
lady went, in place of the lady Murasaki, to serve [as her daughter's guardian] in the Shigeisa. ("Fuji no uraba" 3: 440–41; S.
531)

A KEY TO *GENJI*

I have no idea who compiled this list of high points in *The Tale of
Genji*. As I leaf through it I find any number of passages at which I
nod in perfect agreement. And if there are some that seem to me to
miss the mark, well, people do not all think alike. In any case, this
work has afforded me so many moments of mirth that, for the sheer
fun of it, I have made a copy. Should there be further points that catch
my fancy, I may see fit to add them.[11]

The Very Best in Genji

Man (*otoko*). General Kaoru.
Woman (*onna*). Aoi.
Nun (*ama*). The Third Princess.
Monk (*sō*). Bishop of Yokawa.
Good Looks (*sugata*). Oborozukiyo.
Pretty Face (*mime*). Akikonomu.
Hair (*kami*). The safflower lady's. It says it was longer than her height
    and lay in thick waves upon the hem of her robes. ("Sue-
    tsumuhana" 1: 367; S. 124)
Disposition (*kokoro*). The Akashi lady.
Beautiful Voice (*koe yoki hito*). Kōbai, the boy who sang "Takasago."
    ("Sakaki" 1: 133–34; S. 210)
Good Karma (*kahō*). The Kiritsubo lady.
Best Chapter (*suguretaru maki*). "New Herbs." ("Wakana")
Extraordinary Scene (*koto naru tokoro*). The Ōmi Lady playing Go
    whilst [her father] the minister watches. ("Tokonatsu" 3: 234–35;
    S. 448–49) [In fact she is playing backgammon.]
Poem (*uta*).

> *Yogatari ni hito ya tsutaen taguinaki*
> *ukimi o samenu yume ni nashitemo.*
> ("Wakamurasaki" 1: 306; S. 98)
> "Were I to disappear in the last of dreams
>   Would yet my name live on in infamy?"

Sight to be Seen (*miru koto*). The Picture Competition. ("Eawase")

Sounds to be Heard (*kiku koto*). The Ladies' Musicale. ("Wakana ge" 4: 177f.; S. 599f.)

Joyful Event (*ureshiki koto*). The safflower lady is taken into Genji's household. ("Yomogiu" 2: 344; S. 302)

Heartbreaking Thing (*itōshiki koto*). The Suzaku emperor's poem to the Third Princess: "Though you follow after me down this way, away from the world. . . ." ("Yokobue" 4: 335; S. 658)

> [*Yo o nogareirinamu*[12] *michi wa okuru tomo*
> *onaji tokoro o kimi mo tazuneyo.*
> Though you follow after me down this way, away from the world,
> search out the same place (in Paradise).]

Vulgar Thing (*nikuki koto*). Yūgao writes her "I need not guess" poem on a fan. ("Yūgao" 1: 214; S. 59)

> [*Kokoroate ni sore ka to zo miru shiratsuyu no*
> *hikari soetaru yūgao no hana.*
> I need not guess whose it is, that face in the evening,
> shining with the brilliance of the dew upon the *yūgao*.]

Forlorn Moment (*kokorobosoki koto*). When Genji ponders the fact that he might not be present for the next year's invocation of the holy names. ("Maboroshi" 4: 534; S. 734)

Moment of Amazement (*mezurashiki koto*). When the secret of his birth is revealed to the Reizei emperor. ("Usugumo" 2: 439f.; S. 340f.)

Unacceptable Behavior (*ukerarenu koto*). The lady of the locust shell continues to mix in society after she has become a nun. ("Hatsune" 3: 149–51; S. 415)

Perfection (*aramahoshiki koto*). The lady Murasaki's dwelling.

Ineptitude (*kokoro okuretaru koto*). The safflower lady's behavior, no matter what she does.

Immoderation (*setsu naru koto*). Genji goes to the Fujitsubo empress. ("Wakamurasaki" 1: 305–6; S. 98–99)

Splendid Thing (*imijiki koto*). The lady of the orange blossoms becomes Yūgiri's guardian. ("Otome" 3: 61; S. 379)

Place of Elegance (*yū naru koto*). Among those of all the ladies Genji called upon that New Year's Day, the apartments of the Akashi lady. ("Hatsune" 3: 143–45; S. 412–13)

Deplorable Deed (*wabishiki koto*). Genji forces himself upon the Fujitsubo empress while she is visiting her home. ("Wakamurasaki" 1: 305–6; S. 98–99)

Agitating Scene (*mune tsubururu*[13] *koto*). After the lady Murasaki dies, Yūgiri sees her and recites the poem, "As a dream in the darkness before dawn." ("Minori" 4: 498; S. 720)

[*Inishie no aki no yūbe no koishiki ni*
ima wa to mieshi akegure no yume.
"I remember an autumn evening long ago
As a dream in the dawn when we were left behind."]

Thing of Beauty (*omoshiroki koto*). The Festival of the Cherry Blossoms. ("Hana no en")

Matter of Anxiety (*obotsukanaki koto*). As the time of the birth of the Akashi princess draws near, Genji worries, "Surely by now. . . ." ("Miotsukushi" 2: 275; S. 273)

Time of Anguish (*urewashiki koto*). When Kashiwagi lay helpless in his yearning for the Third Princess. ("Wakana jō/ge" 4: 139f./209f.; S. 585f./611f.)

Grief (*kanashiki koto*). Ukon's feelings when she realizes that Yūgao[14] is dead. ("Yūgao" 1: 240–43; S. 72)

Amusing Thing (*okashiki koto*). The wording of the Ōmi lady's letter. ("Tokonatsu" 3: 240–41; S. 451–52)

Shame (*hazukashiki koto*). Ukifune's feelings on reading Kaoru's "engulfed in waves" poem. ("Ukifune" 6: 168; S. 1003) [The poem by which Kaoru lets her know that he knows of her affair with Niou:

Nami koyuru koro to mo shirazu sue no matsu
matsuramu to nomi omoikeru kana.
Never did I imagine they would be "engulfed in waves."
They would wait, I thought, the pines of Sue no Matsuyama.
(cf. *Kokinshū* 1093)]

Affecting Scene (*aware naru koto*). Genji, just before he is to leave for Suma, sets out to pay his respects at the grave of the late emperor, and on the way visits Fujitsubo, now become a nun. ("Suma" 2: 170–72; S. 226–27)

Irritating Incident (*modokashiki koto*). The battle of the carriages when the Rokujō lady goes to view the procession. ("Aoi" 2: 16–18; S. 160–61)

Wretched Situation (*kokoro uki koto*). Tō no Chūjō writes to the Second Princess [Ochiba], "I felt pity for you—and now resentment." ("Yūgiri" 4: 471; S. 710)

[*Chigiri are ya kimi o kokoro ni todomeokite*
aware to omou urameshi to kiku.
For some bond? You were always on my mind.
I felt pity for you—and now resentment.]

Wondrous Occasion (*medetaki koto*). The Akashi Lady, when Genji makes his pilgrimage to Sumiyoshi to give thanks for prayers answered, is taken back to the capital by him. ("Miotsukushi" 2: 292–98; S. 281–84) [It is not until the following chapter, "Matsukaze," that she actually comes to the capital.]

Deplorable Deed (*urameshiki koto*). Genji allows Murasaki to see only the outside of the letter from Akashi. ("Miotsukushi" 2: 286–87; S. 278)

Shocking Behavior (*asamashiki koto*). The Minister of the Right walks straight into the room when Genji is with Oborozukiyo. ("Sakaki" 2: 136–38; S. 211–13)

Absolutely Perfect Response (*tsukizukishiki*[15] *koto*). When the guardsman says, "That flower is called the 'Evening Face.'" ("Yūgao" 1: 210; S. 58)

Embarrassing Thing (*katawaraitaki koto*). The safflower lady's poem about the "Chinese robe." ("Suetsumuhana" 1: 372; S. 127)

> [*Karakoromo kimi ga kokoro no tsurakereba*
> *tamoto wa kaku zo tobochitsutsu nomi.*
> This Chinese robe: because of your cold heart
> its sleeves are ever soaked like this.]

Fretful Time (*omoiwazurau koto*). When Nakanokimi moves from Uji to Prince Niou's mansion. ("Sawarabi" 5: 342f.; S. 876f.)

✓ Fright (*osoroshiki koto*). Yūgao's feelings at that "certain mansion." ("Yūgao" 1: 233f.; S. 68f.)

Surprising Thing (*omowazu naru koto*). When Genji goes to Suma he does not take Murasaki with him.

Satisfying Occasion (*kokoro yuku koto*). When the Akashi nun moves to the capital. ("Matsukaze" 2: 391–97; S. 320–22) [The old woman herself is very sad; the satisfaction must be that of the writer.]

Anguish (*kokorogurushiki koto*). Nakanokimi's feelings when Prince Niou becomes Yūgiri's son-in-law. ("Yadorigi" 5: 373–402f.; S. 890–903f.)

Deplorable Thing (*urameshiki koto*). Akikonomu wins the picture competition. ("Eawase" 2: 375–78; S. 314–15)

Keian 3 [1650], Eleventh Month, Sixteenth Day

EXEMPLARS FROM *GENJI*

Man (*otoko*). "Almost too grand a name. Yet he did not escape criticism. . . ." : Genji. ("Hahakigi" 1: 129; S. 20)

Woman (*onna*). Akikonomu.

Pretty Face (*mime*). The Kiritsubo lady.

Disposition (*kokoro*). The lady Murasaki.

Good Karma (*hō*). The Akashi lady.

Chapter (*maki*). "Kashiwagi."

Poem (*uta*).

> *Ima wa tote moen keburi ni mo musubōre*
> *taenu omoi no na o ya nokosan.*[16] ("Kashiwagi" 4: 281; S. 637)
> "My thoughts of you: will they stay when I am gone
> Like smoke that lingers over the funeral pyre?"

Prose Passage (*kotoba*). *Suma ni wa kokorozukushi no akikaze*[17] *ni umi wa sukoshi tōkeredo Yukihira no Chūnagon no seki fukikoyuru*[18] *to iiken uranami no yoru yoru wa ito chikō kikoete.* ("Suma" 2: 190; S. 235) ["At Suma, melancholy autumn winds were blowing. Genji's house was some distance from the sea, but at night the wind that blew over the barriers, now as in Yukihira's day, seemed to bring the surf to his bedside."]

Extraordinary Event (*koto naru tokoro*). When construction of the Rokujō mansion, with its gardens of the four seasons, is completed and Genji's household moves in. ("Otome" 3: 72f.; S. 384f.)

Wondrous Event (*medetaki koto*). When the Akashi princess goes to court, she is permitted to ride in the lady Murasaki's hand-drawn carriage. ("Fuji no uraba" 3: 442; S. 531)

Moment of Joy (*ureshiki koto*). At Hatsuse, where the uncertainties of her life often take her, Ukon finds Tamakazura. ("Tamakazura" 3: 98f.; S. 394f.)

Sight to be Seen (*miru[beki] koto*). The evening when [the dance] "Waves of the Blue Ocean" put to shame even the tints of the autumn leaves.[19] ("Momiji no ga" 1: 387; S. 133)

Heartening Feeling (*tanomoshiki koto*). Genji's feelings when the late emperor appears to him in a dream and tells him to "leave this shore behind." ("Akashi" 2: 219; S. 250)

Desolate Feeling (*wabishiki koto*). Kashiwagi's feelings on the day of the rehearsal for the celebration of the former emperor's birthday; he is summoned to the Rokujō mansion, where Genji "made him empty the wine cup under his own careful supervision each time it came around." ("Wakana ge" 4: 262–71; S. 630–34)

Heartbreaking Scene (*itōshiki koto*). When the Akashi princess is about to board the carriage to go to the lady Murasaki, she clutches her mother's sleeve and says, "You too, mother." ("Usugumo" 2: 423–24; S. 333–34)

Disgusting Thing (*nikuki koto*). [Kumoinokari's] nurse "mutters" about [Yūgiri] being "fated to the Sixth Rank." ("Otome" 3: 51; S. 374)

Moment of Gloom (*kokorobosoki koto*). When at dawn Genji sets out to pay his respects at the late emperor's grave, the moon goes behind a cloud. ("Suma" 2: 173–74; S. 227–28)

Incredible Thing (*mezurashiki koto*). Ōmyōbu somehow contrives to arrange [Genji's] dreamlike meeting with the Fujitsubo empress. ("Wakamurasaki" 1: 305; S. 98)

Perfection (*aramahoshiki koto*). If only Tamakazura could have been married to Prince Hotaru.

Unacceptable Behavior (*ukerarenu koto*). Old Naishi's "you called me Mother's mother" poem. ("Asagao" 2: 474; S. 355)

> [*Toshi furedo kono chigiri koso wasurarenu*
> *oya no oya*[20] *to ka iishi hitokoto.*
> "I do not forget that bond, though years have passed,
> For did you not choose to call me Mother's mother?"]

Difficult Matter (*muzukashiki koto*). General Kaoru's advances toward Nakanokimi after she has become the wife of Prince Niou. ("Yadorigi" 5: 412–18; S. 907–9)

Ineptitude (*kokoro okuretaru koto*). Tayū gives Genji the garment box. ("Suetsumuhana" 1: 371f.; S. 126–28)

Magnificent Thing (*imijiki koto*). General Kaoru, in preference to all the princes, is granted the cup of betrothal as the emperor's son-in-law. ("Yadorigi" 5: 462–63; S. 926–27)

Grief (*kanashiki koto*). Genji's feelings at that "certain mansion" when Yūgao is possessed by a tree spirit and he waits for Koremitsu to respond to his summons. ("Yūgao" 1: 242–44; S. 72–73)

Longing (*koishiki koto*). On that moonlit night in Suma, [Genji recalls past evenings of] music at court. ("Suma" 1: 194; S. 238)

Shock (*mune tsubururu koto*). The first time Genji goes to court to see the [future] Reizei emperor, his father remarks how much the child resembles him. ("Momiji no ga" 1: 401; S. 140)

Heartless Words (*kokoronaki koto*). When [Genji] says, "How touching that [the *yamabuki*] blooms more brilliantly than ever, as if it had no idea that 'this spring its mistress is no longer with us,'"[21] the Third Princess replies, "'No spring comes to my dark valley.'"[22] ("Maboroshi" 4: 518; S. 727)

Disheartening Situation (*ajikinaki koto*). The Rokujō lady's distress at her own "weakness in waiting for the procession of the man who had caused her such unhappiness," though "he passed her by as if she were no 'bamboo by the bend in the river.'"[23] ("Aoi" 2: 17; S. 160–61)

Deep Emotion (*aware naru koto*). Genji's feelings as he takes out the heartrending letters that Murasaki wrote while he was in exile in Suma, writes in the margin of one of them, ". . . may the smoke join her in distant heavens," and burns them. ("Maboroshi" 4: 533–34; S. 734)

> [*Kakitsumete miru kai mo nashi moshiogusa*
> *onaji kumoi no keburi to mo*[24] *nare.*
> "I gather sea grasses no more, nor look upon them.
> Now they are smoke, to join her in distant heavens."]

Moment of Shame (*hazukashiki koto*). "'I hate to think that you would grieve less for me [the Suzaku emperor] gone forever than for him [Genji] gone so briefly such a short distance away.' . . . Tears were streaming from Oborozukiyo's eyes. 'And whom might you be weeping for?' he said, now smiling at her." ("Suma" 2: 189–90; S. 235) [In extant texts of *Genji* he does not smile.]

✓ Moment of Fright (*osoroshiki koto*). At that "certain mansion," as they waited in the "dim, flickering light of the lamp," "there was a persistent creaking, as of someone coming up behind them." ("Yūgao" 1: 243; S. 72–73)

Unfortunate Development (*hoi naki koto*). Though the retired [Suzaku] emperor had gone so far as to drop hints concerning the Third Princess, General Yūgiri coldly passes her by, only to "take the fallen leaf" that Kashiwagi had never loved. ("Wakana jō/ge" 4: 18–19/185; S. 539–40/603) [The quotation is from Kashiwagi's poem lamenting the fact that he had married the Second Princess (Ochiba) rather than the Third Princess:

> *Morokazura ochiba o nani ni hiroikemu*
> *na wa mutsumashiki kazashi naredomo.*
> "Laurel branches twain, so near and like.
> Why was it that I took the fallen leaf?"
> ("Wakana ge" 4: 224; S. 616)]

Wretched Situation (*kokoro uki koto*). Genji's note is discovered by Oborozukiyo's father, the Minister of the Right. ("Sakaki" 2: 137–39; S. 212–13)

Deplorable Deed (*urameshiki koto*). When Murasaki speaks, as if to herself, of "the boat far out from shore,"[25] Genji pretends his sighs are but for the scenery, and lets her see only the outer wrapping of his letter. ("Miotsukushi" 2: 286–87; S. 278)

Astonishment (*asamashiki koto*). The thoughts that pass through Kojijū's mind when Genji sees the pale green letter. ("Wakana ge" 4: 240–41; S. 623–24)

Absolutely Perfect Response (*tsukizukishiki*[26] *koto*). When [Genji] stops and speaks of her as a flower he would be "loath to pass without plucking," Chūjō treats his words as if they were intended for her mistress. ("Yūgao" 1: 222; S. 63)

[Genji:

> *Saku hana ni utsuru chō na wa tsutsumedomo*
> *orade sugiuki kesa no asagao.*
> "Though loath to be taxed with seeking fresher blooms,
> I feel impelled to pluck this morning glory."

Chūjō:

> *Asagiri no harema mo matanu keshiki nite*
> *hana ni kokoro o tomenu to zo miru.*
> "In haste to plunge into the morning mists,
> You seem to have no heart for the blossoms here."]

Surprise (*omowazu naru koto*). Tamakazura suddenly marries General Higekuro, for whom she claimed to feel no love, instead of the elegant and handsome Prince Hotaru, whose "love for her burnt as a silent fire."[27] ("Makibashira" 3: 341–44; S. 491–92)

Mortification (*kuyashiki koto*). Kaoru's feelings when, with his heart set on Ōigimi, he relinquishes Nakanokimi to Prince Niou, no sooner than which Ōigimi dies. ("Agemaki")

Desperation (*kokorozukushi naru koto*). "All through the day, . . . he [Genji] sat gazing off into space, and in the evening he would press Ōmyōbu to be his intermediary." ("Wakamurasaki" 1: 305; S. 98)

Regrettable Thing (*ushirometaki koto*). [Niou's] resentment of that unmistakable "scent upon your sleeve that sinks into the bones." ("Yadorigi" 5: 424; S. 911)

> [*Matahito ni narekeru sode no utsuriga o*
> *waga mi ni shimete uramitsuru ka na.*
> "Most friendly it was of him to give to your sleeve
> The scent that maddens, sinks into the bones."]

Time of Anxiety (*kokoromotonaki koto*). In Suma Genji awaits replies to letters sent by messenger to the capital. ("Suma" 2: 180; S. 231)

Rare Persons (*arigataki koto*). Tō no Chūjō, who went to Suma with no thought for the problems it might create for him at court. ("Suma" 2: 204–5; S. 243–46) Ukifune, who actually worried about being loved by two men. ("Ukifune" esp. 6: 176f.; S. 1005f.)

Thing of Beauty (*omoshiroki koto*). Tō no Chūjō's dance, "Garden of Willows and Flowers," which he had practiced with more than the usual care. ("Hana no en" 1: 424; S. 151)

Humiliation (*kuchioshiki koto*). The Rokujō lady's feelings when she is pushed out of the way in the battle of the carriages. ("Aoi" 2: 16–18; S. 160–61)

Curiosity (*yukashiki koto*). What must have gone through Yūgiri's mind on the morning after the typhoon when he went to Rokujō, found the shutters not yet raised, and heard indistinct voices, first that of a woman and then his father laughing in response? ("Nowaki" 3: 262–64; S. 460)

Embarrassing Scene (*katawaraitaki koto*). The Ōmi lady confronts that "very proper young man" [Yūgiri] with her "just tell me" poem. ("Makibashira" 3: 390; S. 510)

> [*Okitsufune yorube namiji ni tadayowaba*
> *sao sashiyoramu tomari oshieyo.*
> "If you're a little boat with nowhere to go,
> Just tell me where you're tied. I'll row out and meet you."]

NOTES

1. *Roppyakuban utaawase*, Winter, Round 13.
2. *Meigetsuki*, entry for Karoku 1.II.6 [1225]. "Stolen in the Kenkyū era [1191–99]."
3. Text in Shigematsu Nobuhiro, *Shinkō Genji monogatari kenkyū shi* (Tokyo: Kazama Shobō, 1961), 142–45. The same manuscript is printed in Abe Akio, Oka Kazuo, and Yamagishi Tokuhei, eds., *Kokugo kokubungaku kenkyū shi taisei 3: Genji monogatari, jō* (Tokyo: Sanseidō, 1960), 112–14.
4. Text in Shigematsu, 145–47, and Abe, et al., 115–17.
5. Text and brief discussion thereof in Inaga Keiji, "Meiō ninen okugaki mugedai *Genji shō* shoshū '*Genji monotatoe* (kadai)' kaisetsu, honkoku," *Kokubungaku kō* 33 (1964): 35–39. Text alone reprinted in Inaga, *Genji monogatari kenkyū* (Tokyo: Kasama Shoin, 1967), 601–13. This printing of the text is collated with twenty-eight fragments of what appears to be another copy of the same text, which is appended to a copy of *Genji kokagami* owned by Professor Katagiri Yōichi. These fragments are extremely useful in resolving some of the textual difficulties in the Inaga text. The entire *Genji shō* is printed in Teramoto Naohiko, *Genji monogatari juyō shi ronkō, zoku hen* (Tokyo: Kazama Shobō, 1982), 769–98. As the title of Inaga's article indicates, the list itself bears no title. That attached to the translation is Inaga's provisional title.
6. Shigematsu, 134–35.
7. Inaga, "Genji monotatoe," 35–37. This article contains a useful list displaying the correlation of categories in the three texts.
8. In the preface to his *Kokinshū tōkagami.*
9. Only forty-six survive.
10. This and all subsequent comments enclosed in brackets are added by the translator.
11. Someone has indeed made additions; there are two entries entitled *urameshiki koto.*

12. Extant texts of *Genji* read *wakareirinamu.*
13. The *Taisei* text reads *tsuburu. -ru* is emended from Shigematsu.
14. The *Taisei* text here reads "Yūgiri." The translation follows the Shigematsu text, which, correctly, reads "Yūgao."
15. The *Taisei* text reads *tsukizukishi. -ki* is emended from Shigematsu.
16. *NKBZ* 4:281 reads *mo* for *ni mo, nao* for *na o,* and *nokoran* for *nokosan.*
17. *Kokinshū* 174.
18. *Shokukokinshū* 868.
19. Cf. "Hana no en" 1: 434: "Hana no nioi mo keosarete."
20. Cf. *Shūishū* 545.
21. *Kokinshū* 851.
22. *Kokinshū* 967.
23. *Kokinshū* 1080.
24. All texts of *Genji* read *o* in place of *mo.*
25. *Kokin rokujō* 1888.
26. The text here reads *tsurezurenaru(shiki).* The emendation follows Inaga's suggestion. *Kenkyū,* 609.
27. "Hotaru," 3:193; S. 432.

Wasabigaki

Edwin A. Cranston

In a little-noted passage of *Hyakureishō*, the monkish author Jōken (1293–1367) mentions his discovery of "several tens" of previously unknown *waka* written in angular calligraphy on thick Michinoku paper and carefully wrapped in a stiff crimson fabric inserted into a lacquer box of apparent antiquity.[1] His account is disappointingly brief, but he does describe the distinct scent of sandalwood that emerged from the box once its elaborately decorated cover had been removed. He states that the discovery was made during the course of the annual autumn *mushiboshi* at his temple in the Eastern Hills, in the sixteenth year of the Shōhei era (1361) of the true succession of divine sovereigns, during a period of particularly fine weather and excellent moonlit nights. The origin of the box, and how long it had been in the temple archives, were equally unknown to Jōken, but an inspection of the contents led him to speculate about a source in a once-affiliated nunnery. Inquiries in that quarter were useless, however, as the nunnery had fallen victim to the flames of civil war a generation or two earlier.

Jōken was unusual, if not unique, among the scholar-monks of his sect for his firm belief in the authenticity of *Genji monogatari,* which he sometimes referred to as *Yomo no hikari* (Light from the Four Directions), and regarded as both historically true and spiritually efficacious—in short, as a kind of secular scripture. (See especially *GRR:* 299–301.) In this way he defended the author against accusations of mendacity with resultant assignment to hell in the afterlife. His "Hundred Proofs," a positivistic work well ahead of its time, has as its aim the biographical verification of the existence in historical time of the characters in what others have considered Murasaki's fiction. Unfortunately, it has only come down to us in fragments.

Extant portions of *Hyakureishō* do, however, include the afore-mentioned account, and an appended document (*GRR:* 318–26) providing the texts of the discovered poems interspersed with occasional comments by Jōken himself. There is a hint in Jōken's more than slightly obscure *hentai kanbun* preface that he suppressed an indeterminate number of the poems, or set them aside for a "separate transmission." Lamentably, this excised body of verse has failed to surface in any of the private or public collections in which Japan abounds, and one can only assume it to have been lost. Even some of the remaining poems are fairly startling, and many decidedly odd. It is my hypothesis that we have Jōken to thank for their present order, as it is known that he was a serious student of *Shinkokinshū* and other classical anthologies with their exquisite harmonies of association and progression. I also believe that he attached the title *Wasabigaki*, which like the text proper is in *kana*, and which I assume can be interpreted "Rakings of the Early Ebb," but which I fear could also be understood, *man'yōgana*-style, as "Writings of a Japanese Nose." Admittedly these hypotheses are based on little more than intuition.

Jōken immediately recognized the persona—to him, the author—of the poems as the unfortunate daughter of Prince Hitachi known to *Genji* readers as Suetsumuhana ("Safflower"). Her chief physical distinction among Genji's loves is only too well known, but her alleged poor taste in clothes and lack of poetic ability are as frequently held up to ridicule, and must have provided a cruel amusement for the well-dressed and poetically adept original audience of the *Tale*. Murasaki ascribes only six poems to her, and often shows her nonplussed by the need to frame a reply. Thus, one can imagine Jōken's excitement at finding that *in actual fact* she was the author of dozens of poems, all apparently hidden away and never shown. His comments, however (when he is not elucidating points of doctrine), usually limit themselves to a scholar's puzzlement at the peculiarities of her style and diction. My own interest in translating *Wasabigaki* has been fueled by the hunch I have long cherished that a character like the Hitachi princess would be rich in unexploited possibilities for an inner life kept hidden out of shame, and more particularly by the gothic fascination of her house. Whatever the true source of the poems, they do reveal unexpectedly strong, if confused, emotions, and an attachment to ruin that is ultimately Romantic.

While the modern reader will hardly feel that the verses in *Wasabigaki* are likely to establish their author as a distinguished voice among Japanese poets, and while I have only with great trepidation ventured to put forward highly tentative versions, I have been rash enough to assume that people in books have real lives, and that we cannot help wanting to know all about them. (This assumption may put me in pretty much the same intellectual company as Jōken.) Unfortunately, *Wasabigaki* (at least in its expurgated state) is a frail reed, or perhaps one might say, a crushed mugwort. Be that as it may, I have chosen to proceed with this project, adding occasional comments of my own to those of the erudite monk. I have numbered the poems and romanized them in five-line form for the convenience of the reader.[2]

1. Uta ni nao   Always until now
    na ga kokoro kome   you have put your heart in songs—
      mushi kueru   so shall you still,
    furuki kotonoha   though the words you rake together
    kakiatsumetsutsu   are but old, worm-eaten leaves.

Jōken comments of this poem only that it is in an unfamiliar style (*ito mishiranu sama nari*). One might suspect him of writing it himself as an opening verse. The reader has no doubt already considered the possibility that Jōken is in fact the author of the entire document. Future research may cast more light here.

2. Yomogiu ni   In my fox-haunted
    kitsune madoeru   wormwood patch there roam about
      ushi no ko no   the young of cattle,
    itazura areba   and their naughtiness pains me so
    uchinagametsutsu   that I stay inside and brood.

Jōken: Wild things are strange to *waka*; the poet's heart must have been such. (*Ayashiki kedamono wa waka ni awazu, utayomi no kokoro ni ya arubeki.*)

3. Kusagusa no   "Weeds," they say, and "trash,"
    kigi o kuzuki to   of the grasses and the trees
      iu hito wa   so various in kind—
    mori mo aezaru   such people are pale monkeys
    mashira narikeri   who cannot abide the forest.

Jōken: No comment.

EAC: It is clear that Jōken could not cope with this poem, which embodies precisely the kind of savage Romantic proto-environmentalism associated with house-owners who take a perverse pride in the unkemptness of their properties. The likelihood of a scholar having authored this poem is remote. The use of language is, however, quite rich.

4. Tsuyu shigeki   Where the dew lies thick,
    mugura no yado o   on a house all creeper-clad,
      tare ya tou   oh, who will call?
    matsumushi naku na   Pining insect, do not cry,
    hitori nuru to mo   though drops soak your lonely bed.

Jōken: This is in a familiar [or "well-heard"] style. (*Kore zo yoku kikoetaru sama naru.*)

EAC: The lady reveals her softer side.

5. Yūgure wa   No one comes along
    tare mo kayowanu   my narrow path in the gloaming,
    hosoki michi   all is blotted out;
    taehatenureba   even were one to wander by,
    ari to mo madou   an ant would lose its way.

Jōken: The "narrow path" is the worldly way, often known as the "dark path." Those that enter it go astray. (*Hosoki michi to ieru wa, kono yo no michi nari. Aruiwa, kuraki michi to iu. Ireru wa madou nari.*)

EAC: The learned monk misses the *kakekotoba* in the last line. Note how obsessed with nature the poet is.

6. Makekazura   The jungly mugwort,
    yaemugura nomi   bindweed and the stinging vine
    kuru to ni mo   alone come calling,
    uchi ni mo furite   coiling in and out of doors
    akisame no koro   too old to fend off autumn rain.

Jōken: The "stinging vine" [*makekazura*] is not identifiable; perhaps the reference is to *hikage no kazura* ["club moss"]. However, the latter does not fit the line. (*Makekazura to wa, ika naru mono ya shiranu. Aruiwa, hikage no kazura ka. Shikashi, ku ni awazu.*)

7. Koyoi mo ya   Tonight once more
    hito minu sode ni   on this sleeve so long unseen
    tsuki sayuru   will the moon shine clear,
    noki no shinobu ni   and the wind rise, ruffling through
    kaze wataritsutsu   the fern along my eaves?

Jōken: A fine poem. The moon, clear, awakens all. (*Yoki uta nari. Tsuki saete, hito kotogotoku samasubeshi.*)

EAC: The moon may shine "on" the sleeve because of its glossy surface, but more likely due to tears. The usual term is *yadoru* ("lodge").

8. Tare narade   'Tis not another,
    ware koso koto o   no, 'tis I who all alone,
    hikisusabe   idly strumming strings,
    tsuki iru made ni   lie until the moon goes down
    hitori tamakura   on the pillow of my arm.

Jōken: The line *Tare narade* ["'Tis not another"] is questionable. Does one play the koto with another's hand? (*Tare narade to ieru ku, ito ayashi. Hito no te nite koto o hiku koto ya wa aru.*)

EAC: The poem surely suggests that the lady imagines a listener intrigued by a music whose source he does not as yet know. But can one play the koto while lying down?

9.	Izayoi no	In the hazy light
	kage no oboro ni	of this hesitating moon
	hito towaba	should someone call,
	izuko mo sorane	would the sound of ghostly strings
	hiku koto to ka ya	draw him whither he knew not?

Jōken: *Śunya* is *rūpa*, *rūpa* is not other than *śunya*. It is a fine poem. But the moon is clear, not hazy. (*Kū sunawachi kore shiki nari. Shiki kū ni kotonarazu. Yoki uta nari. Tada, tsuki wa oboro ni arazu. Sumeru nari.*)

EAC: Jōken's doctrinal knee-jerk must have been triggered by *sora*. The reader's attention would better be directed to the lady's intensifying fantasy.

10.	Momoshiki no	Were such strings as these
	ōmiyahito ni	to be fingered by a dweller
	hikareba ya	of the mighty court,
	ne no ito takete	with what lofty, antique strains
	koyoi kikoemu	might yet the night rejoice?

Jōken: No comment.

11.	Koto no ne wa	The sound of a koto
	ito kikigurushi	is a strain to hear so far:
	hikade koso	night after night
	yoruyoru matsu no	with no plucking the pining
	mushi no koe sure	insect keeps raising its voice.

Jōken: The content and diction are both poor, but the love affair of the Hitachi princess and Hikaru Genji begins to appear. That is interesting. (*Kokoro kotoba tomo ni waroshi. Tada, Hitachi no miya hikaru kimi aiomou no den arawaresomuru, omoshiroshi.*)

EAC: The translation is also nothing to write home about. That aside, it becomes apparent that the princess was aware of Genji's presence, probably from his first surreptitious visit. It seems a pity she consigned her reaction to the lacquer box.

12.	Akane sasu	Madder-root-shining
	hi mo tokenikeri	sunbeams, and the last ice melts,
	shitamoyuru	for him who entered
	fukaki morimichi	the deep ways of my woodland
	wakeiru hito ni	smoldering with undergrowth.

Jōken: The season should be autumn, not early spring. Most peculiar. The forest path is where the travelers wander before reaching the Magic City. (*Kono niimakura wa, aki nite arubeshi. Hatsuharu no sama aru wa ayashi. Morimichi to ieru wa, tabibito no kejō ni itaranu ma ni madou narubeshi.*)

EAC: Enter the Hero, evidently impressively enough to bring about a conflation of seasons in the lady's mind.

13. Honobono to	Faintly, faintly
akatoki no sora	does the red dawn streak the sky—
kakushikemu	surely it concealed
kosode no ura ni	in my sleeve's crimson lining
someshi kurenai	what I dyed to hide behind.

Jōken: The connection with the bodhisattva Samantabhadra is most holy. (*Fugen Bosatsu no yukari ari. Ito tōtoshi.*)

EAC: One suspects that *ura* in line 4 is an *engo* suggesting "pain." Such elephantine remarks as Jōken's provide ample reason for the lady's blush.

14. Akigiri no	In the autumn mist
tachinishi sode no	he rose and went out, leaving
wakare kana	sleeves reft in parting,
kokorobososhi to	too narrowly cut to hide
kakushiwazurau	the frail new bloom in my heart.

Jōken: No comment.

EAC: Princess Hitachi's obsession with clothing images has often been remarked.

15. Karakoromo	A Chinese garment—
kigi no hayashi ni	worn out in the underbrush,
madoikoshi	you braved my grove:
kimi yue sobotsu	now for you these sleeves are drenched—
sode na yari so ne	pray, do not abandon them.

Jōken: In the grove were two *śal* trees. There was much weeping and wetting of sleeves. (*Hayashi no naka ni sara sōju ariki. Iki to shi ikeru mono, naku koto hanahadashi. Sode no kuchitsuru nomi.*)

EAC: One assumes that this poem accompanied one of Princess Hitachi's gift packages to Genji, all of which Murasaki Shikibu depicts him as scorning. Jōken (here off on another scriptural tangent) has placed it too early in the series, however, if the following refers to the lady's disappointed waiting for her lover's "next morning" poem.

16. Mori no shita	Under the grove
shigereru kusa no	heavy grows the grass with dew—
tsuyu omomi	see how it bends,
nabikinikerashi	crushed to earth although no foot
fumi o minu yo wa	comes bearing word tonight.

Jōken: The poem has a touch of the antique. Not bad. (*Yaya furumekitaru uta nari. Warokarazu.*)

EAC: Jōken tends to be distracted by individual lexical items, here apparently the use of -*rashi*. He was an early student of *Man'yōshū*, and the author of a brief *karon* entitled *Sanshishō* (Notes on the Mountain Persimmon; *GRR:* 174–91). It will be noted, however, that the poem is typically mid-Heian in its imagery and use of *kakekotoba*, not to mention the allegorical mode so prevalent in *Wasabigaki*. Jōken's understanding of Man'yō style is questionable. It would be in dubious taste to point out the latent sexuality of this poem and #15. These matters are best passed over in silence. The lady is crushed because Genji has sent no poem all day.

17.   Tōnari to   A distant sounding
     kane no ikutabi   fades away into silence . . .
       kikoyu to mo   let the bell be struck
     shijima ni makuru   when the evening hour comes,
     iriai tsukazu wa   lest the ringing be in vain.

Jōken: The evening bell is the voice of the Law. Let it resound in all hearts. (*Iriai no kane wa nori no koe nari. Bosatsu bonpu nari to mo kokoro ni hibikubeshi.*)

EAC: A metaphorical reading of "bell," "strike," etc. would fall into those faults of overinterpretation so prevalent in certain quarters at present. The scholar should avoid seeing too much in a poem. It would be safer to stick with Jōken if one simply must "interpret."

18.   Hi kurureba   When the day grows dark,
     sasuga yomogiu   sunlight fails the wormwood patch
       utokaramu   so alien to you,
     kurenaibana mo   though a crimson flower smiles
     hitomoto emedo   the sad welcome of its bloom.

Jōken: "The wormwood patch" has an inner meaning. It should not be mentioned. This is a very worldly poem. I am shocked, ashamed. (*Yomogiu to ieru wa oku no i arubeshi. Iubekarazu. Ayashiku zokumekitaru uta nari. Asamashi. Hazukashi.*)

EAC: *Kurenaibana* ("a crimson flower") refers to the *benibana* (safflower, *Carthamus tinctorius*), also known as *suetsumuhana* ("the flower plucked at the end"), the source of a rich red dye.

19.   Momiji senu   Without fall colors,
     aki ya wa kuru to   how could autumn ever be?
       ho ni izuru   Openly in plume,
     obana mo koyo to   the tailflower bends to the wind,
     kurenai maneku   beckoning, "Crimson, come!"

Jōken: No comment.

EAC: *Obana* ("the tailflower") refers to the *susuki* (*Miscanthus sinensis*), also known as *hanasusuki*, often translated "flowering plumegrass."

20.	Suetsumu to	Though plucked at the end,
	hito ni tsumaredo	pulled, mauled, dragged up by the root,
	nekoji nite	now she lies alone:
	itsu sakisomuru	when can any flower bloom
	makegi no hana zo	on the broken lacquer tree?

Jōken: The poet is physically and emotionally a mess. A case of lacquer poisoning? (*Yomibito wa, mi mo kokoro mo, midaretaru sama nari. Aruiwa, urushi ni maketaru yue ya?*)

EAC: *Makegi* ("the . . . lacquer tree") refers to the *urushi no ki* (*Rhus verniciflua*), whose sap is highly poisonous.

21.	Kuchinashi to	"Mute Jessamine,"
	sue o tsumaruru	said he to the safflower,
	benibana no	plucking off her head;
	someshi kinuginu	but the whispering silk she dyed,
	otozure ya senu	parting, will yet draw him back.

Jōken: A strange poem. (*Ayashiki uta nari.*)

EAC: Perhaps Jōken intended *iyashiki*, "a base poem." I think it rather fine, however, despite the violence it shares with #20. The lady is clearly put on her mettle by teasing and neglect. *Kuchinashi* ("Mute Jessamine") refers to the gardenia, jessamine, or cape jasmine (*Gardenia Jasminoides Ellis*). Its fruits do not open their mouths even when ripe, so lexicographers inform us. It produced a gamboge dye often blended with safflower red. *Tsuma-* must be an *engo* here and in #20.

22.	Hitohana ni	One flower's dyeing—
	somenishi sode mo	do not say the hue is pale
	usukarazu	on the sleeves she sent:
	ura mo omote mo	inner and outer, cheek and heart,
	tada no kurenai	left and right pure crimson.

Jōken: There is an Inner and Outer in Śākyamuni's teaching as well. But the Flower is one. (*Saka no mioshie ni mo ura omote ari. Tadashi, hana wa hitotsu nomi.*)

EAC: To "dye with one flower" means to immerse the fabric only once. The princess was fond of heavy, solid colors such as could only be produced by repeated dippings. I shall refrain from pointing out the repressed inner metaphor.

23. Ikutabi mo   Over and over
    fukazome ni seshi   she dyed deep this Chinese cloak,
      karakoromo   only now, alas,
    ima ya hitoshio   for another drenching tide
    kurenai masaru   to encrimson it again!

Jōken: Loss of blood through excessive lacrimal involvement can be life-threatening. An infusion of the above-mentioned "mute jessamine" is a specific for this condition. (*Ketsurui nado tashō arawaruru baai tomokaku, nagaku idesuguraba inochitori narubeshi. Kuchinashi to saki ni yomaretaru koso kono yamai ni yoku kiku yakusō nare. Senjite nomubeshi.*)

EAC: Jōken's medical treatise *Hyakunichisōsōroku* (Browsing the Garden Catalogue) has regrettably been lost. The above excerpt is thus all the more precious.

24. Yomosugara   All night long she dyes
    karakurenai ni   in the finest crimson hue
      furiizuru   with such outpouring
    shiruki akegata   of bright droplets as at dawn
    kosome no koromo   shine red on her deep-stained sleeve.

Jōken: It is the long night without hearing the Buddha's name. We wait the dawn. (*Hotoke no na o kikazaru nagaki yo nari. Akegata o matsu nomi.*)

25. Karakoromo   A Chinese garment—
    somenishi sue no   after I had dyed for you,
      matsuyama ni   clinging to Pine Hill
    ada naru iro no   what was left but seaweed trailing
    mosuso kakarite   skirts of a false lover's hue?

Jōken: *Rūpa* is *śunya*. (*Shiki sunawachi kore kū nari.*)

EAC: This poem appears to mark the high tide of the lady's passion for the clothing *mitate*. Her "weeds" (*mo*), which are also "seaweed" (*mo*), are left dripping at Sue no Matsuyama. In the present expurgated state of the document it is impossible to tell how many—apparently few—billows she has shared.

26. Komu komu to   "I'll be back!" barked he,
    tanomeshi kitsune   a fox full of promises—
      megitsune to   alas, the vixen
    ana mezurashiku   finds his coming a strange tale
    soine suru yo ya   when she sleeps whole nights alone.

Jōken: These animals are very odd. But Śākyamuni too was an animal in a former life. Wearing animal skins is sinful. (*Ke no mono tote ito ayashi. Aruiwa, Saka no zense naru ya. Kawagoromo tote wa, hanahada tsumi fukashi.*)

EAC: Reenter the Hero.

27. Fuyuchidori   Plover in winter,
     kawa ni ya asaru   what streambeds do you forage?
     asahi sasu   For a dripping beak
     taruhi tsurashi to   shining in the morning sun
     kuchibashi mo mizu   is hardly an icicle.

Jōken: "The morning sun" alludes to *Light from the Four Directions.* (*Asahi to ieru wa, "Yomo no hikari" o mitatsuru nari.*)

EAC: The lady's hardy wit belies the melting tone of her earlier poems. Actual encounters with her lover seem to have brought out this side of her personality. No doubt the manner can be traced back to roots in the *utagaki,* the sex picnics of old. In any case, it is not likely to please a lady if you liken her to an icicle, even if she does in fact have a cold.

28. Yukiyaranu   Not yet gone: he leaves
     sue no matsu o mo   snow still on the jealous pine
     e ni omoi   boughs deeply bound
     wa ga tachibana no   we too long waited to have seen
     amari mirarete   our now flowering mandarin.

Jōken: They who pillow together a single night do well to think of karma. (*Makura o tomo ni sureba, hitoyo nari to mo, en fukakarubeshi. Omoubeshi.*)

EAC: The procrustean tensions of the translation fail to convey the ineffable grace of the Japanese. There is also a possibility that the main point has been missed.

29. Yukiyaranu   Out by the stiff gate
     kadomatsu mo kare   pines, neglected, die in snow,
     shizu no ko no   and a peasant child,
     kanoko madara ni   mottled like a little fawn,
     murahada miyuru   shows skin all blains and blotches.

Jōken: My fur coat would be warm. Where did I put it? (*Kawakoromo atatakarubeshi. Izuko ni osameokikemu.*)

EAC: The poem is particularly fine, both in sentiment and phraseology. The fourth line in particular has a classic ring to it.

30. Sashimogusa   Moxibustion grass
     kogaretsutsu nomi   smoldering alone I twist
     katayori ni   my single thread;
     ito moetaemu   when the fire burns to the end,
     sue no yomogiu   I'll still have my wormwood patch.

Jōken: Moxa is good for stiff shoulders, so are massage and acupuncture. No thread, even if single, should be used with the needle.

(Katakori ni mogusa, momi, hari, izure mo yokaramu. Katayori nari to mo, ito fuyō to subeshi.)

31. Miotsukushi   The end of my rope?
      naniwa namiji no   But Naniwa, Tsukushi sound
         ukarebune   such a wave-tossed way;
      ushi to mo kitsune   in my fox-haunted forest
      komu hi morimimu   let me wake and watch for day.

Jōken: Foxes are devilish creatures; don't let them touch you. But the Dharma Boat carries all to salvation. Drifting boats are useless. (*Kitsune wa mamono nari. Sawarubekarazu. Tadashi, nori no fune ni noraba, arayuru mono kano kishi ni todokubeshi. Ukarebune wa ikade ka.*)

EAC: Princess Hitachi's finest hour.

32. Ito taete   The lines are broken,
      tanomishi suji mo   all the threads that bound us cut,
        kayowaneba   and you come no more:
      hanarejima naru   the wrecked vessel of my hopes
      kataware obune   lies stranded on a desert isle.

Jōken: You should have taken the Dharma Boat. (*Nori no fune ni norubekariki.*)

33. Haru sugite   Spring has slipped away,
      natsu kinikerashi   summer seems upon us now—
        shizuku yori   from ceaseless dripping
      yane no koborete   the roof sags, begins to spill
      ana hototogisu   through its gaps the cuckoo's song.

Jōken: Not bad. It has the good old Man'yō cadence. (*Warokaranu uta nari. Yoki inishie no Man'yō no shirabe ari.*)

EAC: From this fragmentary collection it is impossible to determine how many seasons went by in this fashion. Murasaki's account provides no assurance that her hero did other than neglect the princess for several years before his exile.

34. Shinobugusa   Climbing fern ran wild,
      haemidaretsutsu   emblem of my old longing,
        karesomete   but began to droop
      wasuregusa tsumu   then at twilight, as I plucked
      tasokaredoki ni   grasses of forgetfulness. . . .

Jōken: *Shinobu* ["longing"] and *wasure* ["forgetting"] are opposites. Two grasses should not be picked in the same poem. What is the meaning of this? (*Shinobu wasure aitagaeri. Isshu nisō to wa ikade ka. Fushigi nari.*)

EAC: This heartrending cry comes across the gulf of time unmuted. The last line of the poem deserves particular attention.

35. Matsumushi no
     oshi to serareshi
     naku koe o
     nochinochi made mo
     komewazurainu

The pining insect,
made out still to be a mute,
for long afterward
wearied as she tried in vain
to hold her stifled cries.

Jōken: The *Lotus Sutra* tells us dumbness and stammering are punishment for blasphemy. (*Oshi kotodomori to zo, Daijō soshiritaru tsumi ni mo, kazoetaru kashi.*)

EAC: The learned monk's familiarity with the best versions of the great Heian classic is evident here.

36. Omoiyare
     shika naku yama no
     yayoshigure
     iro koso miene
     shitaba momizuru

Give a thought to us—
on the deer-crying mountain
nights of chilly rain:
though the colors are not seen,
the underleaves are turning.

Jōken: *Rūpa* being *śunya*, it is not seen. (*Shiki kū nareba mienu nari.*)

EAC: One might suspect an ingenious allegory here, but its explication eludes me.

37. Tsuta kaede
     mugura yomogiu
     kuzu no ha no
     uramite kurasu
     kokoro naki kana

Vines in the maples,
creepers in the wormwood patch,
leaves of arrowroot:
peering out from under, bitter . . .
no, darkness has not touched my heart.

Jōken: "Monks are heartless/mindless, but not as numb/dumb as they look," in the words of the saintly Saigyō. (*Sō wa kokoro naki mi naru ni mo kakawarazu, aware wa shirarekeri to, Saigyō Shōnin no on'uta ni.*)

EAC: Jōken displays his admirable erudition once again. The modern reader will be more concerned with the liminality of psychotic semiosis in this poem than with questions of mere intertextuality.

38. Furi furare
     kozo no fuyu ni mo
     kasanarite
     kōreru sode ni
     yuki no uwaginu

Falling in flurries,
this year too on the wintry sleeve
left alone to freeze,
coating the old unmelted year
comes my overcloak of snow.

Jōken: I must have given it back to my sister. (*Kawagoromo o imōto ni kaeshitsuran ka.*)

EAC: This poem is in the worst *Kokinshū* style.

39. Kusagakure
     arenishi sato no
     kuzure yori
     akugareizuru
     tama yukue nashi

Hidden in the grass,
the ruined village lies fallen;
from rotted timbers
a foxfire floats out, away—
a soul with nowhere to go.

Jōken: No comment.

EAC: It is somewhat surprising that Jōken does not comment on this poem. Perhaps its redolence of the native cults made it seem inappropriate. Or perhaps he was still thinking about his fur.

40.	Yukue naku	Once the soul has flown,
	tama tobisarite	whither no one can tell you,
	naki kara wa	what remains, a shell,
	dokudami museru	is the rondure of a skull
	dokuro naruramu	grown over with deadly must.

Jōken: In the age of the End of the Law, corpses and skulls are everywhere. (*Mappō ni iritareba, izuku mo naki kara, dokuro, chirijiri sanzan miyuru nari.*)

EAC: *Dokudami* ("deadly must") is a foul-smelling perennial, *Houttuynia cordata*, whose medicinal properties seem to have escaped Jōken's attention. This poem and #39 suggest that Princess Hitachi is undergoing intermittent possession by the spirit of Ono no Komachi. It is intriguing to suppose that she suffered a concomitant delusion as to her beauty.

41.	Shigekereba	Here in my jungle
	hirune no yume mo	even dreams in broad daylight
	kasuka nite	come only faintly,
	noki no shinobu no	and I startle, yearning, chilled
	shizuku yori samu	by drops from the fern-grown eaves.

Jōken: It has been observed, and rightly so, that the world is frailer than a dream. (*Yo no naka wa yume yori hakanashi to, yoku yoku ieru koto nari. Aruiwa, kano Shikibu ga monogatari o tsukuritaru wa kono miya ni ya.*)

EAC: The reader's attention is directed to the lovely series of *s-* sounds in this poem. Middle Japanese would have had *sige-*, *sinobu*, and *sizuku* to go with *samu*. The pluvial onomatopoeia is masterful. Or is there a hint that someone is frying fish for the princess's supper?

42.	Kotogotoku	Had all my pine-trees
	matsu mo kareseba	one by one turned brown and died,
	fujinami no	where would he have seen
	naminami naranu	the waving emblem of my faith
	shirushi wa izuko	trailing its wisteria bloom?

Jōken: No comment.

EAC: The Return of the Hero. Jōken is definitely asleep at the switch, or else has abandoned the biographical interests so evident elsewhere in *Hyakureishō*.

43. Kuru toshi no
     mugura no yado o
     mimu hito ka
     nakibito kouru
     kodama nokoru to

In the coil of years,
he who looks upon this house
   all creeper-clad,
will he weep where once I yearned
for one lost, in the echoing wood?

Jōken: This is a fine poem. It well expresses Princess Hitachi's regret at leaving her birthplace, despite the decay into which it had fallen since her father's demise. Possibly she was not totally enamored of being a kept woman. (*Ito yoki uta nari. Hitachi no miya no, chichimiya nakunarinitaru yori arenitari to wa iu mono no, sasuga ni umaresodateraretaru tokoro nari tote, ima wa izuru o, yamu o ezu shite, kokoro nokorikeru o, yoku shirushiarawaseru nari. Aruiwa, hikari ni sasaremu o, yaya tameraikeru tokoro aru o ya.*)

44. Yashioginu
     mukashi somenishi
     kurenai no
     nado mata michite
     furiidetsutsu mo

To our deep dyeing
long ago eight times you came
   in Chinese crimson;
whence again must this welling
pour its drops on my narrow skirts?

Jōken: Even ink-black sleeves grow moist at such suffering. (*Sumizome no sode tote mo, mukashi no kanashimi o saguru nite nurenikeri.*)

EAC: *Kurenai* (= *kure no ai*) should mean "indigo from Kure." "Kure," the Japanese name for the ancient Chinese state of Wu, according to one school of thought derives from *kul*, the Korean word for a written character. Another theory holds that *kure*, "evening," is the source. This is likely to have been the case: the sun sets in the west, and China is west of Japan. The meaning of *ai* ("indigo") was probably altered to "crimson" in *kurenai* because of the flaming sunsets that are immortalized in the ancient Chinese hymn "The West is Red" (*Xi shi hong*). A variant of #44, however, reads *karaai*. *Karaai*, unlike *kurenai*, means "Chinese indigo" (or "Korean indigo," or "the indigo of realms beyond the sea"). To simplify matters, the princess may have intended to say that she had often experienced "blue" periods while "dyeing."

45. Natsukashiku
     aranu hana nite
     nado somemu
     nagaruru namida
     hinemosu akashi

Why should I dye them
with a flower that you find
   lacking in allure?
These my endless, streaming tears
are red the whole day through.

Jōken: Flowers are red, violets are blue. (*Hana wa akaku, sumire wa aoshi.*)

EAC: Jōken's astute, if terse, comment is best understood in the light of a passage in his *Sanshishō* (*GRR:* 176) in which he establishes that the "violets" (*sumire*) in *MYS* 8: 1424 are not violets, but young women drying their indigo garments on a streamside meadow.

46.	Karakoromo	From Chinese garments
	karakau koro mo	you tease out your foreign fun—
	ari to kiku	priceless mockery:
	sono oriori wa	may it pleats you, see my pique
	uraminu mo nashi	all underlined in fustian.

Jōken: Should I scrap this one too? (*Kore o mo kirinokubeki ka.*)

EAC: Only think with what regret the shy princess must have hidden such a gem in her lacquer box. It is plain that age and custom have not dulled her wit.

47.	Shirakete mo	Bleach them as I may,
	nao hitohana no	from the single flower still
	tada no iro	the one true color,
	asezu kosode ni	never fading, sinks deeper
	shimi koso masare	to stain the fabric of my sleeves.

Jōken: "The One Flower" is the Buddha's Way; "stains on the sleeves" are sins. Right reason seems not to run through. Perhaps an example of Zen folly? (*Hitohana to ieru wa, hotoke no michi nari. Kosode ni shimi tote wa, tsumi no koto narubeshi. Dōri no tsūzenu uta nari to omowaru. Aruiwa, Zenshū no irihoga to ka.*)

EAC: Does Jōken hint that these poems are not by the princess at all, but the doodlings of a Zen master in his off hours? I for one find that hard to accept. To me their idiom is indelibly Heian, and deeply feminine.

48.	Toshi nagaku	Over the long years
	mizu no kagami no	I have never cared to glance
	narai to ya	at water mirrors—
	koboruru kushi no	spilling tresses ere I knew
	hikata shiranami	dropped white with the drying tide.

Jōken: No comment.

EAC: If Jōken fails to comment because of offense at the Shinto solar symbol of the mirror, he is showing surprising prejudice for a Buddhist of his age, and a Man'yō scholar at that. In any case, the pathos and rhetorical finesse of the poem speak for themselves. (Of the translation, by the same token, the less said the better.)

49.	Ikue ni mo	Add on more layers
	kasanete shita ni	to my underclothes, you say,
	kinu kiyo to	keep warm at night;
	koto mutsumashiku	ah, how intimate your words,
	kokoro munashiki	but how empty is my heart!

Jōken: Garments padded with silk floss must be warm. Too bad I don't have any. I miss that fur. (*Wataire no kinu mo atatakarubeshi. Araba koso. Kawagoromo yo, koishi, natsukashi.*)

EAC: Tsurayuki would have praised the fine balance between *kokoro* and *kotoba* in this poem. It is in the best *Kokinshū* style.

50.	Awanu yo ni	On those nights alone
	ikue mo hedate	many an estranging layer
	kasanenemu	would I lie beneath,
	usuwarai seshi	who shiver on my pallet, clutching
	toko no kinuginu	the thin straw of your parting smile.

Jōken: It's already three months since I found this manuscript. This winter is the coldest we've had in years. (*On'utahogu o mitsukuru yori, haya mitsuki tateri. Fuyu no samuki wa reinen ni naki hodo nari.*)

EAC: This poem is an early example of *yōen*, the style of shimmering, illusory beauty, and is thus the forerunner of the intense lyricism of *Shinkokinshū*. Note how the *omokage* or retinal image of the absent lover hovers over the recumbent, shivering lady.

51.	Tamakazura	Garlands for her brow . . .
	hau kuzu no ha no	no, I shall not stoop to pry,
	urami seji	all pale with envy;
	arashi no mae ni	withered leaf before the storm,
	kareha fukare yo	fly wherever you are blown!

Jōken: The wilting of the garland signals the final decrepitude of the angel in the World of Desire. (*Tamakazura no shiorureba, yokukai no tennin no tsui ni otoruru shirushi to su.*)

EAC: Here we see the lady's last twinge of jealousy (hardly hinted to Murasaki's readers) and final resignation after years of luxurious neglect at Nijō. Note how she remains obsessed with botanical images.

52.	Oihatete	Aged utterly
	wasuraregusa ni	forgotten grass on the hillside
	yamai ari	brooding and unwell:
	karete mo shinobu	withered, still ferns of longing
	yado no yomogiu	stir memories of the wormwood house.

Jōken: Those who suffer from physical complaints should consult *Hyakunichisōsoroku*. This staying up all hours in winter has put an ache in my bones. I must have that young Daitoko heat the bath. (*Manbyō ni nayameru mono wa, gusō no "Hyakunichisōsoroku" o miru ga yoroshikaramu. Shikaredomo, fuyu no yo no fukuru made inishie no hito no fumidomo o yomu waza, hanahada kuruoshi. Ana, kurushi. Ano wakaki Daitoko o shite, furo o takasemu.*)

EAC: One cannot but admire the skill with which Jōken has arranged these fifty-two poems, beginning with "song" and ending with "wormwood patch." Perhaps one may also be forgiven for preferring them, give or take a few, as the authentic voice of the "hidden flower" of old Heian, to the work of such other notable practitioners of the *waka* form as O. Komachi and I. Shikibu. At the very least, surely *Genji monogatari*, great and compendious *speculum amantis* though it is, shows nothing quite like them.

Apparently Jōken did not attach a colophon to *Wasabigaki*; at least, none is to be found in the text in *GRR*. The circumstances of the discovery and copying seem to be adequately dealt with in the *kanbun* preface. However, the document is followed by a note, in what must have been another hand, to the effect that Jōken was bedridden for several weeks in the early spring of 1361 with what looks to have been an attack of acute bronchitis, no doubt brought on by his nocturnal labors. It was accompanied by bouts of explosive coughing that caused him to levitate off the floor, "*sugyōza no tobu yō nite.*"

A final note: Could the number of poems selected by Jōken for *Wasabigaki* be taken as a cryptic hint as to his calculation of Princess Hitachi's age when she finally cut her "spilling tresses" and left the world? I must leave this intriguing problem for the young generation of *Genji* scholars to ponder.

NOTES

1. *Hyakureishō*, in *Gunshū ranjō ruijū*, ed. Kanawa Chūrō, 63 vols. (Tokyo: Saitei Shoseki Kabushiki Kaisha, 1932) [hereafter *GRR*], 19: 317. This volume also contains other extant works by Jōken. Parenthetical references are to this edition, specifying page but omitting volume number.
2. The *kanbun* preface, frankly beyond my competence, has been left to challenge some future specialist.

The Case of the Plagiaristic Journal: A Curious Passage from Jōjin's Diary

ROBERT BORGEN

A Japanese sinologist, discussing the increasing popularity of tea during the Song dynasty (960–1279), notes that it was even cultivated at Buddhist monasteries. Another Japanese scholar, a prolific specialist in Japanese cultural history, writes of the introduction of tea to Japan. He describes how a Japanese monk went to China in 1072 and found "a forest of tea trees" growing there at the holy mountain where his sect had been founded. Both of these scholars cite the same source: the diary kept by that Japanese monk during his travels. It offers a vivid description, and, coming from a firsthand observer, it certainly seems to be an authentic account. We assume the diary to be truthful, in part because our common sense tells us that, even though diaries may be partial and subjective, at least they ought to be reliable in such impersonal matters as tea cultivation. Moreover, even the most secular of us would probably assume a devout monk to be reasonably trustworthy when discussing this doctrinally neutral matter. In short, most readers are unlikely to question a description of vegetation that appears in a diary.

Perhaps we exaggerate the artlessness of diaries. One American authority, Donald J. Winslow, defines a diary simply as "a daily record of matters affecting the writer personally, or which come under his personal observation."[1] Students of Heian literature, however, will recognize that diaries must be treated more critically. They may constitute a major genre of Heian literature, but they rarely meet the criteria offered by Winslow. The only familiar example that takes the form of a daily record—*Tosa nikki* (The Tosa Diary)—is, in fact, highly fictionalized: its author, a man, invented the character of a woman to serve as his imaginary diarist. And, although the story no doubt is loosely based on its true author's experiences, many of its incidents certainly seem to be made up. It is a good story masquerading as a diary.

Other important "diaries," such as *Kagerō nikki* (The Gossamer Years), include long sections of personal memoirs that seem more autobiographical than diary-like. Then again, some autobiographical works that resemble these "diaries" are labeled "anthologies" (*shū*), for example, *Kenreimon'in Ukyō no Daibu shū* (The Poetic Memoirs of Lady Daibu). The categories are sufficiently confused that a single work can have alternate labels. What we usually call *The Diary of Izumi Shikibu* (*Izumi Shikibu nikki*) is, in most of its manuscripts, known as *The Tale of Izumi Shikibu* (*Izumi Shikibu monogatari*). And indeed, a tale is what it seems to be, as it is written in the third person and follows the ritualized patterns of courtly love as established in poetic anthologies.[2] These highly diverse texts perhaps have only two things in common: first, since their content is determined by literary convention as well as by actual events, the reader can presume a certain degree of fictionalizing in all of them; and second, they are written in classical Japanese.

The "diaries" discussed so far have been literary diaries. The Heian period also produced many not-so-literary diaries written in Chinese, or at least something that looks remarkably similar to Chinese, the writing system that is often known as *kanbun*, although that term also refers to true Chinese. These texts differ from their literary cousins not only in language but also in content, for generally they do fit the definition offered by Winslow. They are daily records of events that their authors experienced directly or learned of indirectly. In them, one can find some very personal comments. In his *kanbun* diary, for example, Emperor Uda (867–931, r. 887–97) reported both a bout of impotence and the name of the drug that cured it. *Shōyūki* is quite opinionated, for its author, Fujiwara Sanesuke (957–1046), was an unsuccessful rival to the great politician Fujiwara Michinaga (966–1027), whose portrayal in the diary is unflattering. It records, for example, Michinaga's boastful poem:

Kono yo o ba	This world, I think,
waga yo to zo omou	is indeed my own,
mochizuki no	when I think that,
kaketaru koto mo	like the full moon,
nashi to omoeba	it lacks nothing.

In the diary, this Japanese poem is written out in Chinese characters with just enough Japanese script used to make it intelligible. Sanesuke notes sarcastically that no one was able to produce a suitable poem to answer this bit of pomposity, as Michinaga had requested, and so the assembled courtiers simply repeated Michinaga's "masterpiece."[3]

Colorful passages such as these, unfortunately, are the exception in *kanbun* diaries. More typically, they offer unadorned accounts of daily events. The very absence of obviously literary flourishes makes us believe that they are reliable. Historians such as our sinologist and tea enthusiast consult them regularly, and students of literature too may read them as sources of background information, but it is a rare scholar who showers on them the loving attention that the greatest of the literary diaries commonly receive. They are regarded as valuable sources of information, not texts to be studied and admired for their intrinsic literary merits.

In violation of the general rule, this paper will closely examine a few entries from one of these *kanbun* diaries and suggest that they are less "accurate" and more "literary" than they seem. The diary in question comes from a specialized sub-genre, the *kanbun* travel diary, that is distinctive in subject matter but not in style. It is *San Tendai Godai san ki*, literally, "The Record of a Pilgrimage to the Tiantai and Wutai Mountains," the account by the Tendai monk Jōjin (1011–81) of his pilgrimage to China accompanied by seven disciples.[4] It covers a period of approximately sixteen months in the years 1072–73. These were eventful months. After crossing the sea to China, Jōjin arrived at Hangzhou and made a pilgrimage to the nearby Tiantai Mountains, where his sect had been founded. Then he went to the Song capital of Kaifeng, where he had an audience with the emperor, observed the imperially sponsored sutra translation project, and successfully prayed for rain to end a drought. He also made a pilgrimage to the Wutai Mountains, where he witnessed a miracle: a manifestation of the bodhisattva Mañjuśrī. Finally, Jōjin and his party returned to the region where they had originally landed. There, five of Jōjin's disciples boarded a ship and returned to Japan, carrying with them the manuscript of Jōjin's diary. Jōjin himself remained in China and eventually was buried there.

The diary is a precious document. It is more detailed than Ennin's diary describing a similar pilgrimage over two centuries earlier and made familiar through the work of Edwin Reischauer.[5] To those interested in Japan, it offers a firsthand account of how Sino-Japanese relations were conducted in a day when Japan is sometimes said to have isolated itself from Chinese influences. Jōjin demonstrates this view to be an oversimplification at best. For sinologists, the diary is a treasure trove of information on diverse topics, ranging from religion and art to court ritual and bureaucratic practice. Its description of Song transportation systems is particularly detailed. And it makes frequent references to tea drinking, which is why tea enthusiasts value it. It is, in fact, the diary quoted to show that tea was cultivated at the Tiantai Mountains during the Song dynasty. Coincidentally, this description of tea cultivation occurs in one of the entries to be examined more closely. These will be the passages recounting Jōjin's arrival at the Tiantai Mountains and exploration of the monasteries there on the thirteenth, fourteenth, and eighteenth days of the Fifth Lunar Month in 1072. A full translation of these entries is appended to this essay. The three days omitted were uneventful and have only brief entries of little interest.

In general, the diary's tone is matter-of-fact. Most entries are brief and unadorned statements of the events that took place on a given day. Occasionally, however, Jōjin will offer fuller descriptions of noteworthy places or events. For example, as a Buddhist monk, he is inclined to record the appearance of great monasteries in minute detail. Simple curiosity results in an equally careful description of a camel. Other things that impressed him range from the marketplace at Hangzhou to his audience with the emperor. Some of the more spectacular sights were, he noted, beyond his powers of description. And, although most of his narrative seems objective and unemotional, Jōjin was often moved to tears, usually by sights of religious significance—relics of Buddhist patriarchs, for example—or occasionally by objects that stirred thoughts of home, such as portraits of previous Japanese pilgrims and letters from Japan.

The laconic declarative sentences that predominate in the diary make the detailed entries—usually written in equally simple declarative sentences—seem vivid by comparison. Consider, for example, the entry for the thirteenth day of the Fifth Month. It begins in typical fashion:

> Clear skies. At the hour of the rabbit [6:00 A.M.] we left our lodgings. After continuing for five li, we rested at the home of Min Shisan in Yongbao township. Next, continuing for five li, we reached Feiquangou and rested. Next we continued five li until we reached the home of Chen Qishu, where we rested and everyone drank tea. Although we offered money, the head of the household refused to accept it.

This is what most of Jōjin's entries have to offer on days when he was traveling: distances covered between obscure places. In this case, the recitation of distances and place-names is enlivened by the fact that his host declined payment for tea. Still, the only readers likely to be interested in such a passage would be Heian monks who wished to follow in Jōjin's footsteps—and they were probably his intended audience—or modern historical geographers.

The day that began so routinely, however, turned out to be an auspicious one, for that afternoon Jōjin arrived at Guoqingsi, the principal monastery in the Tiantai Mountains and one of the main objects of Jōjin's pilgrimage. The tone of Jōjin's writing changes abruptly:

> We traveled five li through the mountains until, at the first quarter of the hour of the sheep [1:30 P.M.], we reached the Great Gate of Guoqingsi. At last I saw the bridges and halls! Around the monastery aged pines flourished profusely. For ten li, gem trees glistened along the sides of the path. The five peaks enveloped the monastery, and the two valley streams flowed together. This is truly one of the four wonders!

This passage goes well beyond the usual examples of Jōjin's more detailed accounts that merely increase the number of facts recorded. The translation does not do justice to the poetic quality of his description of the scenery around the monastery, for the original is written in neatly balanced four-character phrases employing terms far more elegant than Jōjin's ordinarily colorless vocabulary. Having waxed poetic, Jōjin soon turns maudlin. When he visits a hall dedicated to the patriarchs of his sect and filled with statues of them, he exclaims: "Overwhelmed, I could not hold back my tears. Now I saw what in the past I had only heard of. It matched reports precisely!"

In part, Jōjin's sudden burst of rhetorical flourish and emotion can be explained by circumstance. Even today, the scene as one approaches the monastery is roughly as Jōjin described it. And we are not surprised that he was moved to tears upon seeing images of the patriarchs at the holy mountain where his sect was founded. After all, for twelve years he had been praying for the opportunity to make this pilgrimage.

The problem is that, although the scene may have been real and the tears may have been Jōjin's, many of the words he uses to describe them—the ones underlined in the translations—are borrowed. The description of the trees and brooks, the phrase about at last seeing what previously he had only heard of, both of these passages are taken verbatim from the writings of the monk Enchin (814–91).

More than two centuries earlier, in 853, Enchin had made a pilgrimage to China. After his return, his disciples and in turn their followers and their followers' followers—including, eventually, Jōjin—came to form a faction that contended for power with monks in Ennin's lineage within the divided Tendai sect. Enchin too had kept a diary. Unfortunately it survives only in a highly abbreviated version, but a memorial to the Japanese court in which he describes his journey to China has been preserved. The phrases Jōjin borrows appear in it. Jōjin, however, was not quoting directly from the memorial, for the same material was also used in an early biography of Enchin, and at one point Jōjin specifically cites the biography as the source of a brief quotation. Presumably it was the source for all his borrowings from Enchin, since he does not seem to have brought with him a copy of either Enchin's diary or the memorial.[6] Jōjin knew he was using Enchin's own words, for in another place, he correctly attributes a quote found in the biography to Enchin himself. His treatment of another source, *Tiantai shan ji*, an important early ninth-century Chinese account of the Tiantai Mountains, is similar: he cites it only once but borrows two additional passages from it.[7] In other words, he reveals the identity of his sources but not the degree to which he has relied on them.

The appended translation reveals the extent of Jōjin's borrowings. Were Jōjin a modern author writing for publication, we would surely find him guilty of plagiarism. He was, however, a devout monk and not a thief, literary or otherwise. In part, he may be offering us the literary equivalent of a familiar phenomenon: the tourist sees what is expected rather than what is there. His writing reflects a vision highly colored by extensive reading.

That alone, however, does not fully explain Jōjin's technique of composition. We must recognize that he was working within literary traditions that did not seek the same sort of originality we do today. Looking at roughly contemporary Japanese prose, one finds large sections of Murasaki Shikibu's diary expropriated by the author of *Eiga monogatari* (A Tale of Flowering Fortunes). Poets were already employing the technique of allusive variation (*honkadori*) in which layers of meaning were added to new poems by incorporating into them language from familiar ancient works. In Chinese literature, too, using the language of the masters in one's own writings was common practice, and certainly Japanese did this extensively when they wrote in Chinese.[8] For Jōjin, borrowing language was an accepted practice that served legitimate functions. The function varied with the form of the borrowing, acknowledged or unacknowledged. Even the unacknowledged borrowings, however, should be treated as a form of allusion, not plagiarism. Although we may thus summarily dismiss the charge of verbal theft, the implications of Jōjin's borrowings pose an interesting question.

Most of the diary's quoted passages are clearly labeled as such. In the section under consideration, Jōjin identifies and transcribes for us texts ranging from roadside distance markers to an ode hymning the praises of Tiantai. The ode not only makes good reading, it also reminds us that Tiantai was indeed a holy place, worthy of the effort required to visit it. All citations of this sort, even the road signs, lend an air of authenticity to the text. Somewhat like modern tourists' snapshots, regardless of their artistic merit, they help verify that the traveler has actually been there. In a different vein, Jōjin also quotes himself. Apparently, he kept a record of his dreams—a rather specialized sort of diary—and one of the sights at Tiantai recalled for him a dream of eleven years earlier that he noted down. He reproduces his account of it for us.[9] The dream, it turns out, suggests that his successful pilgrimage was a reward for his religious merit. We may find this immodest, but Jōjin probably regarded it as an affirmation of the significance of his journey.

In addition to these acknowledged quotations, the skeptical reader will suspect that, when Jōjin recounts the history of a monastery, for example, he occasionally lifts material from other written sources, even though the sources remain unknown and the final version ends up in Jōjin's typically laconic style. In the translation that follows, his summary of the history of Guoqingsi—replete with precise names and dates accurately recorded—almost certainly was copied from a written source, but one that remains unidentified. If we cannot locate the source, we can at least surmise that it was written during the Tang dynasty (618–907). Customarily the honorific "great" was applied only to the current dynasty, and so, since Jōjin's account speaks first of the "Sui" (581–618) and then of the "Great Tang," with no mention of later periods, evidently he was copying from a text written during the Tang.

Jōjin also offers a version of the life of the semilegendary poet Hanshan, including a poem by Hanshan's purported mentor, Fenggan. This material is significant because, although most of the phrases Jōjin uses come from familiar Chinese accounts, his arrangement of them is unique. Possibly he copied them from a source that is no longer extant, and thus may offer us valuable material for the study of the Hanshan legend.[10] But, precious though this passage may be, as a writing technique it is simply another example of presumed copying from an unidentified source. Like the acknowledged quotations, this type of borrowing is hardly remarkable. When noting down facts (or at least what Jōjin regarded as facts, such as the story of Hanshan), copying them faithfully, as Jōjin probably did, is preferable to attempting to improve upon them. In effect, Jōjin was taking useful background material directly from reliable sources.

Neither of the two types of borrowings discussed so far violates our sense of what a diary ought to be. If Jōjin happened upon an interesting text, his copying it into the diary seems perfectly reasonable.

Similarly, a traveler cannot observe historical background directly. It has to come from another source, and Jōjin's literary tradition did not demand that he rewrite such material to put it in his own words or provide a footnote. The third type of borrowing that appears in the Tiantai entries, however, is more problematic and, unlike the first two, can be identified later in the diary only once: near the end of his stay in Kaifeng, when Jōjin requests permission to return to Tiantai, he re-recycles Enchin's poetic description of the approach to Guoqingsi.[11] Only in the passages under review (or a reiteration of them) does Jōjin employ the technique of adopting the words of another to narrate what would seem to be his own personal experiences. In some places, he is borrowing elegant language to make his description of the setting—the scenery and the monasteries—more vivid, more poetic. But also, in the one extreme case quoted above, he uses someone else's thoughts to explain why he was moved to tears. Thus, Jōjin's arrival at Tiantai results in a few days of distinctive entries in his diary, passages that conflict with our notion of what a diary ought to be by using someone else's words to describe what would appear to be his own experiences, observations, and even feelings.

The borrowing of poetic language begins with Jōjin's first view of Guoqingsi in one of the passages quoted above. The writing here is doubly allusive: Jōjin was using the words of Enchin (as quoted in the biography), who in turn was alluding to an even earlier account of the Tiantai Mountains, *You Tiantai shan fu* (A Poetic Essay on a Visit to the Tiantai Mountains) by the Taoist Sun Chuo (314–97), the source of the four rather obscure characters translated as "the gem trees glistened."[12] Enchin's allusion would have been familiar to an educated Japanese, for the original poetic essay appears in *Wen xuan* (Literary Selections), one of the principal Chinese anthologies studied in early Japan. These characters had come to be associated with Tiantai and can be found in various writings about the mountains there. Jōjin thus begins his account by placing himself squarely in the orthodox traditions of pilgrimage to Tiantai and of conventional literary description of the mountains.

Somewhat later—about eighteen sentences in the original, depending on how it is punctuated—we come to the passage in which Jōjin uses Enchin's words to explain his tears. Here, he gives us Enchin's description of the statue of the sect's founder, a few of his own words, and then some more of Enchin. In the original biography, the passage describing the gem trees appears directly before that describing the image of the patriarch that moved him to tears. Only a phrase describing a spring that Jōjin would not see until the next day is omitted. In other words, Jōjin took a single passage from Enchin, divided it into four shorter ones, rejected an irrelevant one, and worked the other three into his own narrative at appropriate places. The first quotation, with its flowery language, stands out from its otherwise prosaic setting and thus serves as an effective introduction to the diary's distinctive Tiantai entries. The other two phrases fit perfectly Jōjin's usual style. Had the first quotation not sent us to Enchin, we would assume that the other two were Jōjin's own words.

On his second day at Tiantai, Jōjin tells us the story of Hanshan and, toward the end of his entry, cites two of his sources—first *Tiantai shan ji* and then the biography of Enchin—and gives quotations from each of them. After three uneventful days, Jōjin devotes a day to sightseeing in the mountains behind Guoqingsi. Once again, many of the sights are described in a mixture of Enchin's and his own words, with material from *Tiantai shan ji* used to describe the Stone Bridge, one of the scenic wonders of Tiantai. *Tiantai shan ji* is a doubly appropriate source, for it is not only a classic account of Tiantai, it is also a text that Enchin had introduced to Japan. As before, the borrowing is not strictly mechanical. Although most of the material from Enchin is still in its original order, it is broken up into units that alternate with Jōjin's own writing. Where a monastery's name has changed in the intervening centuries, Jōjin updates a passage otherwise identical with Enchin's original. This similarity of language allows us to "correct" Jōjin's perplexing description of a rock formation known as the "Stone Elephant." Jōjin's diary claims that it was so named "because its appearance does not resemble that of a real elephant." One character is different in Enchin's version, which says, "Its appearance is no different from that of a real elephant," and is obviously the "correct" version. Either Jōjin or a later copyist of his diary changed the character. If it was indeed Jōjin himself, we are further warned of the danger in assuming his diary to be an accurate description of his experiences. In this instance, he may be offering us nothing more than a botched attempt at copying what someone else wrote.

Jōjin's borrowing, in particular his abrupt stylistic shift to elevated, allusive writing, produces several effects. Most obviously, it lets the reader know that something important has happened. Jōjin was also impressed by the imperial palace and the Wutai Mountains, both of which he would subsequently visit. Neither, however, resulted in such lofty prose as he used—or rather borrowed—at Tiantai. Clearly, Tiantai was special, even though among holy mountains Wutai was perhaps even more important. Tiantai was unique both because Jōjin's sect had been founded there, and because it was the holy mountain visited by the head of his lineage within the sect. Enchin, whose words he copied, never got as far as Wutai. That was the Buddhist center visited by Ennin, founder of the rival faction. Enchin's itinerary simultaneously made Tiantai all the more important to Jōjin and also, coincidentally, deprived him of a good source of flowery phrases to describe other sights.

The tone of Jōjin's writing not only tells us that Tiantai was particularly important to him, his use of Enchin's language helps legitimate Jōjin's own status as a member of the small but esteemed fraternity of monks who had made the pilgrimage to China. Throughout his diary, Jōjin refers to earlier Japanese pilgrims to China. Along with the biography of Enchin, he carried with him the travel diaries of Ennin and Chōnen (d. 1016), a Shingon monk who had visited China in 983–86. Since Chōnen's diary is now lost, we cannot say whether Jōjin borrowed from it, but he does refer to Ennin's once when, during his voyage to China, he sees a bird similar to one Ennin had mentioned. In China, Jōjin made a point of visiting monasteries where Japanese monks had resided and recording information about their experiences in China. At Tiantai, he was moved to tears when shown the portrait of an earlier Japanese pilgrim, and he had the precise answers when an official asked when two other Japanese monks had come. Rather than suggest that his own trip is unique, he thus placed himself securely within an ongoing tradition of Japanese pilgrimage to China.

Since Enchin was especially important to him among these travelers, Jōjin's use of Enchin's words at a key point in the journey does more than simply establish his ties with the founder of his lineage. It also honors Enchin. If no other place was as sacred to him as Tiantai, no other source was as treasured as Enchin's writings. His use of Enchin's language, as noted, lent a poetic quality to his text. Perhaps it might be compared to allusive variation, the technique used in Japanese poetry when a poet adopted some of the language of an earlier poem and, more importantly, elaborated on its meaning. That technique is possible only because it can presume a corpus of familiar poems. Here, familiarity breeds esteem, for allusive variation calls respectful attention to the old poem. Jōjin in fact wrote poems in Japanese; six survive. He must have been familiar with allusive variation. Although his borrowings from Enchin may lack much of the subtle complexity of that technique, they do have the same side effect of calling our attention to Enchin's writings and telling us that his words merited emulation, as did his deeds. Using his language was one way Jōjin acknowledged his spiritual debt to Enchin.

One remaining problem is why Jōjin did not use this technique elsewhere when he witnessed impressive sights. This question cannot be answered conclusively, but various explanations are possible. In the case of Wutai, although Enchin may not have gone there, Jōjin could have turned to other sources for materials to borrow, texts such as Ennin's diary. Perhaps, however, he chose to call less attention to the mountain associated with an opposition patriarch. But the brevity of his stay there was probably a more significant consideration. A busy three days at Wutai in the dead of winter may not have allowed the opportunity for attempts at elegant composition. In Kaifeng, however, he had ample time. He was there for five months and described the imperial palace and various great monasteries. His account is detailed, but hardly poetic.

This suggests another possible reason: without convenient models to imitate, perhaps Jōjin lacked the literary skills necessary to produce anything more elegant than his usual prosaic narrative. In his diary, he notes that, as a form of religious abstention, he had renounced poetry. Enchin, he explains, had come to regret having wasted time on the frivolity of writing verse. Presumably this refers to poetry in Chinese, since, as noted, Jōjin did write poetry in Japanese. The cynic, after reading Jōjin's diary, may speculate that he avoided composing Chinese poetry not for religious reasons but simply because he was no poet. For Jōjin, elegant composition may have required great effort that only sufficient inspiration could motivate. His arrival at Tiantai was indeed inspiring, but he gradually came down with a mild case of sensory overload. What at first had been profoundly inspirational eventually became merely very impressive. Just as modern tourists during their first few days abroad may photograph everything they see, only to leave their cameras packed away toward the end of their trip, so Jōjin could have become gradually satiated with wonders and chosen to describe them less elaborately. The fact that he continued to make daily entries throughout the period covered by the diary may be more remarkable than his dropping the use of flowery language. He did better than Ennin, who must have suffered from the same problem and, in the later portions of his diary, made only sporadic—albeit sometimes quite lengthy—entries.

In treating Jōjin's borrowings as allusions, we thereby acknowledge that he employed a literary technique in his diary, an otherwise prosaic, matter-of-fact specimen from a generally prosaic, matter-of-fact genre. By alluding to more polished, self-consciously literary works, Jōjin is cautioning us that even his generally unadorned and apparently hastily written collection of daily entries cannot be read simply as a record of "matters affecting the writer personally," to repeat our American definition of a diary. Jōjin was writing for an audience: he had his diary sent home to Japan, presumably to serve as an incentive and practical reference that subsequent pilgrims might carry to China as he had taken Ennin's and Chōnen's diaries. In fact, in 1082 another Japanese monk, inspired by Jōjin, made a similar pilgrimage.[13] Jōjin's intended readers would have recognized his allusions easily, for they came from the works a monk planning a pilgrimage to China would have studied just as Jōjin did.

The problem is that modern readers, less familiar with Enchin and Heian writing techniques, may easily overlook the significance of Jōjin's literary flourishes and mistakenly assume that Jōjin is simply describing what he saw. In fact, what he writes is based in part on what he observed, and in part on what he read. Ignoring this fact puts our modern Japanese scholars on shaky ground when they cite Jōjin to prove that tea was grown at Tiantai in the Song dynasty, for the passage they refer to is one of those taken verbatim from Enchin, who had been there more than two centuries earlier. Tea was probably still cultivated there in Jōjin's time, as it is even today, but his diary is not the best possible source to prove the point. Historians must read at least this passage with the same caution they would bring to a more obviously literary diary.

INTRODUCTION TO THE TRANSLATION

The following is a translation of three entries from the first fascicle of Jōjin's *San Tendai Godai san ki* (The Record of a Pilgrimage to the Tiantai and Wutai Mountains). They recount his activities on the thirteenth, fourteenth, and eighteenth days of the Fifth Lunar Month in 1072. I have attempted to minimize notes. Although most of the places, historical figures, buddhas, and other proper nouns mentioned can be identified, I have provided notes only on the most essential. Also, I have been flexible in treating proper nouns in the text: those that go into English well have been translated ("Great Buddha Hall" instead of "Dafodang"), whereas those that would merely sound exotic have been transliterated ("Guoqingsi" rather than "Monastery of National Purity"). Buddhist terms that cannot be translated—proper nouns, for example—have been put into their original Sanskrit pronunciations, which may sound unfamiliar to those of us who are not buddhologists, but offer the only reasonable solution to the problem of choosing between Chinese and Japanese versions. Chinese governmental terminology is translated following Charles O. Hucker, *A Dictionary of Official Titles in Imperial China* (Stanford: Stanford University Press, 1985).

In Jōjin's day, distances were measured in li, a unit defined as 360 paces and equal to roughly 1,890 feet. Days were divided into twelve units, each approximately two hours long and identified by an animal in the Chinese zodiac. "The hour of the rabbit" is in fact the period in the middle of which the sun rose, but for the sake of simplicity, I have identified it as 6:00 A.M. The equivalents given for other "hours" are similarly approximate. All quoted material, acknowledged or otherwise, is underlined, with the sources indicated in brackets for the unacknowledged quotations. "Enchin" refers to Enchin's biography, and "*Tiantai*" to *Tiantai shan ji*. The precise source for the material here attributed to "Hanshan" is problematic, as discussed in the preceding essay.

EXCERPTS FROM *THE RECORD OF A PILGRIMAGE TO THE TIANTAI AND WUTAI MOUNTAINS*

Thirteenth Day:

Clear skies. At the hour of the rabbit [6:00 A.M.] we left our lodgings. After continuing for five li, we rested at the home of Min Shisan in Yongbao township. Next, continuing for five li, we reached Feiquangou and rested. Next we continued five li until we reached the home of Chen Qishu, where we rested and everyone drank tea. Although we offered money, the head of the household refused to accept it. Next we continued three li until we reached Jingfu Cloister, where we rested. We worshiped the eight-foot image of Śākyamuni in the Golden Hall. Shinken[14] selected two texts from among the old sutras: *The Curing Hemorrhoids Sutra* and *The Eight Brilliant Kṣitigarbhas and Ten Kings Sutra*. Next, continuing two li we reached Xuanjia Bridge and rested. A marker stated "Twenty Li to Tiantai District; Twenty Li from Guanling." Next, continuing five li, we saw a stone pagoda about fifty feet high named Hefangyang Pagoda.

Next, continuing five li, at the hour of the horse [noon], we saw Mount Chicheng. Atop the mountain is a pagoda. From afar we worshiped the spot where Great Master Zhizhe [538–97] passed away.[15] Seeing it for the first time, I was so deeply moved that I could hardly control my tears. Next, continuing five li, at the hour of the sheep [2:00 P.M.], we reached the Qing household and rested. Palace Monk Raien[16] provided 158 cash so the thirteen bearers could drink some wine. A marker stated "Taiping Township: to the East, Guoqingsi, Ten Li; Jing District, Five Li."[17] The head of the household, a religious man, offered us tea to drink. For a while we gazed at the south face of Mount Chicheng [Red Wall], which looked just like a wall made of red stone.

Next, continuing five li, we entered the mountains of Guoqingsi, where we saw a five-story stone pagoda fifty feet high. We traveled five li through the mountains until, at the first quarter of the hour of the sheep [1:30 P.M.], we reached the Great Gate of Guoqingsi. At last I saw the bridges and halls! Around the monastery aged pines flourished profusely. For ten li gem trees glistened along the sides of the path. The five peaks enveloped the monastery, and the two valley streams flowed together. This is truly one of the four wonders! [Enchin]

A large group of monks—several tens of them—came out to welcome us. They were headed by the abbot, Recipient of the Purple Robe Zhongfang; the assistant abbot, Recipient of the Purple Robe Lixuan; and the director, Recipient of the Purple Robe Zhongwen. Then we entered together through the Great Gate, sat in chairs, and drank some tea. Next we all went to the quarters where we were to be lodged. The Chinese monks spent considerable time greeting us kindly, just as if we were old friends. Again we drank tea. The Great Master who served as abbot took out a Chinese calendar to determine whether or not the day was auspicious. Since today was indeed auspicious, we then went to burn incense in the various halls.

First we went to the Imperial Arhat Cloister. In it were life-size wooden statues of the sixteen arhats and three-foot statues of the five hundred arhats.[18] In front of each was a tea vessel. Led by the abbot, each of us in turn burned incense and worshiped. I was so moved that my tears were beyond restraint. Next we entered the refectory, worshiped Qilangtian,[19] and burned incense. I cannot adequately describe the refectory's manner of construction. It was amazing. Next we went to the Great Master Hall. Its inscription said "Great Master Zhenjue Fagong Cloister." A true representation of Zhizhe was seated on the meditation platform. [Enchin] A statue of Dingguang was seated on the Treasure Pedestal. Lining three sides were seated statues of the Great Masters of the Tiantai sect. I burned incense and worshiped. Overwhelmed, I could not hold back my tears. Now I saw what in the past I had only heard of. It matched reports precisely! [Enchin] Next we went to the Great Buddha Hall which contained a sixteen-foot golden statue of Śākyamuni and, seated to its left and right respectively, sixteen-foot statues of Amitābha and Maitreya. I burned incense and worshiped. Next I went to the Ordination Platform Cloister. Its marvelous decoration was beyond description. I burned incense and worshiped. On a later day, I will visit the various other cloisters to burn incense and worship.

Guoqingsi was founded during the Sui dynasty [581–618] in the eighteenth year of the Kaihuang era [598], on the twenty-ninth day of the First Month when the emperor dispatched Adjutant Wang Hong there in response to the last request of Great Master Zhizhe. In the Great Tang dynasty [618–907], during the reign of Emperor Wuzong [841–47], the monastery was abolished in the fifth year of the Huichang era [845], in the Third Month. Subsequently, during the reign of Emperor Xuanzong [846–59], in the fifth year of Dazhong [851], it was rebuilt in accordance with an imperial decree. Altogether it has eight hundred major buildings of various types. The monastery is ten li north of the Tiantai district capital.

Next we returned to our quarters and rested. At the hour of the monkey [4:00 P.M.], the abbot provided a splendid banquet. The dining table was wonderfully decorated. At the seven hours I performed the rites and, in addition, I recited six chapters of the sutra while riding in the palanquin.[20] At the hour of the rooster [6:00 P.M.], I went to the Bath Cloister and washed. The water is said to be heated daily.

Fourteenth Day:
At the hour of the dragon [8:00 A.M.], the abbot came, sat down, and greeted me. I presented him with a rosary made of soapberry seeds and ornamented with glass. All the other monks also came to greet us and check the official document appointing me *ācārya*.[21] At the second quarter of the hour of the snake [9:30 A.M.], a meal was served in the abbot's quarters. Seven of us Japanese monks went together; the postulant alone stayed behind. The Great Master Zhizhe Repentance Hall serves as the abbot's cloister. It is known as the Site of the Teachings Cloister. First we entered the Zhizhe Repentance Hall and worshiped several tens of statues that the Great Master had personally venerated: a three-foot Śākyamuni, an Amitābha, an Avalokiteśvara, and so forth. Next we worshiped and viewed the Great Master's own sutra, fascicle seven of *The Lotus Sutra* in his own hand, with a colophon containing the date and his name, also in his own hand. I was so moved that my tears were difficult to restrain. All the other fascicles, I was told, had been destroyed by fire. Behind the buddhas were hung paintings of the Great Master, the sixteen arhats, and the Priest of Sizhou.[22] Next we reached our dining place. Its decoration was marvelous. The assistant abbot and director ate with us.

At the hour of the horse [noon], we went to worship at the Three Worthies Cloister. The three worthies are the meditation master Fenggan, the bodhisattva Shide, and the bodhisattva Hanshan, who are manifestations of Amitābha, Samantabhadra, and Mañjuśrī. The meditation master is beside a tiger; the other two great beings are in lay costume. During the Zhenguan era [627–50] of Taizong's reign in the Tang dynasty, the three worthies appeared at Guoqingsi. First, the meditation master Fenggan resided in a hut at the northwest corner of the monastery's Great Storehouse. Then, one day as he was strolling on a path through the pines, he saw a child about ten years old crying beside the Chicheng Road. When Fenggan asked, the child said he had neither home nor surname. The master led him back to the monastery warehouse and raised him. He was called Shide [i.e., picked up and obtained]. Later there was another sage who came from Hanyan [Cold Crag] and so came to be known as Hanshanzi [The Cold Mountain Gentleman].

   In the seventeenth year of Zhenguan [643], the Grand Master for Court Discussion, Envoy, General Commander and Acting Prefect of Taizhou, Supreme Pillar of the State, and Recipient of the Scarlet Robe and Fish-Seal Sack, Lüqiu Yin, said to the meditation master Fenggan, "I am not yet familiar with Tiantai. What worthies reside here whom I can revere as teachers?" The Master replied, "See them and you will not know; know them and you will not see. If you wish to see them, ignore their appearance and then you will see them. Hanshan is Mañjuśrī who has fled the world to Guoqingsi, and Shide is Samantabhadra dressed as a pauper." The prefect finally reached Guoqingsi, where in the kitchen, before the hearth, he saw two men facing the fire and laughing boisterously. The prefect bowed to them. In unison, the two men yelled at the prefect. They took each other's hand, laughed loudly and shouted, "Fenggan talks too much, the blabbermouth Amitābha! We don't know why you bow to us!" [alternate translation: You didn't recognize Amitābha. Why bow to us?] The two left the monastery hand in hand, ran off, and did not return to the monastery. The prefect then went to the meditation master Fenggan's cloister and opened the chamber, but all he saw were the footprints of a tiger. Then he asked the monk Shide Daojiao, "On days when the Meditation Master is present, what religious practices does he engage in?" The monk replied, "On days when Fenggan is present, his only merit is hulling rice to make offerings. At night he sings songs and enjoys himself."

   The following is a poem by Fenggan:

> Since I came to Tiantai
> I have experienced several myriad turns.
> A single body like the clouds and waters,
> Calmly, it comes and goes at will. [Hanshan]

Details can be found in the biographical records. Hanshan is seventy li west of Tiantai district and is also called "Hanyan." Shide Rock is one *chō*[23] east of the Great Gate of Guoqingsi through a pine forest.

Next I worshiped at a well that the Meditation Master Puming made with his staff. Known as Puming Fountain, it is in the northwest corner of Great General of the Desert Hall,[24] which is located at the northeast corner of the Great Buddha Hall. I burned incense. Next I worshiped Meditation Master Fenggan at the Daily Abstinence Hall, within which were several small statues of buddhas. In each of the two rear corners were wooden statues of the Three Worthies. I burned incense as an offering.

Next I worshiped the Senior Immortal who is Master of the Land, King of the Mountain, and Chief Minister. The Senior Immortal is Wang Zijin, son of King Ling [r. 572–45 B.C.] of the Zhou dynasty [1122?–256 B.C.]. The monastery is the site of the prince's residence. He became an immortal and, after hundreds of years, had an audience with Zhizhe, took vows, and entrusted this land to him. He is just like the Mountain King at Japan's Mount Tendai.[25] *Tiantai shan ji* states, "The immortal was Qiao, the eldest son of King Ling of Zhou. His style was Zijin. He enjoyed playing the mouth-organ and producing the cry of the phoenix. In the region between the Yi and Luo Rivers, he met with the Taoist Fu Qiugong, climbed Mount Song, and stayed there more than thirty years. Afterward, he appeared riding on a white crane, bid farewell to the people and departed. He was given the immortal offices of Sage of Tongbai and Supporter on the Right of the Office of the Five Peaks of the Royal Domain. He serves as attendant when the emperor comes to perform the rites at this mountain."

Next I worshiped at Dinghui Cloister. According to *The Biography of Great Master Chishō*,[26] "Using the thirty ounces of gold dust that the Minister of the Right [Fujiwara Yoshifusa] had given him for travel provisions, he bought lumber to construct a Concentration Hall at the Guoqingsi Concentration Cloister and provided for lectures in perpetuity. He also built a three-bay chamber to fulfill the patriarch Saichō's vow. Then he asked the monk Qingguan to serve as chief intendant." Therefore, I burned incense and worshiped.

Next I went to the Enlightened Mind Cloister. It is a sutra storehouse from Zhizhe's time and contains several tens of sutra boxes. The resident intendant monk Xianning is eighty-two years old and reads *The Lotus Sutra*. The keeper of sutras Zheming prepared tea and mountain peaches. Next I worshiped at the Revolving Tripitaka Repository. Sutras are stacked layer upon layer on all eight sides. Since a person can enter beneath it and make it turn, it is called the Revolving Tripitaka Repository. It is like a pagoda, about twenty feet high, constructed inside a two-story building. I burned incense.

At the hour of the rooster [6:00 P.M.], I returned to my quarters. I gave the abbot's disciple Yugui a soapberry seed rosary ornamented with glass in response to his sincere request. At the seven hours I performed the rites.

Eighteenth Day:

Clear skies. At the hour of the dragon [8:00 A.M.], I entered the palanquin to ascend the mountain. Palace Monk Raien and Postulant Chōmei stayed behind, but all the others accompanied me. The abbot came and told me that I should bring along some of my gold and silver to present at the various cloisters, and so I took four ounces of silver when I went up the mountain. Climbing the precipitous slope east of the monastery, we proceeded thirteen li to Jindi and visited Dinghui's True Body Stupa Cloister. A plaque inside said, "Imperial Cloister of True Enlightenment." This cloister contains the stupa of the Tiantai Great Master's true body.[27] The stupa has an underground chamber within which sits the Great Master's true body. I burned incense and worshiped. My tears were all the more difficult to restrain. In the past I had only heard the name of the cloister; now I was worshiping here in person. To what might I compare the joy in my heart? The resident intendant, an aged monk, came out and prepared tea. I presented him with one ounce of silver.

I left the tomb in which Great Master Zhizhe's body rested [Enchin], entered the palanquin, and at last headed for the monastery Dacisi. To the north and south rose the peaks of Jindi and Yindi; to the east and west flourished pines and bamboo of the human world. Amid these, the road passed. [Enchin] Proceeding two li, we arrived at Dacisi. During the Chen dynasty [557–89], on the sixth day of the Second Month in the tenth year of Dajian [578], Emperor Xuan established the monastery for Great Master Zhizhe and named it Xiuchansi. From the first year of Renshou [601], after Guoqingsi had been established nearby, this monastery naturally declined. Subsequently it was rebuilt and named Chanlinsi. After it was destroyed during the Huichang era [i.e., in 845], it was again reconstructed. Its buildings altogether have two hundred and nineteen rooms. During the third reign of the Great Song, on the third day of the Seventh Month in the first year of the Dazhong Xiangfu era [1008], by imperial edict, the name Chanlinsi was changed to Dacisi. This is where Zhizhe transmitted the dharma. It is also called the Yindi Place of Religious Practice. [Enchin] During the Chen dynasty, in the seventh year of Daqian [575], Great Master Zhizhe, summoned by a portent, journeyed to the east and arrived at this mountain in the Ninth Month. Thereupon he met the Meditation Master Dingguang. He spent the night at Jindi, but the meditation master said, "The northern peak, Jindi, is where you ought to dwell." Thus he first entered the site of the present Dacisi.

First I went to the Great Buddha Hall, where I burned incense before sixteen-foot statues of Śākyamuni, Amitābha, and Maitreya. Next I went to the Great Master Zhizhe True Body Cloister and burned incense. Next I went to the Great Master Dingguang Hall and burned incense. Next I went to the Lotus Repentance Cloister, where, inside the hall, there is a great sculpture of a white elephant. It is a statue of the elephant upon which the bodhisattva Samantabhadra was riding when he appeared before Great Master Zhizhe, just as the master was performing the Repentance Rite. Here I also saw the three jeweled stairways. The plaque on the Great Master Hall is in the calligraphy of Great Master Fagong. The hall has a plaque imperially bestowed by the Zhu imperial family of the Great Liang dynasty [907–23]. During his lifetime, Great Master Zhizhe taught the Sui emperors; posthumously, he was granted the title Great Master Fagong by the emperor.

Next I worshiped at the Ordination Platform Cloister, which was just as magnificent as the Ordination Platform at Guoqingsi. There are two ordination platforms only fifteen li apart. The Dacisi Ordination Platform was constructed by imperial order of Emperor Xuan of the Chen dynasty. The Guoqingsi Ordination Platform was constructed by imperial order of Emperor Yang [r. 605–17] of the Sui dynasty. Next I worshiped at the Folong Place of Religious Practice. The assistant abbot showed me to his chamber to have tea. He greeted me by prostrating himself three times. I returned his bows. For a while afterward, he wiped away tears. My interpreter Chen Yong said, "Your face resembles that of Great Master Zhizhe, and so he thought that perhaps the Great Master had reappeared. This is why he bowed to you." He presented me with copies of *The Sudden Enlightenment Collection of the Zen Sect* in one fascicle and *A Commentary on "The Song of Enlightenment"* in one volume. Once more, he bowed to me three times and I returned his bows as before. Again, he wiped away tears and repeated that I resembled Zhizhe.

Next we went to the refectory for a vegetarian banquet, which was truly delicious. I gave the functionary monk one ounce of silver. An aged monk brought forth a portrait of the Japanese monk Gentō Shōnin,[28] on which was written his title "Recipient of the Purple Robe Great Master," and a eulogy. I was too startled to copy the text, but seeing the image of a Japanese moved me to profuse tears. Southeast of Dacisi is the Stone Elephant Place of Religious Practice. This is where Great Master Zhizhe was enlightened by Samantabhadra, who descended on an elephant and touched his head, predicting he would attain Buddhahood. It has been passed down from ancient times that Samantabhadra's white elephant changed into a great boulder. Because its appearance is no different from that of a real elephant,[29] it is known as the Stone Elephant Place of Religious Practice.

Furthermore, on the west side of a stone cave south of the elephant, there is a boulder that, when struck, produces a sound just like an actual drum. People say that when Zhizhe preached, he struck it to summon the monks. Facing each other to the east and west of the elephant are stones shaped like screens. Between them is a stone receptacle in the form of a large box about eight feet high. It is said that the ancient worthies gathered the essential writings from throughout the empire and placed them in the receptacle. Only Zhizhe opened it and looked at them; other than him, there has not been such a person.

Then, proceeding north from Dacisi for twenty-five li on a mountain path, there is a pavilion called Menluoding. It was built by the Surveillance Commissioner of Zhedong and Vice Censor-in-Chief Meng Jian, and so it is also known as "Vice Censor Meng Pavilion." From there, going about thirty-five li, we reached the highest point in the Tiantai Mountains. This peak is named Huading. It is where Zhizhe retired, defeated the Heavenly Demons, and received the revelation from the mysterious monk. The rock where Dingguang summoned him with his hand still exists, and the site where Dingguang dwelled is preserved for eternity as if it were new. The bamboo grows darkly; there is a forest of tea trees, beside which is a pavilion named Daojingding. Water from a sweet spring flows by it and people rested there. Next we descended Huading following a stream to the foot of the mountain until we reached Buyunding pavilion. Again we followed a stream until we reached Stone Bridge [Enchin], where there is an enormous place of religious practice. First I worshiped a life-size golden statue of the Venerable Baidaoyou. On three walls of the hall were hung paintings of the sixteen arhats. The Venerable Baidaoyou was a man from the land of Anagamin. Long ago, at the beginning of the Jin dynasty [265–420], the monk Baidaoyou from Great Nālandā monastery in Central India crossed the vast drifting sands, worshiped at the Wutai Mountains, and reached Mount Chicheng at Tiantai. After overcoming the mountain gods, he then came here, crossed Stone Bridge, and personally saw the five hundred great arhats, whom he worshiped and made offerings to. Therefore, an image of the venerable one is enshrined here.

The master of the hermitage, Yincheng Ācārya, together with the functionary, came out and offered tea. The monks' hall and dormitories were connected by numerous corridors. Next I went to Stone

Bridge. A corridor of more than twenty bays had been constructed on the path up the hill. After passing through it, I arrived at the pavilion by Stone Bridge. It is a large building of five bays at which the court makes annual offerings to the five hundred arhats. Next I went up to the bridge, burned incense, and worshiped. The bridge is pale green in color and about seventy feet long. The east side is two feet wide; the west side, seven feet. Its dragon form, its tortoise back, are as if a rainbow-shaped beam crossed over the water. Two valley streams flow together, pass beneath the bridge, and produce a waterfall. The stream then flows west to the border of Yan district. Gazing up at it from below, one sees a rainbow on a clear day drinking the valley stream. The bridge towers spectacularly; the sound of the waterfall is like thunder. [*Tiantai*, Enchin][30] About twenty feet from the west end of the bridge is a boulder ten feet high. No one without special powers can cross it unaided. In recent times, people who only go as far as the middle of the bridge say that they have crossed Stone Bridge. This is very strange! Within the long corridor are three teak trees, about ten feet high. The Venerable Baidaoyou brought the seeds from India and planted them. Their leaves resemble those of a rhododendron. Above the bridge are two or three small cascades.

At the hour of the monkey [4:00 P.M.] we returned to the hermitage, where a delicious vegetarian banquet was prepared. Others again went to the Stone Bridge, but I stayed in my quarters. This monastery is named Stone Bridge Monastery. The monk who serves as monastery administrator has already taken two ounces in silver. Great Master Chishō stated, "Every time I unroll a picture of the Tiantai Mountains, I gaze at the features of Huading and Stone Bridge, but I have not yet met with the good fortune of having a chance to visit them. I had long thought this." [Enchin] Finally he crossed the sea. Now, this insignificant monk too has followed in the footsteps of the Great Master, carried out his old wish, and worshiped the Stone Bridge. I was moved to limitless tears. At the seven hours, I performed the rites.

Looking now at my *Dream Record*, for the night of the thirtieth day of the Seventh Month in the fourth year of Japan's Kōhei era [1061], I find the following entry: "Tonight I dreamed of a great river with a white stone bridge. This insignificant monk Jōjin began to cross the bridge, but there was a gap in it. Before I reached the gap, a man appeared with a board, which he used to walk over the open area. He then allowed Jōjin to cross over it successfully. In the dream, I thought 'This is the Stone Bridge of Tiantai.' A person without an enlightened mind could not cross it. In my heart, I was very pleased." Today I saw the form of the Stone Bridge and it matched the dream of an earlier day.

Stone Bridge of the Tiantai Mountains
Introduction and Ode

Composed by the monk Yuanfu, Scribe of Baoshousi Monastery
in the Right Division of the Tang Capital, the Imperially Appointed
Palace Monk, and Most Virtuous Recipient of the Purple Robe

Calligraphy by the Monk Lijian from Tiantai, the Capital of the
Immortals

The scenery of Tiantai is incomparable. Since ancient times, it has
been the dwelling of gods and immortals. Only a regional dignitary
with a sightseeing carriage could visit it. At the end of the Yuanhe era
[806–21], I, Yuanfu, came to Stone Bridge. I saw all the scenic wonders: Flower Peak [Huading], White Sand, Double Tower, and Jewel
Platform. At Stone Bridge I composed an ode:

Before the primeval chaos had been ordered,
Who wrought the transformations,
Kneaded the clay of Tiantai, the Heavenly Terrace,
That powerfully supports the sky's blue arch?
Its rocks form a bridge:
A rainbow on a clear day.
Neither sculpted nor polished,
Neither smoothed nor burnished,
Truly it is the earth's bones,
Truly it is a natural achievement.
The stars drift in their cobalt pool;
The moon hangs in its heavenly void.
Enclosed by precipitous cliffs,
It links the myriad valleys.
The Venerable Baidaoyou,
The ancient immortal Prince Zijin,
Each strode the precipices
As lightly as the wind.
A young dragon suddenly flies forth:
The water wells from overflowing fissures.
The surging rapids loudly thunder,
Rushing furiously, shouting, calling,
Then head for the sea,
Boundless, boundless,
Uprooting boulders, moving mountains,
Shattering cliffs, destroying river banks.
A jade screen opens on the mountains;
Strings of pearls link the trees.
It aroused the talent of Sun Chuo,
Stirs one to write as Xiangru.[31]
So that this bridge will be remembered forever,
I record this hymn of praise.

The monk Zexi of Jiwangsi Monastery erected this stele in the Intercalary Fifth Month of the year Yiya [1045] in the Jingli era.

Yang Hongju of Hongnong carved the characters.

Tiping, Functionary of Shouchangsi Monastery in Charge of the Imperial Writings, and Recipient of the Purple Robe

Fangyan, Abbot of Shouchangsi Monastery in Charge of the Imperial Writings, and Recipient of the Purple Robe

Qingxu, Tiantai Assistant Registrar of Monks and Supervisor of the Ordination Platform, Specially Selected Recipient of the Purple Robe, wrote the heading in the seal style.

Lige, Imperially Appointed Tiantai General Registrar of Monks and Supervisor of the Ordination Platform, Specially Selected Great Master Zongjiao, re-erected it.

NOTES

1. "Glossary of Terms in Life-Writing: Part I," *Biography* 1.1 (1978): 72.
2. The works mentioned are all available in good translations with critical introductions discussing these issues. For *Tosa nikki*, see Earl Miner, trans. and intro., *Japanese Poetic Diaries* (Berkeley and Los Angeles: University of California Press, 1969); for *Kagerō nikki*, Edward G. Seidensticker, trans. and intro., *The Gossamer Years* (Rutland, Vt., and Tokyo: Tuttle, 1964); for *Kenreimon'in Ukyō no Daibu shū*, Phillip Tudor Harries, trans. and intro., *The Poetic Memoirs of Lady Daibu* (Stanford: Stanford University Press, 1980); and for *Izumi Shikibu nikki*, Edwin A. Cranston, trans. and intro., *The Izumi Shikibu Diary* (Cambridge: Harvard University Press, 1969). For the relation between a "diary" and poetic anthologies, see Janet A. Walker, "Poetic Ideal and Fictional Reality in the *Izumi Shikibu nikki*," *Harvard Journal of Asiatic Studies* 37.1 (1977): 135–82.
3. The passage from Uda's diary is quoted in *Fusō ryakki*, vol. 12 of *Kokushi taikei* (Tokyo: Yoshikawa Kōbunkan, 1965), entry for Kanpyō 1.VIII.10; Michinaga's poem appears in the entry for Kannin 2.X.16 of *Shōyūki*, in *Zōho shiryō taisei bekkan* (Kyoto: Rinsen Shoten, 1965). The only *kanbun* diary available in English is Edwin Reischauer's *Ennin's Diary: The Record of a Pilgrimage to China in Search of the Law* (New York: The Ronald Press Co., 1955). Francine Hérail has recently published a French version of Michinaga's diary, *Notes journalières de Fujiwara no Michinaga, ministre à la cour de Hei.an (995–1018): Traduction du Midô kanpakuki* (Geneva and Paris: Librairie Droz, 1987, 1988, 1991).
4. Some readers may be surprised at how the title of this diary has been translated, since, in English, we are used to hearing of "Mount Tiantai," a term I used myself in earlier publications. However, a glance at a topographical map of China will reveal that the name "Tiantai" refers not to a single mountain, but rather to a mountain range of modest proportions. The case of Wutai is similar, hence the translation.

     This diary is available in four printed editions. It first appeared in vol. 26 of *Kaitei shiseki shūran* (Tokyo: Kondō Kappanjo, 1902). The eminent buddhologist Takakusu Junjirō edited a version that was included in *Dai Nihon Bukkyō zensho*. Both of these editions have been reprinted, the latter many times, with the diary appearing in vol. 72 of the 1972 edition (Suzuki Gakujutsu Zaidan). Takakusu's notes are particularly valuable. The same volume of *Dai Nihon Bukkyō zensho* also includes Takakusu's edition of the earliest commentary on the diary, *Sanpo Tendai Godai san ki,* by Narushima Chikuzan, circa 1840. The most fully annotated edition is in Shimazu Kusako, *Jōjin azari no haha shū, San Tendai Godai san ki no kenkyū* (Tokyo: Daizō Shuppan, 1959). The most recent is Hirabayashi Fumio's *San Tendai Godai san ki: kōhon narabi ni kenkyū* (Tokyo: Kazama Shobō, 1978). The oldest extant manuscript, dating from 1220, was reproduced in 1937 (Tōyō Bunko Sōkan, no. 7). For a complete discussion of the diary's textual history and manuscript versions, see Hirabayashi, 399–440. Each of the printed editions has useful features, but also numerous typographical and factual errors. All are worth consulting, but, if possible , they should be read in conjunction with the reproduction of the manuscript.

For a fuller description of the diary, see my article *"San Tendai Godai san ki* as a Source for the Study of the Sung Dynasty," *Bulletin of Sung Yuan Studies* 19 (1987): 1–16. I am currently working on a complete translation of the diary, a project that has been supported by grants from the National Endowment for the Humanities, Fulbright Commission, and Social Science Research Council, which permitted me to do the research on which this study is based.

5. In addition to his translation (see note 3 above), Reischauer also wrote a study of the diary, *Ennin's Travels in T'ang China* (New York: The Ronald Press Co., 1955).

6. Jōjin claims to have carried to China over six hundred fascicles worth of religious texts, and he mentions many of them in his diary, but not the one in which these passages originally appeared. For a detailed study of the texts Jōjin carried with him, see Fujiyoshi Masumi, "Jōjin no motorashita higa no tenseki: Nissō bunka kōryū no hitokusari," in *Bukkyō shigaku kenkyū* 23.1 (1981): 33–48. The extant fragment of Enchin's diary (*Gyōrekishō*), a modern compilation of his writings that includes his memorial (*Chishō Daishi yohō hennen zasshū*), and the early biography of him (*Tendaishū Enryakuji Zasu Enchin den*) appear in *Dai Nihon Bukkyō zensho* 72: 188–92, 198–224, and 145–52, respectively. For a detailed study of the diary, see Ono Katsutoshi, *Nittō guhō gyōreki no kenkyū,* 2 vols. (Kyoto: Hōzōkan, 1981–82). The sources used in writing the biography are discussed in Tokoro Isao, "Enchin Kashō den no sozai to kōsei," *Bukkyō shigaku* 14.3 (1969): 162–80. The fact that Jōjin brought only the biography, not the diary, of Enchin, supports the theory that by his day, the full diary was already lost. Perhaps he took the biography because it was more polished than the available abbreviated version of the diary.

7. *Tiantai shan ji* appears in vol. 51 of *Taishō shinshū daizōkyō* (Tokyo: Taishō Shinshū Daizōkyō Kankōkai, 1973), item 2096, pp. 1052–55.

8. For Murasaki Shikibu and *Eiga monogatari,* see William H. and Helen Craig McCullough, trans. and intro., *A Tale of Flowering Fortunes* (Stanford: Stanford University Press, 1980), 50–63; and Richard Bowring, trans. and study, *Murasaki Shikibu: Her Diary and Poetic Memoirs* (Princeton: Princeton University Press, 1982), 22. For *honkadori,* see Robert H. Brower and Earl Miner, *Japanese Court Poetry* (Stanford: Stanford University Press, 1961), 14–15, 231–33, 287–91, and 316–18. Borrowing as a technique in Chinese literature is generally recognized, but has been little studied. One relevant article is James R. Hightower, "Allusion in the Poetry of T'ao Ch'ien," *Harvard Journal of Asiatic Studies* 31 (1971): 5–27. Kojima Noriyuki has produced two multivolume studies of Chinese sources of Japan's literature in Chinese, *Jōdai Nihon bungaku to Chūgoku bungaku,* 3 vols. (Tokyo: Hanawa Shobō, 1962–65); and *Kokufū ankoku jidai no bungaku,* 4 vols. to date (Tokyo: Hanawa Shobō, 1968–). In English, some material on this topic appears

in my book *Sugawara no Michizane and the Early Heian Court* (Cambridge: Harvard University Press, 1986); see 187–89 and 295–96 in particular.

9. Arthur Waley, in an essay, "Some Far Eastern Dreams," cites this dream and offers a more colorful interpretation of it than my own (see his *The Secret History of the Mongols* [London: George Allen and Unwin, 1963], 72–73).

10. For the Hanshan legend and poems, see Robert G. Henricks, trans. and annot., *The Poetry of Han-shan* (Albany: State University of New York Press, 1990). The most familiar source for the Hanshan legend is the introduction to the poems attributed to a murky figure, Lüqiu Yin (translated in Henricks, 29). Jōjin offers a rearranged version of material found in that introduction, combined with passages from an account of Shide, another of Hanshan's legendary friends, plus a few connecting phrases for which a source cannot be identified. The connecting phrases could have been added by Jōjin as he combined materials from two sources, but, given his inclination to copy verbatim, more likely he was working from a source that is no longer extant. At least to a modern Western reader, Jōjin's rendition makes a more coherent story than does the familiar Chinese version. Although largely unknown to sinologists, Jōjin's account may be based on an early textual tradition now lost in China. For details, see my "The Legend of Hanshan: A Neglected Source," *Journal of the American Oriental Society* 111.3 (Fall 1991): 575–79.

11. See the entry for Xining 6.III.23, in fascicle 7. Note that Jōjin is using Chinese era names by this point.

12. For translations of *You Tiantai shan fu*, see David R. Knechtges, trans., *Wen xuan, or Selections of Refined Literature, Volume Two: Rhapsodies on Sacrifices, Hunting, Travel, Sightseeing, Palaces and Halls, Rivers and Seas* (Princeton: Princeton University Press, 1987), 243–53; and Richard B. Mather, "The Mystical Ascent of the T'ien-t'ai Mountains: Sun Ch'o's *Yu-T'ien-T'ai-Shan Fu*," in *Monumenta Serica* 20 (1961): 226–45. The phrase in question appears on p. 251 of Knechtges, who renders it, "Gem trees, glittering and gleaming," and on p. 242 of Mather, who translates it "alabaster orchards gleam and glow."

13. This monk, Kaikaku, also left a brief diary that was unavailable to scholars until 1960. It has been published, with a detailed introduction by Ono Katsutoshi, as "Kaikaku no Tosōki" in *Ryūkoku Daigaku ronshū* 400–1 (1973): 507–31.

14. One of the seven disciples who had accompanied Jōjin to China. Among them was a postulant who had not yet taken his final vows.

15. The founder of the Tiantai sect, also known as Zhiyi.

16. Another of Jōjin's disciples.

17. Guoqingsi was the principal monastery at Tiantai.

18. An arhat is a Buddhist sage who has attained liberation from the cycle of rebirth. Arhats are commonly represented in groups of sixteen or five hundred.

19. A Taoist deity.

20. Jōjin performed specific Buddhist rites at seven set times each day. Occasionally, as on this day, he also read chapters from *The Lotus Sutra*, the principal text of his sect.

21. Originally meaning simply "a teacher," the term came to be a title granted by the government to distinguished Buddhist monks, including Jōjin.

22. A Central Asian monk who arrived in China around the year 700, established himself in the city of Sizhou, and came to be a popular object of worship.

23. A Japanese unit of measure; approximately 360 feet.

24. A Central Asian deity that had entered the Buddhist pantheon.

25. In other words, from Jōjin's perspective, the Taoist tutelary deity of Tiantai corresponded to the Shinto tutelary deity of Mount Hiei, the headquarters of the sect in Japan.
26. Enchin's posthumous title.
27. Here Jōjin is describing the monument ("stupa") that contained Zhizhe's mortal remains ("true body"), which seem to have been preserved as a mummy in seated, meditating posture.
28. A Japanese monk who had gone to China in 1003.
29. This translation follows Enchin, as discussed in the preceding essay (see p. 71).
30. Here, Jōjin takes two passages from *Tiantai shan ji*. Between them, he places the phrase, "as if a rainbow-shaped beam crossed over the water," which combines elements from that source and from Enchin. He then concludes with another phrase modified from Enchin, "the sound of the waterfall is like thunder."
31. Sun Chuo (314–71) described Tiantai in his famous poetic essay discussed above; Xiangru is probably Sima Xiangru (179–117 B.C.), who is renowned for his florid poetic essays, but does not seem to have had any direct ties with Tiantai.

Aisatsu: The Poet as Guest

HARUO SHIRANE

It is tempting to read and interpret Matsuo Bashō's (1644–94) poems either in a lyrical or expressive mode, as an expression of the speaker's subjective state, or in a descriptive, mimetic mode, as a reflection of the external world as it is perceived by the speaker. This tendency, however, overlooks the crucial fact that much of Bashō's prose litera-ture and poetry originated as *aisatsu,* or greetings, which function in a highly performative mode, the primary objective being to fulfill a specific social or religious function such as complimenting a host, expressing gratitude, bidding farewell, making an offering to the land, or consoling the spirit of a dead person.[1] Despite the eremitic image that he cultivated in his later years, Bashō was constantly meet-ing people, particularly on journeys to various parts of Japan. Almost all these encounters resulted in *aisatsu,* in poetry that acted as saluta-tions or as other forms of direct address. Indeed, almost half of the roughly two hundred and fifty poems in Bashō's three most famous travel accounts—*Nozarashi kikō* (Records of a Weather-Exposed Skel-eton), *Oi no kobumi* (Records of a Travel-Worn Satchel), and *Oku no hosomichi* (The Narrow Road to the Deep North)—can be considered *aisatsu.*[2] In contrast to what Jonathan Culler calls the apostrophic mode, in which the speaker of a Romantic poem addresses a dead or absent person ("O thou with dewy locks"), or speaks to an abstract notion or object as if it were alive ("O Rose, thou art sick!"), these *aisatsu* often appear in a lyrical mode—with the speaker, to borrow Northrop Frye's phrase, turning "his back on the audience"—even as the poem functions as a form of direct address.[3]

Poetry has enjoyed a long history as a form of extemporaneous dialogue in Japan. *Mondōka,* the "poems as dialogue" in the *Kojiki* (712) and other ancient narratives; *sōmon,* the "love poems" in the *Man'yōshū* (749); and *zōtōka,* the "exchanged poems" popular in the

Heian period, were all written in expectation of an immediate poetic reply. From the time of its emergence in the ancient period, the thirty-one-syllable classical poem (waka) served as a form of direct address. In the world of the Heian aristocracy, for example, it would have been almost impossible to pursue the opposite sex without waka. Renga (classical linked verse) and haikai (comic linked verse), both of which required group composition, inherited this tradition of poetic dialogue. Sōgi shogakushō (Sōgi's Instructions for Beginners), a renga handbook attributed to Iio Sōgi (1421–1502), states:

> First of all, composing linked verse is like having a dialogue in which individuals speak to each other about various aspects of life. If someone says, "Wasn't yesterday's wind fierce!" one must answer with a phrase such as: "Indeed, the cherry blossoms have been completely scattered, leaving nothing."[4]

As Hattori Dohō's Sanzōshi (Three Books, 1702), a record of Bashō's teaching by one of his leading disciples, suggests, Bashō followed the tradition established by his renga and haikai predecessors.

> From long ago it has been said that the host is supposed to compose the wakiku, or second verse, though that should depend on the circumstances. From the distant past, the hokku—called the "guest's opening verse"—was always composed by the guest as a greeting. The author of the second verse then returned the greeting. In the words of the Master, "The wakiku is composed by the host and is, in this regard, a greeting." He taught us that even verses strictly on snow, moon, or cherry blossoms should include the spirit of greeting. (NKBZ 51: 536–37)[5]

The word aisatsu, which originally referred to an exchange of letters, came to mean the exchange of greetings necessary to establish a social relationship. The word further evolved to mean the ritual of composing a hokku (or any other verse in a linked-verse sequence) that expressed the guest's or the host's respect or affection for the other. Typically, the main guest would be invited to compose the hokku, and the host would reply with the wakiku, the second verse of the haikai sequence.

The following hokku, which appears in Oku no hosomichi, is a typical aisatsu to a host.

Upon my arrival at the post station at Sukagawa, I visited a man named Tōkyū, who insisted that we stay for four or five days and who immediately asked how I had fared at the barrier at Shirakawa. I replied that I had not been able to compose any poetry: I had been exhausted from the long journey, the beauty of the landscape had overwhelmed me, and I had been torn by thoughts of the past. However, feeling that it would be a pity to cross the barrier without producing a single verse, I wrote:

Fūryū no	The beginnings of
hajime ya oku no	poetry!—In the Deep North
taue uta	songs of rice-planting.

We added a second and third verse to my verse, and in the end we composed three linked-verse sequences. (*NKBZ* 41: 351)[6]

Bashō wrote this poem shortly after passing the barrier at Shirakawa, considered to be the entrance to the Deep North. Commentaries differ on whether the opening lines—*Fūryū no hajime ya* ("The beginnings of poetry!")—refer to the origins of poetry or to the first poetry that the speaker has encountered since entering the Deep North. In either case, the poem is a greeting to Tōkyū, who is providing Bashō with lodgings. Arriving at the time of rice-planting and hearing the rice-planting songs (probably in the fields owned by Tōkyū), Bashō greets the host with a poem that is the equivalent of saying: "The rice-planting songs of the Deep North are quite refined, aren't they!" thereby complimenting the host on his home. The *hokku* is the opening verse of a *kasen*, a thirty-six-link *haikai* sequence, the first composed by Bashō since entering the Deep North. The poem can thus also be construed as an expression of Bashō's joy and gratitude at being able to compose *haikai* linked verse for the first time in the Deep North (the *fūryū* referring to the linked-verse session).

The *wakiku*, which was composed by Tōkyū, is also an *aisatsu*.

Ichigo o orite	Collecting wild strawberries,
waga mōkegusa	my only offering to you.

In response to the *hokku*, which expresses the guest's admiration for the Deep North, the second verse implies that, being in the country, the host has nothing to offer his cultured guest: the most he can do is collect and serve some wild strawberries. Unlike the *hokku*, which flatters the host, the *wakiku* is self-effacing and humble. Following poetic protocol, the *wakiku* refers to the same season as the *hokku*: both *ichigo* ("wild strawberries") and *taue uta* ("rice-planting songs") belong to summer.

The following two verses open a *kasen* composed in the Third Month of 1686 by six people at the residence of Suzuki Seifū.

Hana sakite	The cherry tree blooms,
nanuka tsuru miru	for seven days, I watch the crane
fumoto kana	at the mountain foot.

(Bashō)

Ojite kawazu no	Frightened, a frog
wataru hosobashi	crosses a narrow bridge.

(Seifū)[7]

The *hokku* expresses the pleasure of simultaneously enjoying the cherry trees, which were said to bloom for seven days, and the crane, which was thought, once it landed, to stay for seven days. Bashō's *hokku* praises both the elegant setting and the host, Seifū, a *haikai* poet and a native of the Deep North, who is symbolized by the crane, which migrates annually from the north. Seifū's *wakiku* returns Bashō's greeting, humbly depicting himself as a frightened, uncertain frog and apologizing for his provincial origins.

In principle, any one of the thirty-six verses in a *kasen* can function as an *aisatsu*. The *ageku*, or closing verse, must, by convention, be auspicious, suggesting an atmosphere of peace. It can at the same time be, as in the "rice-planting" sequence, another greeting to the host.

Kogai suru ya ni	At the silkworm grower's house
kosode kasanaru	the robes of fine silk stack up.

(Sora)

Sora's verse describes the abundance of *kosode*, the narrow-sleeved robes of fine silk (which were worn especially on New Year's Day), thereby suggesting the opulence of Tōkyū's residence and offering an auspicious New Year's greeting to the host, who was a successful silkworm grower.

A *jihokku*, an autonomous *hokku*—as opposed to a *tateku*, a *hokku* in a linked-verse sequence—can also function as an *aisatsu*. Bashō wrote the following *jihokku*, which appears in *Nozarashi kikō*, when he visited the country villa of Mitsui Shūfū, a wealthy resident of Kyoto.

> I went to the capital and visited Mitsui Shūfū's mountain home in Narutaki.

A Forest of Plum Trees

Ume shiroshi	White plum blossoms—
kinō ya tsuru o	could it be that the crane
nusumareshi	was stolen yesterday?

The poem is a greeting to Shūfū, whose residence (particularly its plum blossoms) and character remind Bashō of Lin Hejing, a Song sage and recluse who lived on a solitary mountain near a lake and who is said to have looked after his plum trees as if they were his spouse and raised a crane as if it were his child. The *hokku*, which playfully attributes the lack of a crane at Shūfū's residence to theft, expresses Bashō's deep admiration for his host's reclusive lifestyle.

The poem as *aisatsu* is by no means limited to greetings to a host or guest. The following passage from *Sanzōshi* indicates some other types.

> From long ago it has been said, "When one composes a *hokku* to celebrate the opening of a new building, one must be careful to avoid words related to fire such as 'burning' and 'frying.' When it comes to composing poems of mourning, one must be careful not to use words like 'dark road,' 'wandering path,' 'sin,' and 'guilt.' And when composing a *hokku* on board a ship, one must avoid words such as 'overturning,' 'sinking,' and 'wind-swept waves.'" ("Shirazōshi," *NKBZ* 51: 536)

A *hokku* can celebrate an important birthday (longevity), the completion of a new residence, or any other prominent social occasion. Or it can mourn the loss of an individual's life. Another significant form of *aisatsu*, particularly for Bashō, was the parting poem, composed either by the departing traveler (usually Bashō himself), or by the person left behind. Bashō often offered a poem to a disciple about to embark on a journey. Most typically, however, the *aisatsu* is an expression of gratitude toward one's host, a situation that Bashō constantly encountered in his many travels.

"INDIRECT EXPRESSION"

In an *aisatsu*, the speaker stands in a close relationship to another, whom he or she addresses directly. As a consequence, a number of Bashō's *aisatsu*, particularly in his earlier poetry, are cast in the form of a question, a plea, or a command.

Upon being invited to someone's hermitage.

Aki suzushi	Coolness of autumn.
tegoto ni muke ya	Everyone, peel them yourselves!
uri nasubi	Melons and eggplant.

(Oku no hosomichi, NKBZ 41: 377)

In this impromptu and lighthearted *hokku*, the guest's enthusiasm and joy at the prospect of being treated to a fine meal in such a relaxed,

cool setting are so great that he playfully orders everyone to join in
and help peel the fruit and vegetables.

In contrast to this kind of direct address, which distantly resembles the apostrophe in Romantic poetry, Bashō's well-known *aisatsu*
are more subtle and lyrical, with the speaker, in Frye's words, turning
"his back on the audience." Most of these *aisatsu* are some form of
allegorical or metaphorical expression, in which a particular word or
image implicitly represents the object or person to be greeted. In
Sanzōshi, Hattori Dohō (1657–1730), one of Bashō's leading disciples,
comments on this process.

Toginaosu	Polished once more,
kagami mo kiyoshi	how the sacred mirror shines!
yuki no hana	Flowers in the snow.
Ume koite	Longing for plum blossoms,
unohana ogamu	I bow before a hydrangea
namida kana	with tears in my eyes.

The poem on snow was composed on the occasion of the
reconstruction of the Atsuta Shrine. The first five syllables,
"Polished once more," gently express the spirit of rebuilding
and reflect the stature of the shrine. The poem on plum
blossoms was composed on the occasion of the death of
Bishop Daiten of Engaku Temple. The speaker pays tribute
to the deceased by comparing the bishop to plum blossoms
and then bowing before a hydrangea, which was in bloom at
the time. The feelings of the speaker are revealed, not directly, but through a separate object that captures the character and status of the person in question. ("Akazōshi," *NKBZ*
51: 559)

Dohō here selects two representative poems by Bashō (the first appears in *Oi no kobumi* and the second in *Nozarashi kikō*), a poem of
celebration and a lament, both of which demonstrate the same rhetorical technique. Dohō, who closely follows Bashō's teachings, argues
that the *aisatsu,* instead of directly expressing emotion or thought,
should express the speaker's feelings indirectly, through "an object"
(*mono*). In the two exemplary poems, the "objects" are the mirror and
the plum blossoms, representing the shrine and the bishop, respectively. The "object" should function as a metaphor of the subject's
"character and status" (*kurai*). The dignity and grace of the newly
reconstructed shrine are embodied in the mirror, which is so pure that
it reflects the blossoms in the snow. The plum flower likewise embodies the refined character and high status of the bishop.

Umoregi (Buried Tree, 1673), a *haikai* handbook by Kitamura Kigin (a disciple of Teitoku and Bashō's teacher) defines two poetic principles—*fū* (Ch. *feng*), "indirect expression," and *ga* (Ch. *ya*), "direct expression"—which are combined in Bashō's *aisatsu*. Kigin gives the following *renga* verse by Shinkei as an example of *fū*:

Na wa takaku	Possessing a voice
koe wa uenaki	without peer, known far and wide,
hototogisu	the cuckoo.

The verse implicitly compares the poet's host to a *hototogisu* (cuckoo), which is admired and well known for its beautiful voice. In *Sanzōshi*, Dohō argues that an *aisatsu* should use this kind of "indirect expression" (*fū*), which had long been employed in classical poetry. A salient characteristic of Bashō's *aisatsu*, particularly in his later poetry, is that it often manages to combine this kind of "indirect expression" (*fū*) with "direct expression" (*ga*). Even as the *hokku* includes within it an allegorical address, it reflects, or at least appears to reflect, a careful, nonconventional observation of nature. The *ga* contains the *fū* fully within it. As a consequence, the reader will often miss the allegorical (*fū*) dimension while still appreciating the *hokku* as a lyrical or descriptive (*ga*) poem.

Sometimes a key word is sufficient to make the poem an *aisatsu*. At a time when there was no air-conditioning, the word "cool" (*suzushi*), a *kigo* (seasonal word) for summer, was the ultimate compliment that could be paid to the host of a summer's lodging. One consequence is that a number of Bashō's *aisatsu*, including the above *hokku* on peeling melons and eggplant, contain this word. A good example from *Oku no hosomichi* is:

> I visited a person named Seifū at Obanazawa. Though he is wealthy, he is not lacking in spirit. Having traveled a number of times to the capital, he understood the tribulations of travel and gave me shelter for a number of days. In various ways he was able to ease the pain of a long journey.

Suzushisa o	Taking some coolness
waga yado ni shite	as my lodging for the night,
nemaru nari	I stretch out my legs.

(NKBZ 41: 367)

Bashō, exhausted from a difficult journey, finds Seifū's residence and hospitality to be coolness itself and relaxes as if he were at home. (Bashō deliberately uses a word, *nemaru*, which, in the local dialect, means to sit or lie down in a relaxed manner.)

Some of Bashō's *aisatsu* are what Kigin would call *ga* ("direct expression"), employing neither allegory nor key words.

Upon visiting the thatched hut of a recluse.

Tsuta uete	Vines in the garden.
take shi go hon no	Four or five bamboo trees stirred
arashi kana	by a storm—

$$(NKBZ\ 41:\ 291)$$

Though this poem from *Nozarashi kikō* eschews *fū* ("indirect expression"), the sketch of the simple garden—the bright leaves of the autumn vine (*tsuta* is a *kigo* for autumn) and the sound of the storm stirring the leaves of four or five bamboo trees—captures the tranquil and refined character of the inhabitant, making it a greeting, an expression of Bashō's admiration for his host's reclusive lifestyle. Indeed, this *hokku* can be taken as an example of a poem that, according to *Sanzōshi*, is on "snow, moon, or cherry blossoms," on nature and the seasons, and yet has the "spirit of greeting."

FROM SOCIAL ACT TO LITERARY ART

The *aisatsu* was composed for a specific person, or audience, who was expected to reply in kind. As a consequence, a poem could fail as an *aisatsu* if it were not composed quickly and spontaneously. Saitō Tokugen gives the following advice in *Haikai shogakushō* (Instructions for Beginners of Haikai, 1641).

No matter how good a poet is, there are times when he cannot produce a poem on the spot. But even on these occasions, it is best to compose spontaneously, on the cherry blossoms or the autumn leaves in the garden, or on something unusual in the setting. Impromptu composition is far more desirable than a verse that you have prepared in advance. Is there anything better than a salutation?[8]

Similar advice appears in *Kyoraishō*, which records an episode in which, as the honored guest, Kyorai was asked by the host to write a *hokku*. When Kyorai encountered difficulty, being unprepared, Bashō presented a *hokku* in his place and then later reprimanded his disciple.

The Master said, "We went to Masahide's residence for the first time today. As the honored guest, you must be ready to present the opening verse. When asked to compose, you cannot spend time pondering the merits or demerits of the verse. Present it as quickly as possible. You did neither. There is only so much time in an evening. Had you continued to take time composing a *hokku,* the session would have been spoiled. The poetic atmosphere would have been lost. That is why I presented a *hokku* in your place." (*NKBZ* 51: 446)

Sanzōshi presents a similar view.

> The Master said, "Always study *haikai.* During a linked-verse session, do not allow even a hair to stand between you and the copying stand. You should immediately express your thoughts, without hesitation. Once the session is over, the verse is no more than trash." ("Akazōshi," *NKBZ* 51: 549)

Bashō stresses that it is far better to present a poem immediately, even if it means composing an inferior verse. The creation and maintenance of proper atmosphere take precedence over literary quality. Like *chanoyu,* the art of tea, a *haikai* session is a performing art, a one-time, spontaneous meeting of its participants, who must interact closely and pay their respects to each other. To fail to observe this social dimension is to fail in the art.

The *aisatsu* was judged by and valued for its appropriateness to the situation. In the Fifth Month of 1694, while on his last journey, Bashō, hearing that his disciple Yasui was building a hermitage, composed the following two *hokku.*

Suzushisa no	For making coolness,
sashizu ni miyuru	it seems to be the right design—
sumai kana	your future dwelling.
	(*NKBT* 45: 78)

Suzushisa o	For making coolness,
Hida no takumi ga	the carpenter of Hida
sashizu kana	has the right design.
	(*NKBT* 45: 77)

"Coolness" (*suzushisa*), in addition to being a key word, suggests the refreshing, ideal nature of the future residence as well as the pure spirit of its planner and future inhabitant. The first *hokku,* which implies that the design alone presages an excellent dwelling, is a poetic prayer for the rapid completion of the building. The second *hokku* playfully suggests that the legendary carpenter of Hida Province (who appears in the twelfth-century *Konjaku monogatari* and who is now reincarnated in the form of Yasui) is about to build another ideal dwelling. After conferring with another disciple, Bashō chose the first of the two *hokku* and sent it to Yasui. In a letter to his friend Sanpū, Bashō subsequently noted that the second poem, on the carpenter of

Hida, was superior to the first. When faced with alternative compositions, Bashō had thus chosen, not the work of superior literary quality,
but the poem best suited to the occasion, the more effective *aisatsu*.

But even as Bashō stressed the importance of poetry as effective
dialogue, he simultaneously pursued the notion of the *hokku* as poetic
art. In contrast to the *aisatsu* poems, which required speed and spon-
taneity, these poems were usually the result of extensive effort and
many revisions.

Karazake mo	Both dried salmon and
Kūya no yase mo	frail begging monks of Kūya
kan no uchi	in the winter cold.

In regard to this poem, the Master said, "In order to
express the essence of that spirit, I agonized for many days."
The poem, it seems, required a gut-wrenching effort. ("Akazōshi," *Sanzōshi*, *NKBZ* 51: 564)

The composition of poetry here is a long, painful, lonely process. The
relatively small number of poems that Bashō wrote (for a *haikai* poet)
and the numerous extant variants reveal a poet who constantly re-
wrote his poems, long after they had served their initial purpose.

If the *haikai* session occurred in the summer, the *hokku* had to
avoid the word "hot" (*atsushi*), and if the poet was invited by a patron
during the winter, he or she could not use the word "cold" (*samushi*).
Bashō was not constrained by such external circumstances in rewriting his *aisatsu* poems. The following *hokku* was composed in 1689,
during Bashō's journey to the Deep North, as part of a *kasen* at the
residence of Takano Ichiei, a wealthy shipping agent who owned a
boathouse on the Mogami River.

Samidare o	Gathering the rains
atsumete suzushi	of summer, it brings coolness—
Mogamigawa	Mogami River.

(Bashō)

Kishi ni hotaru o	Tying fireflies to the bank,
tsunagu funagui	the posts on the river wharf.

(Ichiei)[9]

The *hokku* praises the view of the river from Ichiei's residence by
commenting on the "coolness" created by the sight of the huge
Mogami River gathering in the summer rains. In the *wakiku*, which
associates Bashō with the fireflies and the host with the restraining
posts on a boat pier, Ichiei thanks his distinguished guest for the
opportunity to entertain him. When Bashō inserted this poem into
Oku no hosomichi three or four years later (in 1692 or 1693), he completely transformed it.

The Mogami River originates in the Deep North, with its upper reaches in Yamagata. Along the way there are frightening rapids with names like Scattered-Go-Stones or Flying Eagle. The river skirts the north side of Mount Itajiki and then finally pours into the sea at Sakata. As I descended, passing through the dense foliage, I felt as if the mountains were covering the river on both sides. When filled with rice, these boats are apparently called "rice boats." Through the green leaves, I could see the falling waters of White-Thread Cascade. Sennindō, the Hall of the Wizard, stood on the banks, directly facing the water. The river was swollen by rain, making the journey by boat perilous.

Samidare o	Gathering the rains
atsumete hayashi	of summer, it rushes forth—
Mogamigawa	Mogami River.

(*NKBZ* 41: 369)[10]

After visiting Ichiei, Bashō traveled down the Mogami River, encountering the rapids (considered one of Japan's "three great rapids") at a time when the river was overflowing. The prose passage in *Oku no hosomichi* and the revised version of the poem, both of which stress the power and speed of this large river, appear to reflect this later experience. Whatever the exact cause for the change, the revised version, which drops the key word *suzushi* ("cool"), is no longer an *aisatsu* to Ichiei. Instead it grasps, in *haikai* fashion, the poetic essence (*hon'i*) of Mogami River, an *utamakura* (poetic place) associated by literary tradition with wild rapids.

A different type of transformation occurs in another poem on Mogami River, which Bashō composed in 1689 as a *hokku* in a seven-verse linked sequence at the residence of Terajima Hikosuke, a wealthy merchant.

Suzushisa ya	Such coolness!
umi ni iretaru	Pouring itself into the sea,
Mogamigawa	Mogami River.

(Bashō)[11]

The *aisatsu* praises the view from Hikosuke's house, which overlooks the Mogami River at the point where the giant river flows into the Japan Sea. A revised version of the poem appears in *Oku no hosomichi*.

I left Haguro and went to the castle town of Tsurugaoka, where I was invited to the home of a samurai called Nagayama Shigeyuki. We composed one sequence of *haikai* linked verse. Sakichi, who had accompanied me this far, saw me off. I boarded a boat and traveled down the river to the port of

Sakada, where I lodged at the home of a doctor named En-
nan Fugyoku.

Atsumiyama ya	From Hot Sea Mountain
Fukuura kakete	to Beach of Breezes, we gaze—
yūsuzumi	cooling off at dusk.

Atsuki hi o	Pouring the hot day,
umi ni iretari	the hot sun, into the sea—
Mogamigawa	Mogami River.

                                        (*NKBZ* 41: 371)

The first poem creates the feeling of coolness not only by having
the speaker gaze at the vast coastline from south (Hot Sea Mountain)
to north (Beach of Breezes) at dusk but by lightly punning on the
place names. The "breeze" (*fuku*) from Fukuura blows over the "heat"
(*atsui*) of Atsumiyama to bring "evening cool" (*yūsuzumi*). The Atsumiyama poem, which was initially composed by Bashō as an opening
hokku for a *kasen* and as an *aisatsu* to Fugyoku, appears here in its
original form. The Mogami River poem, by contrast, has been significantly altered. Instead of pouring itself into the sea, the Mogami River
pours *atsuki hi*—which can be read either as "the hot sun" or "the hot
day." The poem suggests both a setting sun washed by the waves at sea
and a hot summer's day coming to a dramatic close in the sea. As in
the other Mogami River poem, Bashō drops the word *suzushi* in order
to create a more artistic poem, one which suggests coolness without
using the word.

    In comparison to Yosa Buson's (1715–83) *hokku,* only a relatively
small portion of which are prefaced by headnotes, the majority of
Bashō's independent *hokku* are preceded by some prose description of
the setting. Unlike Buson, who composed many of his poems in his
study or at *hokku* parties, Bashō's poems were often *aisatsu* that required an understanding of the circumstances of composition for
their full effect. But in rewriting his poems, which he often did, Bashō
was not in the least constrained by the original circumstances or motives. He routinely freed the poems from their initial settings, either
by shortening, changing, or eliminating the original prefaces, or by
altering the poem itself. Sometimes Bashō revised an *aisatsu* for the
purpose of creating another *aisatsu* to someone else. During his journey to the Deep North, Bashō constantly met people, composed numerous *aisatsu,* and produced at least seventeen *hokku* (*tateku*) for
linked-verse sessions. Of the twelve *hokku* which he chose for inclusion
in *Oku no hosomichi,* however, seven are revised.[12] Bashō was both an
intensely "private" poet, for whom poetry was an essential form of

social dialogue, and an extremely "public" writer, for whom the best poetry transcended time and place. Though *Oku no hosomichi* is usually thought of as an intimate and faithful account of Bashō's travels and of his life as a "private" poet, it is in fact a "public" and often fictional work written for a wider audience in which the *aisatsu*, when it does appear, becomes literary art rather than social necessity. And yet, as we shall see, even these seemingly "public" narratives can sometimes be considered "private" *aisatsu*, salutations to specific individuals or disciples.

GREETINGS TO THE LAND

Bashō wrote *aisatsu* not only to people but to the spirit of the land.[13] The "beginnings of poetry!" (*Fūryū no hajime ya*) poem cited earlier is not only an *aisatsu* to Bashō's host Tōkyū, it is a greeting to the region of Michinoku, complimenting the land for its fertility (rice harvest) and culture (song). The revised version of the first Mogami poem ("Gathering the rains/ of summer, it rushes forth—/ Mogami River"), while no longer a salutation to Bashō's host Ichiei, can still be regarded as an *aisatsu* to Dewa Province, home of the Mogami River.[14] *Sanzōshi* comments on this type of greeting:

Wase no ka ya	Fragrance of rice plants—
wakeiri migi wa	wading through fields; on my right
Arisoumi	the Ariso Sea.
	(Bashō)

Hitoone wa	Is a cloud pouring
shigururu kumo ka	rain on one of the ridges?
yuki no Fuji	Snow-covered Fuji.
	(Bashō)

With regard to these verses, the Master said, "When you compose a poem upon entering a large province, you must understand that province. Once a famous person from the capital went to Kaga Province and composed a poem about treading on minnows in a river called the Kunze. Even if this were a superb poem, it would be inappropriate: it does not reflect the dignity and status of that province." The Ariso poem was composed with these considerations in mind.

As for the verse on Mount Fuji, if the vast scale of the mountain is not revealed in the poem, Mount Fuji will become just another mountain. ("Akazōshi," *NKBZ* 51: 556–57)

The poem must reflect the character and size of the province if it is to pay proper tribute. If a poet enters a large province such as Kaga and composes on an obscure place like the Kunze River or on a lowly subject such as minnows, the poem will be an insult to the province. The first exemplary poem opens with the image of the speaker working his way through a field of ripening rice plants, suggesting a bumper crop and a rich province, and ends with Arisoumi (literally, "Rocky-coast Sea"), a famous *utamakura*. The two expansive and felicitous images suggest the grandeur of Kaga Province. In the second poem, a cloud of rain on one of the ridges, indicating that atmospheric conditions differ from one part of the mountain to the next, reveals the awesome size of Mount Fuji, covered with dazzling snow. The result is a laudatory address to the large province of Suruga (Shizuoka Prefecture).

An *aisatsu* to the land will sometimes focus on the products of the locale. The following poem, written in 1694 during Bashō's last journey as a greeting to Bashō's host, Tsukamoto Joshū, is also an *aisatsu* to Suruga Province.

Surugaji ya	Road through Suruga—
hanatachibana mo	even the orange blossoms have
cha no nioi	the fragrance of tea.[15]

The poem praises the province by making reference to two famous local products, oranges and tea. (Both are *kigo* for summer.) The much-admired, strong scent of the orange blossoms is overwhelmed by the fragrance of fresh tea leaves being roasted. The harmonious aromatic mixture becomes a treat for the traveler, a visitor to Suruga.

Sometimes Bashō's *aisatsu* are to a deity or spirit of a particular place. The following passage appears toward the beginning of *Oku no hosomichi*:

> On the first of the Fourth Month, we visited the holy mountain at Nikkō. In the distant past, this holy mountain had been called Futara Mountain. When the Great Master Kūkai built a temple here, the name of the holy mountain was changed to Nikkō, Light of the Sun. Perhaps the Great Master had been able to look a thousand years into the future. Now its holy light shines brightly over the entire land, and its benevolence extends to the most remote corners of the country. The dwellings of the four classes—the warrior, the farmer, the artisan, and the merchant—are safe, and the world is at peace. I have more to write, but out of respect for the deity, I shall stop here.

Ara tōto	Awe-inspiring!
aoba wakaba no	On dark green leaves, light green leaves,
hi no hikari	the light of the sun.
	(*NKBZ* 41: 345)

The *hokku* is, first of all, a landscape poem, which derives much of its beauty from the melodic middle line (with its repeated *a* sound): the speaker is struck by the sight of the sun shining on a rich mixture of dark evergreen leaves (*aoba*) and light-green deciduous leaves (*wakaba*).[16] By incorporating the name of the place into the poem—*hi no hikari* ("light of the sun"), the Japanese reading for Nikkō—the *hokku* also becomes a salute to the deity at Nikkō. The initial version, recorded by Sora, Bashō's travel companion, is:

Ana tōto	Awe-inspiring!
ko no shitayami mo	Reaching the dark beneath the trees,
hi no hikari	the light of the sun.

This earlier version, in which the light of the sun reaches even the darkness beneath the thick trees, directly echoes the prose passage that describes the divine light (of the Tokugawa clan deity) extending even to the distant, inner reaches of the land. The first version is more allegorical and conceptual, paying open tribute to the deity at the Tōshōgū Shrine. By contrast, the final version in *Oku no hosomichi* can—like many of Bashō's best *aisatsu*—be read either as a descriptive landscape poem or as a greeting. The speaker expresses awe at the sight of the rays of the summer sun pouring down on the dark and light green leaves that envelop the mountain. The sunlight is also the divine light that "shines brightly over the entire land." In the words of Kigin, the *fū* ("indirect expression") is contained within the *ga* ("direct expression"). The wonder of nature and that of the divine presence become one. The poem, however, is not necessarily a faithful depiction of Bashō's personal experience. Sora's diary on the journey to the Deep North reveals not only that Bashō conceived of the poem before going to Nikkō but that there was no sunshine on that particular day: "The first of the Fourth Month. A steady drizzle since last night. Cloudy all day. We arrived at Nikkō in the afternoon."[17]

Greetings to the land usually incorporate the name of the place into the poem. As in the Nikkō poem, Bashō's *aisatsu* to a place or its spirit often employ the kind of complex wordplay reminiscent of Teimon and Danrin *haikai,* specifically *kakekotoba* (puns) and *engo* (associative words), which interweave the name of the place with a description of the locale. Since these *aisatsu* to the land must reflect the tone or character of the particular place at which the poet now resides as a guest, these poems are often indistinguishable from poems on *utamakura*, poetic places, which also embed the place-name into the poem. As we shall see, *utamakura* poems can be conceived not only as salutations to the place (and its spirit) but as *aisatsu* to the poets of the past who have become, through their poetry, associated with that particular place. The "beginnings of poetry" *hokku*, for example, is not only a greeting to the region of Michinoku (not to mention the host Tōkyū), it is an *aisatsu* to those ancient poets closely associated with Michinoku—Nōin, Saigyō, Sōgi—who are the symbolic "beginnings of poetry" for Bashō.

PROSE LITERATURE AS *AISATSU*

Many of Bashō's *haibun*—his elliptical, poetic prose vignettes, of which there are over sixty—were originally written as *aisatsu*, as greetings of the kind found in his poetry.

Minomushi no	Come and listen
ne o kiki ni koyo	to the sound of the bagworm!
kusa no io	My grass hermitage.

In response to this *hokku* by Bashō, Yamaguchi Sodō wrote "Minomushi no setsu" (Comment on the Bagworm). Moved by the beauty of Sodō's poetic prose, Bashō then wrote "Postscript to 'Comment on the Bagworm,'" a *haibun* in which he praises Sodō's writing. The result is an extended dialogue (not unlike *haikai* linked verse) in which Bashō and Sodō alternately meditate on the nature of reclusion.

Some of Bashō's *haibun*, such as "Mourning for Matsukura Ranran" ("Matsukura Ranran o itamu"), are laments. Others, such as "On Parting from Kyoriku" ("Kyoriku ni ribetsu no kotoba"), are the prose equivalent of a parting poem. "Paper Blanket" ("Kamibusuma no ki," 1689) is a record of appreciation. On the last leg of his journey through the Deep North, Bashō rested at the house of a disciple (Jokō) in Ōgaki, where another disciple, Chikuko, offered his services as a masseur to the exhausted master. Bashō was so grateful to Chikuko that, as a memento of his long journey, he left him his treasured "paper blanket" (*kamibusuma*) together with "Paper Blanket," a *haibun* that reveals Bashō's buoyant *haikai* spirit as well as his affection for Chikuko.[18]

As with Bashō's *aisatsu* poetry, a typical *haibun* was written as an expression of gratitude to one's host. The well-known "Tower of Eighteen" ("Jūhachirō no ki," 1688), for example, was written when Bashō was invited to the house of Kashima Zen'eimon, in Gifu, on his way back from his *Oi no kobumi* journey.

There is a stately tower on the banks of the Nagara River, in Mino Province. Kashima is the owner's name. Inaba Mountain rises up to the rear, and mountains high and low, neither too near nor too far, stand to the west. A cedar grove hides the temple in the middle of the rice fields, and the dwellings along the shore are wrapped in the deep green of bamboo. Water-bleached cloth has been stretched out to dry here and there, and to the right a ferryboat floats on the water. The villagers walk back and forth ceaselessly; the houses of the fisherfolk stand side by side; and the fishermen pull in their nets and cast out their lines—each one working as if to enhance the setting of the stately mansion.

The vista is enough to make one forget the heat of the lingering summer sun. The moon at last replaces the rays of the setting sun, and the light of the flares entangled in the waves gradually comes closer as the residents begin cormorant fishing at the base of the mansion—a startling sight! In the cool breeze, I find the famous Eight Views of Xiao-xiang and the Ten Sights of Xihu. If one were to give this tower a name, Eighteen Sights would be appropriate.

Kono atari	From this single spot
me ni miyuru mono wa	all things that meet the eye
mina suzushi	bring coolness.

(NKBZ 41: 456–57)

The *haibun* is an elegant homage to Bashō's host, a kind of hymn of praise, climaxing with the image of "coolness" (*suzushi*) in the *hokku*. Though the social function of this work as a "private" *aisatsu* is obvious, its compact structure, terse style, and gentle poetic overtones quickly turned it into a "public," literary work that was widely admired and repeatedly anthologized.

Another *haibun* salutation to a host is "The Pure Dwelling" ("Sharakudō no ki," 1690), which was written when Bashō, residing in Zeze (Gifu Prefecture), visited the home of Chinseki, a local doctor and one of his most promising disciples.

The mountain is still and nurtures the spirit; the water moves and consoles the heart. Between the stillness and movement is the dwelling of a man called Chinseki, of the Hamada family. Here one gazes forever at the beautiful landscape, composes poetry, and is cleansed of the dust of the world. Hence the name Pure Dwelling. At its gate hangs a warning, "Worldly discretion may not enter," which takes

one step further Yamazaki Sōkan's famous comic poem.[19]
The extremely simple dwelling has two small tearooms,
where Chinseki practices the *wabi* spirit of Sen no Rikyū and
Takeno Jōō without preoccupying himself with their complex rules of tea. In the garden he plants trees, arranges
rocks, and enjoys the fleeting pleasures of life. The Bay of
Omono wears, like two sleeves, Seta on its left and Karasaki
on its right. It embraces Lake Biwa and faces Mikami Mountain. Lake Biwa is shaped like a lute, causing the wind in the
pines to harmonize with the sound of the waves. From an
angle, one can see Mount Hiei and the high peak of Hira,
while Otowa Mountain and Mount Ishiyama rest on one's
shoulder. In the spring, the dwelling wears the cherry
blossoms of Nagara in its hair; and in the autumn, it dresses
in front of the moon at Mirror Mountain. The setting is like
the makeup of a beautiful woman, light one day and heavy
the next, causing the admiring heart to change with the
scenery.

Shihō yori	From all four sides
hana fukiire	cherry blossoms are blown in
Nio no umi	over Lake Biwa.

(*NKBZ* 41: 498)

The first half, which describes the Sharakudō and the origins of its
name, fulfills the *haibun*'s function as an *aisatsu*. Indeed, "The Pure
Dwelling" resembles "Tower of Eighteen" in format, opening with a
description of the natural setting, naming the owner of the dwelling,
comparing the vista to famous places in the Chinese tradition, describing the host's exemplary character, and ending with a felicitous poem.
As in "Tower of Eighteen," Bashō's *haibun* also embodies his spiritual
and aesthetic views: the mountain and water, for example, reflect the
poetics of *fueki ryūkō*, "the unchanging" and the "changing."

The composition of *haibun* was related to the practice of calligraphy and painting, both of which became significant sources of income
for Bashō. To offer someone a poem meant writing it down in an
aesthetically pleasing form. Poems by masters were prized as much, if
not more, for the calligraphy of the author as for the literary contents.
A single *hokku* was sufficient to fill a *tanjaku*, a small rectangular strip
of paper for displaying poetry in the poet's own hand, but for a *kaishi*,
a larger, wider paper, it was usually necessary to add some prose writing to the *hokku*. Sometimes Bashō would copy out a passage from a
Nō libretto next to the *hokku*, but the best solution was usually a sketch

(often an ink-painting) or an original piece of elegant prose, a *haibun*.[20]

Nozarashi kikō, Bashō's first major work of travel literature, draws on at least five such *haibun*. Almost all of the *haibun* that Bashō composed during his visit to the Deep North—there are at least thirteen notable pieces—were later incorporated into *Oku no hosomichi*. The same applies to *Oi no kobumi* and other travel literature. The following *haibun* was given to Bashō's host Tōkyū, using a *hokku* cited earlier, during his journey to the Deep North.

> Looking forward to the various famous places in Michi-noku Province, I traveled north, where I was drawn, first of all, to the ruins of Shirakawa Barrier. I followed the ancient road to that former checkpoint, crossing along the way the present barrier at Shirakawa. I soon arrived at Iwase County and knocked on the fragrant gate of the gentleman Satansai Tōkyū. Fortunately, I was able, in the words of Wang Wei, "to cross the Yang Barrier and meet an old friend."

Fūryū no	The beginnings of
hajime ya oku no	poetry!—In the Deep North
taue uta	songs of rice-planting.

(NKBZ 41: 474)

Compared with the corresponding passage in *Oku no hosomichi*, this *haibun* is far more flattering, comparing the host to a figure in a Chinese poem by Wang Wei and making no mention, as *Oku no hosomichi* does, of the visitor's laborious trek across Shirakawa Barrier. After accumulating a sufficient number of such *haibun*, which were centered on *hokku* and often written for social or professional (financial) purposes, Bashō would integrate them into a larger artistic whole, usually altering the text and the account of the original events.

In the medieval period, *renga* masters frequently traveled great distances, visiting powerful and wealthy provincial patrons, who would invite, treat, and support their favorite poetry teachers in exchange for their company, judgment, and instruction. A *renga* master would often write about his journey and send the *kikōbun* to the provincial host as an expression of gratitude for his patronage and hospitality. Nishiyama Sōin (1605–82), the founder of the Danrin school of *haikai*, and other Edo *haikai* masters continued this tradition. At the end of *Nihon angya bunshū* (Prose Collection of Travels Around Japan, 1690), a collection of travel sketches by the *haikai* poet Sanzenfū (or Michikaze), the author writes,

I dislike most of what is written here. I shortened the original
pieces three times and managed to fit them all into about
seven scrolls. But those who look at even this will be bored.
Since these pieces were written as an expression of appreciation for those who generously offered me lodging and meals,
I have preserved them.[21]

Bashō wrote travel accounts that were more literary than those by
Sanzenfū, but the social aspect that Sanzenfū mentions here, writing
"as an expression of appreciation," is still discernible. Bashō not only
wrote travel accounts as tokens of gratitude, he sometimes illustrated
his own texts, presenting the entire work in an aesthetically pleasing
"picture scroll" (*emaki*) format, one that could, like his *tanjaku* and
kaishi, serve as a memento for his patron or host. The artistically
packaged work was sent, like many of his *haibun*, as a souvenir to those
who had supported him spiritually and financially on his journey.

The most notable example is *Nozarashi kikō*, one of Bashō's most
famous travel works, which was probably written for and sent to Tani
Bokuin, the host and patron who invited him to Ōgaki in the province
of Mino.[22] As his correspondence two years prior to the journey reveals, Bashō initially planned the trip in response to an invitation from
disciples in Ōgaki, particularly Bokuin, a shipping agent, who encouraged him to embark on his first provincial tour as a *haikai* master. The
subsequent death of Bashō's mother (six months prior to the trip) and
the desire to visit her grave became additional motivations, and Bashō
left Edo in 1684. *Nozarashi kikō* comes to a climax with the following
passage.

When I stopped for the night at Ōgaki, I became a guest
at Bokuin's residence. Since I had begun this journey from
Musashi with thoughts of a wind-swept skeleton, I wrote:

Shini mo senu   Not even dead yet,
tabine no hate yo   I come to the journey's end—
aki no kure   the last of autumn.

(*NKBZ* 41: 294)

Bashō's poem, which echoes the opening poem of *Nozarashi kikō*, is an
aisatsu to Bokuin, thanking him for his warm hospitality, which has
saved Bashō's cold, frail body from the death he had anticipated on
the road. The rest of *Nozarashi kikō*, which has little prose and resembles a poetry collection, is different in format and was probably
added later, as a sequel to the main part.[23] As with much of his *aisatsu*
poetry, Bashō first wrote this travel sketch as an *aisatsu* and then later

altered—in this case, added to—the initial version, thereby eliminating much of its original interpersonal function and transforming it into a more "public," literary work.

Bashō's travel pieces, like some of his *haibun*, may also have functioned as a lament or an offering to the spirit of the dead. *Oi no kobumi*, for example, Bashō's second-longest travel account, may have, at least initially, served as a literary prayer to the spirit of Tōkoku, Bashō's disciple and close friend.[24] In the journey described in *Oi no kobumi*, Bashō travels to Hobi, in the province of Mikawa, where Tōkoku is in exile. The journey climaxes with the following scene.

> Honeyama is a place where they capture hawks. It is on the southern peninsula, facing the sea. They say it is the place where the migrating hawks first cross. When I remembered that the Irago hawks appeared in classical poetry, I was even more deeply moved and wrote:

Taka hitotsu	A single hawk
mitsukete ureshi	crosses the sky, to my joy.
Iragosaki	Irago Point.

(NKBZ 41: 316)

At first glance, the poem appears to be a purely lyrical expression of joy that the speaker's journey to a place associated in poetry with hawks has fulfilled his expectations. The *hokku*, however, is also an allegorical greeting, revealing the poet's joy at meeting Tōkoku, who has been exiled to Irago Point and who is, like the solitary hawk in the sky, living a lonely existence on this isolated peninsula. As in the best of Bashō's *aisatsu*, the *ga* ("direct expression") contains the *fū* ("indirect expression") within it. *Oi no kobumi* is a record of a journey that Bashō took in 1687–88, but it was not written until much later, after the journey to the Deep North, around 1690–91, shortly after the death of Tōkoku in the Third Month of 1690—circumstances that strongly suggest that *Oi no kobumi* served, at least in part, as a memorial to his prized disciple.[25]

GREETINGS TO THE ANCIENTS

Perhaps the most intriguing, original, and complex type of greeting in Bashō's literature is that to an "ancient" (*kojin*), a major poet of the distant past, with whom the protagonist often enters into an intertextual dialogue. *Oku no hosomichi*, for example, can be interpreted, among other things, as an offering or tribute to Saigyō on the five-hundredth anniversary of his death. (Saigyō died in 1190, and Bashō embarked on his journey in 1689.) Summoned by the spirit of Saigyō, the protagonist embarks on a distant journey to the Deep North, where he encounters the spirit of his poetic patron.[26] As the ultimate host of Bashō's journey, Saigyō becomes the object of various poems of gratitude, tribute, or remembrance. The primary stage for this interaction is the *utamakura*, the poetic place in which the spirit and poetry of the dead poet resides and which Bashō tirelessly seeks out on his long journey. In these encounters, the narrative often takes on the framework and mood of a "dream structure" (*mugen nō*) Nō play in which a traveling priest addresses and encounters the spirit of the dead in a dream.

> The willow that was the subject of Saigyō's poem "Where a crystal stream flows" still stood in the village of Ashino, on a footpath in a rice field. The lord of the manor had repeatedly offered to show this willow to me, and I had wondered where it was. Today I was able to stand in the shade of this very willow.

Ta ichimai	A whole field of rice
uete tachisaru	now planted, I leave the shade
yanagi kana	of the willow tree.

(NKBZ 41: 350)

The entire passage is an allusive variation on *Yugyō yanagi* (The Wandering Priest and the Willow), a Nō play based on the following poem in *Shinkokinshū* (Summer, 3: 262) by Saigyō.

Michi no be ni	By the road's edge,
shimizu nagaruru	a crystal stream flows gently
yanagi kage	in a willow's shade.
shibashi tote koso	I thought to pause for a while
tachitomaritsure	and stood rooted to the spot.

In the Nō play an itinerant priest (the *waki*), retracing the steps of Saigyō through the Deep North, meets an old man (the *shite* of the first half) who shows him the withered willow about which Saigyō wrote his famous poem. The old man later turns out to be the spirit of that willow. At the end of the drama the priest offers prayers to the spirit of the willow (the *shite* of the second half), thereby enabling it to achieve salvation.[27] When, in *Oku no hosomichi*, the lord of the manor offers to introduce Saigyō's willow to Bashō, the passage takes on the atmosphere of a Nō dream play in which Bashō, who already bears the aura of a traveling priest, encounters the spirit of Saigyō, embodied in the willow.

Most commentators, finding it hard to believe that Bashō would plant rice seedlings himself, interpret the *hokku* as having two subjects:

farm girls, who are planting the seedlings in the rice paddy in the summer, and Bashō, who stands under the willow. Filled with thoughts of Saigyō, who had stood by the same tree and composed the famous poem on the "crystal stream," the speaker loses track of time, and before he knows it, an entire field of rice has been planted by the farm girls. However, the grammar of the poem (which would suggest only one subject, Bashō) and the context provided by the Nō play suggest that it is Bashō, imagining himself as an itinerant monk, who helps plant rice seedlings in the field next to the willow as an offering to the spirit of Saigyō, his poetic host and patron.[28] In either event, the *hokku* quietly echoes Saigyō's poem, bringing the spirits of the two poets together across time.

The "lord of the manor"—*kohō*, a Chinese term reminiscent of medieval Nō librettos—is a reference to Suketoshi (or Mototoshi), an old friend of Bashō's and a wealthy patron. Suketoshi, generally known by his *haikai* name Tōsui, died in the Sixth Month of 1692. *Oku no hosomichi*, one draft of which refers to "the deceased lord of the manor," appears to have been written immediately after Suketoshi's death, three years after the actual journey. The circumstances of composition, which parallel that of *Oi no kobumi*, strongly suggest that this particular passage and poem are also a memorial *aisatsu* to the spirit of Bashō's recently deceased friend and fellow poet.

Bashō's journeys are often thought of as being solitary excursions, but in fact they were often attempts to open up poetic dialogue with other poets in different parts of the country through linked-verse sessions. One of the chief reasons for Bashō's journeys was to avoid the poetic stagnation caused by constantly composing linked verse with the same poets. The journeys also opened up an intertextual dialogue with poets of the past. Many of Bashō's poems that are variations on or allusions to the classical poetry of Saigyō, Nōin, Sōgi, and other traveler poets can be interpreted, at least in part, as greetings to the ancients, who become the wellspring for new poetry. In contrast to the salutations to Bashō's immediate hosts, which are tightly bound by circumstance, these *aisatsu* transcend time and place; or more precisely, they come alive in the context of an extended literary tradition. In *The Anxiety of Influence*, Harold Bloom sees all major Romantic poets as engaged in an intertextual dialogue with their poetic predecessors, engaged in an effort to carve out literary space for themselves, an Oedipal struggle to overcome and "slay" the poetic father.[29] In contrast to Bloom's antagonistic struggle, the dialogue that emerges in Bashō's writings and poetry takes the form of communal, familial greetings, signs of reverence and intimacy, through which the poet attempts to reestablish ties with his poetic ancestors and father figures.

NOTES

1. It should be noted that a number of Japanese modern scholars, beginning with Yamamoto Kenkichi, the first modern critic to stress the notion, have written on the subject of *aisatsu*, though almost nothing has been said about "greetings to the ancients" and the function of *haibun* and prose narrative as *aisatsu*. The following articles and books have been particularly helpful in preparing this essay: Katō Shūson, *Bashō zenku* (Tokyo: Chikuma Shobō, 1975), 2 vols.; Mezaki Tokuei, "Bashō no aisatsu ni tsuite," in his *Bashō no uchi naru Saigyō* (Tokyo: Kayōsha, 1980), 25–72; Miyamoto Saburō, "Bashō haikai ni okeru shū to kō," in his *Bashō haikai ronkō* (Tokyo: Kazama Shoin, 1974), 43–54; Morita Ran, "Bashō no suikōku," in his *Bashō no hōhō* (Tokyo: Kyōiku Shuppan Sentā, 1970), 73–92; Shijō Haku, "Aisatsu ni tsuite," in Kadokawa Gengi, ed., *Hassō to hyōgen, Bashō no hon* 4 (Tokyo: Kadokawa Shoten, 1970), 141–77; Shiraishi Teizō, "Aisatsu ni tsuite," in Inui Hiroyuki and Shiraishi Teizō, eds., *Bashō monogatari* (Tokyo: Yūhikaku, 1977), 120–22; Ogata Tsutomu, *Matsuo Bashō, Nihon shijinsen* 17 (Tokyo: Chikuma Shobō, 1971); Ogata Tsutomu, "Za no bungaku" and "Sakuhin to za," in his *Za no bungaku* (Tokyo: Kadokawa Shoten, 1973), 7–29; Yamamoto Kenkichi, "Bashō," in his *Ikite kaeru* (Tokyo: Kawade Shobō Shinsha, 1973), 280–94; Yamamoto Kenkichi, *Bashō: Sono kanshō to hihyō* (Tokyo: Shinchōsha, 1955), 2 vols.; Yonetani Iwao, "Bashō aisatsu ku no suikō ni tsuite," in *Basho II, NBKSS* (1977), 54–61.

2. Yonetani Iwao claims that forty-six percent of Bashō's *hokku* in his travel literature are *aisatsu*. "Bashō aisatsu ku no suikō ni tsuite," 54.

3. Jonathan Culler, "Apostrophe," in his *The Pursuit of Signs* (London: Routledge and Kegan Paul, 1981), 135–54. According to Frye, "The lyric is the genre in which the poet, like the ironic writer, turns his back on the audience." Northrop Frye, *Anatomy of Criticism* (Princeton: Princeton University Press, 1957), 271.

4. Kidō Taizō, *Renga ronshū II* (Tokyo: Miyai Shoten, 1982), 446.

5. All citations from *Sanzōshi* and *Kyoraishō* are from Ijichi Tetsuo, Omote Akira, and Kuriyama Riichi, eds., *Renga ronshū, Nōgaku ronshū, Haironshū*, vol. 51 of *NKBZ*.

6. All citations from *Oku no hosomichi* and other prose works by Bashō are from Imoto Nōichi, Hori Nobuo, and Muramatsu Tomotsugu, eds., *Matsuo Bashō shū*, vol. 41 of *NKBZ*.

7. The *kasen* is included in *Hitotsubashi*, an anthology edited by Suzuki Seifū, the host and author of the *wakiku*. For text and commentary, see Abe Masami, *Bashō renkushō* (Tokyo: Meiji Shoin, 1978), 5: 86–87.

8. *Teimon haikaishū II*, vol. 2 of *Koten haibungaku taikei* (Tokyo: Shūseisha, 1951), 362.

9. *Hotaru* ("fireflies") is a *kigo* for summer. For text of this *kasen* and commentary, see Abe, *Bashō renkushō* (1981), 7: 172–204.

10. *Samidare* ("rains of summer") is a *kigo* for summer.

11. Scholars are uncertain whether the second line of the poem should be *umi ni iretaru* ("pouring into the sea") or *umi ni iritaru* ("entering into the sea"). Grammatically, the second version is more logical. Both variants exist.

12. For a list of the poems, see Miyamoto Saburō, op. cit., 47–48.

13. According to the folklorist and literary scholar Origuchi Shinobu, when a poet composed a poem on a flower, he or she was also greeting that flower. In the same manner, to compose a poem on a place associated with an *utamakura* was to greet the spirit of that place.

14. Yamamoto Kenkichi, "Bashō," 291–92.

15. Included in the *haikai* anthology *Sumidawara*.

16. *Wakaba* is a *kigo* for spring, but *aoba* is a *kigo* for summer. Bashō visited Nikkō on the first of the Fourth Month, which would make the *hokku* a summer poem.

17. The text of Sora's diary is printed in Ebara Taizō and Ogata Tsutomu, eds., *Shintei Oku no hosomichi*, vol. 490 of *Kadokawa bunko* (Tokyo: Kadokawa Shoten, 1967), 242.

18. *NKBZ* 41: 492–93.

19. Yamazaki Sōkan's comic poem is: "The best guests don't come,/ the second best come but do not sit,/ the third best come and stay for one night/ and the worst stay for two."

20. Imoto Nōichi, "Kaisetsu," in *Matsuo Bashō shū, NKBZ* 41: 31.

21. Cited by Ogata Tsutomu, "Nozarashi sutego," in his *Za no bungaku*, 103.

22. For evidence that *Nozarashi kikō* was written for Bokuin, see Yonetani Iwao, "Nozarashi kikō ni okeru Bashō," *Kinsei bungeikō* 10 (1966), included in *Bashō I, NBKSS* (1969), 76–85; and Ogata Tsutomu, "Nozarashi sutego," in his *Za no bungaku*, 102–19.

23. Yonetani Iwao argues that *Nozarashi kikō* was written in two stages, the second being a kind of sequel. The first part, or original version, was sent to Bokuin as a record of thanks. "*Nozarashi kikō* ni okeru Bashō," 78.

24. Ogata Tsutomu, "Chinkon no ryojō: Bashō *Oi no kobumi* kō," *Kokugo to kokubungaku* (January 1976), included in *Bashō II, NBKSS*, 122–33.

25. On the date of composition and motives for writing *Oi no kobumi*, see Takahashi Shōji, "*Oi no kobumi* no yōkyoku kōsei ni tsuite: *Oi no kobumi* ron josetsu," included in *Bashō II, NBKSS*, 110–21; Ogata Tsutomu, "Chinkon no ryojō: Bashō *Oi no kobumi* kō," 123–33; and Abe Masami, "*Oi no kobumi* no seiritsu," in *Bashō II, NBKSS*, 134–40. All three scholars argue, for different reasons, that *Oi no kobumi* was written long after the actual journey and that the death of Tōkoku was the primary motive for composition.

26. Shiraishi Teizō, "*Oku no hosomichi* no kōsō," *Rikkyō Daigaku Nihon bungaku* (December 1968), in *Bashō I, NBKSS*, 132–40.

27. An English translation of *Yugyō yanagi*, "The Priest and the Willow," appears in Donald Keene, ed., *Twenty Plays of the Nō Theatre* (New York: Columbia University Press, 1970), 220–36.

28. Ogata Tsutomu, *Matsuo Bashō*, 73.

29. Harold Bloom, *The Anxiety of Influence: A Theory of Poetry* (Oxford: Oxford University Press, 1973).

"The Raven at First Light": A Shinnai Ballad

TRANSLATED BY THOMAS BLENMAN HARE

TRANSLATOR'S INTRODUCTION

In the alley outside, the hour being late, he could hear a
wandering musician, and the wooden clappers of a Kabuki
mimic; and presently, from the second floor of a nearby
house, there came a woman's voice singing a Shinnai ballad.
Highly susceptible to the power of music, he was aroused this
evening, by strains from another age, to a nostalgia so intense
that he had to marvel at it himself.[1]

The speaker is a character from Nagai Kafū's early novel *Sneers* (*Rei-
shō*), in Edward Seidensticker's eloquent translation from *Kafū the
Scribbler*. The character has recently come home from study abroad,
and, like Kafū himself, feels alienated from the Japan to which he has
returned. In the strains of Shinnai descending upon him deep in the
night he finds a refuge, a part of the old Japan that has not yet been
completely eradicated in the Meiji rush to modernization. Kafū's
speaker is not xenophobic, and he is not trying to escape the pollution
of Western influence by turning to some indefinable essence of the
Japanese spirit. His appreciation is instead fortuitous and strongly
ambivalent, always tinged by a sense of loss and incompleteness. This
becomes yet clearer in a slightly longer passage from the same work:

Today, along all the handsome main streets of the East, bells
ring forth glad tidings of the age of liberation; but in the back
streets, along the dirty waters of the canals, the whisper of
the samisen is still there, wandering through the darkness.
That voice of civilization, the locomotive, thunders past, but
in the grass along the embankment insects are still singing.
Listen for a moment. In the music of our ancestors, in Take-
moto, Tomimoto, Itchū, Kiyomoto, frail notes from three

thin strings are enough to call up emotions deep as the moment of death. Such music has no need for the complicated structures of Western music, harmony and polyphony and counterpoint. Kōu found it almost unbearable—the loneliness and sadness that were a part of Japanese music, that stemmed from its very inadequacy, its simplicity and its monotony.[2]

Here, the narrator fails to mention Shinnai, naming instead its more theatrical cousins, Kiyomoto and the rest. The ambivalence, however, is spelled out much more distinctly, and it applies just as well or better in the case of Shinnai ballads because it runs a little deeper historically.

Shinnai has a centuries-old association with the licensed quarter and has long been considered improper, or even obscene—not a fit object of approbation, much less study. If the very existence of Shinnai as a viable performing art today is somewhat precarious, it is in considerable degree because of its links with prostitution. But of course, Shinnai would never have come into being at all without the Yoshiwara brothels and their tales of passion and ruin; ironically, it is also true that it would never have come into being without the very censorship and official disapproval that has continually dogged its existence. The ambivalence we mentioned above goes right to the heart of Shinnai.

The origins of Shinnai and several other important genres of Tokugawa ballad music (e.g., jōruri) are intimately connected with the demise of Bungobushi, "Bungo ballads," which had become remarkably popular in the early eighteenth century. A single man, Miyakoji Bungo-no-jō (d. 1740), was responsible for both its success and its infamy. His stories of love suicide and elopement intoxicated the crowds of Edo as much as they infuriated the shogun's moralists. Perhaps not coincidentally, he wore his hair differently from accepted convention, like Franz Liszt and John Lennon. The Confucian Dazai Shundai (1680–1747) speaks for many in excoriating both performers and fans of Bungo-no-jō's then-thriving performing art:

In the beginning of the Kyōhō era [1716–36], jōruri chanters from the Osaka area again appeared here and spread the vulgar style of that region, and, as a consequence, the people of Edo grew more and more enthusiastic about it, abandoning their own vintage jōruri styles to learn only the styles of Kyoto and Osaka. Nor was this trend limited to the lower classes; there were even those among the samurai bureau-cracy and elite who developed a liking for it and learned a bit themselves. In this, they forsook stories about the past and recounted the lascivious goings-on of the common crowd. The language of these pieces is unutterably backward and salacious. It hardly needs mentioning that this sort of thing should not be heard by samurai; in the company of parents and children or elder and younger brothers one should turn one's face away in shame and cover one's ears. Since this kind of *jōruri* has come into fashion in Edo, obscene behavior be-tween the sexes has increased immeasurably, and by the late 1730s has defiled even the residences of the samurai elite.[3]

Dazai speaks in the same threatened voice as other conservatives have in their diatribes against popular arts, from madrigals to waltzes to blues to rock and roll. If there is any difference here from those other cases, it is in the fact that the art under attack was effectively destroyed. In 1736, Bungo-no-jō was banned from teaching his art, and in 1739, he was prohibited from any theatrical performance whatsoever.

But the death of Bungobushi gave birth to a brood of new artistic descendants. Three genres of *jōruri* very important to the Kabuki theater, Tokiwazu, Tomimoto, and Kiyomoto, developed in Edo, while in the Kansai the mournful Miyazono (or Sonohachi) form was born.[4] And then, of course, there is Shinnai.

A disciple of Bungo-no-jō, Miyakoji Kagadayū, continued to en-joy public success but had the discretion to change his artistic name to Fujimatsu Satsuma-no-jō. Among the disciples he attracted were Kaga Hachidayū (1714–74) and Tsuruga Wakasa-no-jō (1712–86). The lat-ter (originally named Takai Masabyōe) had come to Edo to serve in a samurai household, but his dissolute habits got him into trouble, and so he turned to the freer life of a *jōruri* chanter, achieving full profes-sional status in 1748.

Wakasa-no-jō (also known as Tsuruga-dayū) is considered the founder of Shinnai and himself wrote the two great masterpieces in the repertory, *Akegarasu yume no awayuki* (The Raven at First Light: A Faint Snowfall in Dreams) and *Wakaki no adanagusa* (Scandal at Sap-ling [House]), which is more commonly known as *Ranchō*, for its ep-onymous hero. Many other representative pieces in the genre have also been ascribed to him.[5] He managed to attract Kaga Hachidayū away from the tutelage of Satsuma-no-jō into his own new artistic line, and Hachidayū thereafter became known as Tsuruga Shinnai. If

Wakasa-no-jō was the great composer of the genre, Tsuruga Shinnai became its great vocal virtuoso; although he left no compositions of his own, the art itself came to be known by his name, as Shinnai or Shinnaibushi.

As a performing art, Shinnai has enjoyed less success than the other Edo descendants of Bungobushi. Unlike Tokiwazu, Tomimoto, and Kiyomoto, it was not associated with dance, and it garnered neither the professional nor amateur patronage of those other genres. Furthermore, although Shinnai continues to be used occasionally in the theater, it has not nearly so close a connection to Kabuki as do Tokiwazu and Kiyomoto. It is most closely associated with wandering minstrels in Yoshiwara, the licensed quarter in Edo, and although it enjoyed considerable popularity in such a context, it was banned during World War II. Since the end of the war, Shinnai has been unable to attract a large and generous audience.

The piece *Akegarasu yume no awayuki* is one of the two universally acknowledged masterpieces of Shinnai. Inspiration for the piece came from the 1769 love suicide of Iseya Inosuke, the twenty-year-old son of a Kuramae provisioner to the shogun, and his mistress, a twenty-three-year-old Yoshiwara prostitute named Miyoshino. The piece was composed around 1772 and apparently had an immediate success. It was not produced as Kabuki, however, until 1852, when it was given its theatrical debut in Osaka.

By this time a staged version of the story had already been produced in Osaka, but the lead actor, Danjūrō the Eighth, thinking Shinnai too vulgar, commissioned a Kiyomoto adaptation with the title *Akegarasu hana no nureginu* (The Raven at First Light: Robes Dampened in the Flowers, first performance, 1850; Edo debut, 1851). The Kiyomoto version was very successful. It was occasionally inserted into the second act of *Chūshingura*, with the understanding that the hero, Tokijirō, was actually one of the forty-seven retainers in disguise.[6] There are also Tokiwazu and Gidayū versions of the piece.

One critic writing in the early 1960s attributes the success of *Akegarasu* to its skillful depiction of the decadence of the licensed quarter in the 1770s and 1780s; he allows, rather uncharitably, that even the "know-nothing young people of today are struck by its eroticism."[7] If that "eroticism" seems understated three decades later, the piece nonetheless remains remarkably moving. It was never intended to be read, and attains its artistic objectives only in full chanted performance to the accompaniment of *shamisen*, but even in printed form it

provides an intriguing view of the raw materials of *jōruri*. The description of preparations for business in the Yamanaya brothel is finely
detailed; the conversations among the characters are "literary" in that
they contain considerable wordplay, allusion, and wit, while at the
same time remaining plausible. The use of narrative voice is sophisticated, moving seamlessly from description to commentary to direct
quotation. Grammar is flexible; often one "sentence" will pivot into
another without attaining the syntactic stability of more conventional
prose. Vintage literary techniques are deployed from time to time, as,
for example, near the beginning, where a catalog of birds, or
torizukushi (including a rooster, raven, hawk, stork, sparrows, and
cuckoos), is interwoven with the description of someone's arrival in
the licensed quarter.[8] Proverbs and commonplaces from earlier works
find their way into the text. The line *kinō no hana wa kyō no yume*
("yesterday's flowers are a dream today"), for instance, can be traced
from the Nō play *Aoi no Ue* (Lady Aoi), to a *kōwaka* ballad, to a collection of songs from the Genroku period, *Matsu no ha* (Pine Needles),
before it appears in a popular *kouta*, the closest antecedent to
Akegarasu itself.[9]

The piece is melodramatic, to be sure, but the melodrama is
ironically undercut by the last line, which casts the entire experience
into the world of a dream. This final line is the second half of a
framing device that begins with the opening passage of the piece,
where an unspecified (probably male) character is carried into the
bustle of the licensed quarter in a sedan chair. This feature of
Akegarasu has been lost in performance, because the opening passage
is no longer part of the repertory. When performed today, the ballad
is divided into two acts or *dan*; the first is called "Urazato no heya"
(Urazato's Room) and the second is known as "Yukizeme" (Torment in
the Snow). The divisions have been noted in the translation.

Akegarasu yume no awayuki provided the inspiration for the plot of
Santō Kyōden's *sharebon*, *Shōgi kinuburui* (The Fluttering Robes of a
Courtesan), although his characters' names were taken from Chika-
matsu's *Meido no hikyaku* (The Fleet Messenger from Hell). Tamenaga
Shunsui, in his turn, wrote a sequel to the story of Urazato and Toki-
jirō in the early 1820s in his first *ninjōbon*, *Akegarasu nochi no masayume*
(The Raven at First Light: A Dream Come True). A Shinnai sequel,
also entitled *Akegarasu nochi no masayume*, was written by Fujimatsu
Rochū in 1857.

According to this final version, Urazato and Tokijirō make their
escape from the brothel and go to Fukagawa, where they hang themselves. At the time, Tokijirō happens to be carrying a family heirloom,

a precious sword; indeed, his reason for going to Fukagawa in the first place has been to prevent this sword from falling into a stranger's hands. His uncle happens to be the chief priest at a Hokke sect temple in Fukagawa. After Tokijirō and Urazato have killed themselves, he calls upon the magic power of the sword and chants powerful Hokke mantras, succeeding thereby in reviving Urazato and Tokijirō. The master of Urazato's brothel, moreover, turns out to be a parishioner of Tokijirō's uncle; arrangements are made for Urazato's release, and she and Tokijirō are married and presumably live happily ever after.

For the translation I have used the text in *Nihon ongyoku zenshū: Tomimoto oyobi Shinnai zenshū,* edited by Nakauchi Chōji and Tamura Nishio (Tokyo: Seibundō, 1927), 403–13. I have referred as well to texts in *Nihon kayō shūsei* 11, edited by Takano Tatsuyuki (Tokyo: Tōkyōdō, 1961), 396–400; and *Shinnaishū,* edited by Seikyoku Bungei Kenkyūkai (Tokyo: Isobe Kōyōdō, 1911), 15–27. The *Nihon ongyoku zenshū* text contains some annotation and a brief note on the piece.

THE RAVEN AT FIRST LIGHT: A FAINT SNOWFALL IN DREAMS

Heart aloft on the floating clouds each evening in a four-hand palanquin, fleetly borne on well-matched shoulders, running down the road of desperate love, throw yourself into the wager: no sooner have you met than parting springs to mind. The punctual rooster calls the time at dawn, but a raven-haired beauty isn't so heartless; when she crows depends upon the company she keeps.

Filled with restless irritation, you can't force down the lump that catches in your chest. Ah, here we are at last—Bawdytown. Rumor runs rampant on Fifth Street.

Locked out of Yamanaya, Tokijirō prowls about—a sorry plight if he were seen by hawkeyed lookouts, vigilant as storks throughout the night[10]—while Yoshiwara sparrows, window shoppers, prattle on: once you die, you'll hear the songs of Stygian cuckoos, messengers from the abyss . . . but now, before you die, to cast your thoughts to death in a river of tears—no one else could know the depths of his sad heart.

Time to set up shop for the night. A comb box into this room, a mirror stand goes off to that, two or three of the new girls together gossiping, a rumor now and again about a customer; last night's sweet words of love, sighs over the latest tearjerker, a melancholy wish for times gone by. And as always someone's bursting with envy: "I wish I could show off an outfit like that to my own boyfriend, 'specially today."

One of the apprentices, a child, prays in innocence to holy Kannon, "I have a rendezvous with someone I don't like—please don't let him come tonight," and then she tests her fortune with a hairpin on the floor, and when it turns out "He will come," she tries her luck again. Holding back a chuckle at her earnestness, an older girl offers this advice, "It's still too early to say if you like someone or not. You can't be so picky about each and every steady customer you get. After all, success isn't measured by how many times you get to stand in for somebody else." In her embarrassment, the younger girl takes a kimono from the rack and starts to fold it up while yet another girl begins to rush about sweeping the room and carrying away the mirror stand.

Kaya the madam shouts, "Hurry up. It's opening time. Finish your makeup and get down there!" All at once they clatter down the stairs, and silence falls over every room.

Urazato's Room

Wakening to the quiet rain of spring, Urazato already feels the pangs of love's distraction: "What bond is this? Since the first time we met, I've been dominated by this attraction to him; there's no holding out against such tenderness." Heartache when she pulls back bedclothes hiding him from sight: "It must be a load on your mind, Tokijirō, the way they're trying to keep you away from me. I feel so happy that you put up with it all, for my sake. I'm hardly worth it."

Then he puts his arms around her, "No, it's all because of me"; he pulls her close and they lie in wordless embrace, weeping while the time goes by. As his tears stream down gently, "How I wish we could just stay like this. Our love is boundless, but the longer this goes on, the harder it will be for you. I've been telling you all along: there's the two hundred-weight of gold my father sent me for the master here in Edo—so much for that. And I've parlayed everything I can out of the family's business connections. So here I am! I'd like to ask you to put an end to it all with me, but I could never lay a hand on you—I love you too much. I want you to go on without me, and when I'm gone, remember me in your prayers."

He stands up to go, but she holds him fast. "That's too cruel! It's heartless. You could leave me tonight, and still, as long as I knew you were all right, I could hope for a chance to see you again. But what woman could be strong enough to let you go, knowing you'd resolved to die! All those pledges of love we exchanged would turn to bitter enemies. If you've made up your mind to die, then why haven't you asked me to go with you, hand in hand, like this, to cross the triple rapids of the River of Death? Maybe I should be grateful that you don't want me to die too, but I'm not. These days you've grown so pale and thin . . . and then last night, masking plans for death with words of love, lying there half-dressed, in the white gown of a corpse[11] . . . that you could even think of leaving me behind like this, so in love with you. . . . There's something more terrifying than a demon in your heart. I won't release you, I won't let you go. Kill me first, then go!" Clinging tightly to his shoulders, she holds him fast, shuddering with tears.

Kaya the madam scolds, "This girl falls asleep as soon as she sees lamplight." Then she shouts out, "Miss Urazato, Miss Urazato, I'd like to see you for a minute!"

Urazato bolts upright, but casually replies, "Yes, what's the matter?"

Kaya snaps back, "What else would it be but that guest of yours? I hear he's been there all night long, and the younger girls tell me they don't know who he is, but judging from the squabble now, he must be Mr. Tokijirō. Master wants to see you. Come along now." She takes Urazato's hand and drags her off to the next room. The master stands in wait. He grabs her hair and wraps it tightly around his hand.

"Damn you, you just don't get it with words alone." In a rage that might near burst his temples, insensible to any consequence, the whiteheaded old man jerks her down the stairs behind him. A crowd of bouncers follows close on their heels.

"Look at all the trouble Urazato's suffered on account of that man!"

"Deep in debt to the house, he creeps up to the second floor to stay in hiding, the sneak."

"Drag him out and squash him good!"

And from the lightless depths of love's delusion, mercilessly, out they drag him, then they stomp upon him, pound him, rip him right to shreds. And beaten up like that, all he can do is weep and weep and clamber down the back stairs where they pitch him through the entrance, slam the gate shut, and slap the lock down tight: a dreadful sound.

Torment in the Snow

Inside the gate the master ties Urazato to an old tree and picks up a broom to beat her, while gales of snow blow bitterly through the garden. The child Midori cries out, clinging to the master, "Please, sir, let her go!" Thereupon he binds up the sobbing child as well. Urazato raises her tear-stained face. "Punish me as you like, but what's the poor child done? Please, leave her be."

The master feels sorry for the girl, but speaks as harshly as he can. "You look here, Urazato! If we shut out your customer, it's for his own damn good. We have to look after our girls, and the man's own fortune is important, too. Why, he's still young. If we have him coming here too often he's sure to be disinherited . . . if, that is, it's his father's money he's spending; or, if he's in service, then he's sure to botch things with his boss. I hear he's just borrowed more and lengthened his indenture. Next thing you know it'll be either double suicide or a getaway.

"It's my concern for you that makes me do this, even if it turns you against me in the end. I take good care of my girls, no matter what. After all, a woman like you—even as a child you were so pretty that I raised you extra carefully, not like all the others. What do you have to be angry about? You listen here. You had just better get yourself straight and do as you're supposed to."

On and on he lectures her, but she won't hear a word of it. Her mind is set on suffering.

"Your own damn sins condemn you, and that brat Midori is your own damn servant girl. She'll make a good example. Now give him up. Give him up and I'll let you go this very minute.

"Boys, keep your eyes on this bitch." With that, he goes inside. Urazato watches him walk away until her vision clouds with tears.

"Sympathetic words, yes, but don't forget this. Whatever pain and sadness you cause me, I won't give him up. In fact, if I can't live with him, then I want us to die together. Kill me, Tokijirō. I just want to die, I tell you."

Yesterday's flowers are a dream today. When you're swept away by love, there is no right or wrong. Someone bound in service can't have things go her way, and when the time of parting comes, she can't just say goodbye.

"If only I could change this suffering for that shamisen upstairs . . . for Tokijirō staying all night long, pulling me close in my negligée, for all the delights of whispered love—but this is what I get instead. Where is he tonight! What's he doing! What a wretched world when two lovers can't be together.

"How could I deny my life to the man I love? If these dewdrops of my being were to disappear, my anger would die, too, and yet . . .

"Poor Midori, how sad you must feel! How you must hate me! Hold on a little longer. What did you do to deserve this?—you just happened to be in service to a useless whore like me. Please forgive me.

"And tonight of all nights, a snow like this! What could have brought all this to pass? You're awfully cold, aren't you, poor dear?"

"No, no, I'm not cold, but you must be so ashamed, the way they beat up Tokijirō. I'm sad, too, so sad I can't stand it."

"Oh, you're sweet to say so . . . to think so much of your mistress at a time like this—you've seen right through to my heart. What sort of fate could have brought me one so dear? You know, people say 'a beauty knows no truth,' but that could only come from the mouth of a fool, clumsy in the ways of love. The more expert you become, the deeper you fall when you fall in love . . . so tenderly . . . your lover is so dear to you that you're all mixed up by the tenderness. I could melt all away with my love, like a faint snowfall in the sunlight, but I have to meet him once again, see him once again, a final parting in this world." She sobs violently, her emotions frenzied, nearly mad, and in the rain of tears the snow melts and she faints dead away.

Her lover has prepared a short sword in advance. He holds it in his teeth and flexes his body, then sneaks out on a neighboring roof. The branches of a pine bend down as if in sympathy, forming a bridge this single night to carry his quivering legs across. Urazato, seeing him, is overjoyed, and at the same time her thoughts nearly leap with the sadness, the terror and the danger; but bound tightly, like a tree trunk smothered by vines, closed in by the drifts of falling snow, she's trapped, like a warbler fluttering helplessly around its nest.

He descends without mishap and cuts loose the ropes binding the two. "See, Urazato, we could easily die right here, but let's try to get as far away as we can. Luckily, this pine bough lies just low enough for us to climb over the wall together."

They make hasty preparations to escape while Midori pulls at them, imploring them to take her, too.

"And what shall we do with this dear child?"

"Of course. . . ." Tokijirō clutches her underneath his arm and confidently steadies the pine bough so Urazato can climb up while he looks in all directions. He pulls away the sharpened stakes along the top of the wall. The three of them use the pine bough as a staircase and make their way up onto the wall, and when they are about to jump down on the other side, Urazato holds back for an instant; then quieting her palpitating breast, she recalls that she has fully resolved to die. "What have I to fear?"

"Ready now, all together!" Taking hand in hand, they get their balance, nodding in assent, eyes closed, all of a single mind. . . .

And no sooner did you see them jump than you awoke, the dream was gone without a trace—ravens caw at first light and rumor alone lingers on in the aftermath.

NOTES

1. Edward Seidensticker, *Kafū the Scribbler: The Life and Writings of Nagai Kafū, 1879–1959* (Stanford: Stanford University Press, 1965), 39.
2. Ibid., 41.
3. From Dazai's *Hitorigatari*, quoted in Kawatake Shigetoshi, *Nihon engeki zenshi* (Tokyo: Iwanami Shoten, 1959), 616.
4. Kikkawa Eishi, *Nihon ongaku no rekishi* (Tokyo: Sōgensha, 1965), 262.
5. Among them, *Kaerizaki nagori no inochige, Keisei Otowa no taki, Koigoromo tsui no shiromuku, Futaeginu koi no urakata, Ukina no hatsumonpi,* and *Masayume chishio no dakigashiwa.* He also adapted pieces from other styles of *jōruri* for Shinnai, such as *Sekitori senryō nobori* and *Koi musume mukashi hachijō.*
6. Kikkawa Eishi, *Hōgaku kanshō nyūmon* (Tokyo: Sōgensha, 1959), 239–42.
7. Atsumi Seitarō, *Hōgaku buyō jiten* (Tokyo: Fuzanbō, 1961), section 3, pp. 4–5.
8. The identity of the person arriving is unspecified. The social context of the ballad would suggest that the gender is male, but there is no specification of number or person. First or third person, either singular or plural, could of course be read into a translation of the passage, but I have chosen second person because the tone of the passage, its puns and wit, seems to suggest an easy and informal complicity between the narrator and the unidentified subject.
9. Nakauchi Chōji and Tamura Nishio, eds., *Nihon ongyoku zenshū: Tomimoto oyobi Shinnai zenshū* (Tokyo: Seibundō, 1927), 410.
10. *Yoru no tsuru,* "storks at night," is a phrase generally suggesting parental vigilance. Storks were thought to stay awake all night out of concern for their nestlings. Some commentaries suggest that the use of the phrase here alludes to the identity of the child Midori—that she is the child of Urazato and Tokijirō. There is no other indication of this relationship in the ballad as our text has it.

    In any case, the usage of the phrase *yoru no tsuru* here does not seem to speak to the identity of Midori. I think it has merely been included as part of the catalogue of birds in the passage.
11. Having planned to commit suicide, Tokijirō has put on a patternless white silk undergown (*shiromuku*), the customary dress for those about to die.

Romantic Consciousness in *Konjiki Yasha*

CARL F. TAEUSCH II

THE SENTIMENTAL HEROINE

Although largely ignored today by readers of post-Edo fiction, Ozaki Kōyō (1867–1903) was one of the more experimental of the pre-Sōseki Meiji literati, who suggested various themes and styles for later writers to emulate—or to avoid. Kōyō wrote numerous short stories and novels during the last decade of the nineteenth century, which, though perhaps not inspirational, at least titillated a fascinated if unsophisticated audience. *Konjiki yasha* (The Gold Demon), by far his most popular work, kept readers of the *Yomiuri shinbun* in suspense for the five and one-half years of its serialization from January 1897 to May 1902. Though seldom read since its first appearance, *Konjiki yasha* is the one novel for which Kōyō is remembered by the average Japanese. It survives now in song and in dramatic form whose annual performances, whether on television or stage, have achieved almost festival status.[1] Clearly Kōyō's novel captured the spirit of its age. More important, however, in the context of Japan's modern literary heritage, an analysis of its features helps us to define significant themes that appeared in other, more highly regarded works of the time and that have strong parallels in Western fiction.

It is perhaps ironic that Kōyō's undying devotion to sentimental domestic romance began with his own peculiar interpretation of the meaning of literary realism as espoused by Tsubouchi Shōyō (1859–1935) in *Shōsetsu shinzui* (1886). After three years of writing mostly haiku, *dodoitsu* (comic ditties), *rakugo* (comic stories), and travelogues, Kōyō first showed his potential as a reputable novelist with the publication of *Ninin bikuni irozange* in 1889. Direct reference to Shōyō's influence is apparent in the preface to the story, in which the author justifies his motivation to write a "realistic" novel. In an allusion to Shakespeare, whom Shōyō particularly revered, Kōyō notes: "The Englishman Shakespeare is neither a devil nor a god, yet I hear that he can make one laugh or cry by transcribing with a single pen all kinds of human emotion." Later in the same preface he makes his own intentions clear: "Tears are the motif of this novel."[2] In his acceptance of the need for greater attention to character motivation, Kōyō has interpreted Shōyō's call for description of internal emotions as a license for the free expression of sentiment. The author of *Ninin bikuni* becomes deeply involved in his story, like Dickens weeping as he writes, and is firm in his belief that by moving from laughter to melodrama he has made a step toward literary realism.

In his later stories, Kōyō leads his suffering heroines to sacrifice and death, and one finds in these women close parallels with the sentimental heroines of Western fiction. Instead of resignation upon confronting irreversible fate, the heroine is unable to tolerate her plight, and death comes as a most natural culmination to her misery. Harbingers of Kōyō's potential for creating a heroine who evolves naturally from the thematic structure of his novels occur in the short stories "Oborobune" (1890) and "Uzumagawa" (1890), but his characters begin to take on more universal aspects only as he becomes familiar throughout the 1890s with romantic fiction from the West. The developments in Kōyō's fiction up to the writing of *Konjiki yasha* illustrate well how this figure of the sentimental heroine, with which he came to feel so comfortable, was affected not only by his own traditional sensibilities but also by impressions of the Western novel based on his own reading and on the theories expounded by advocates of realism.

There is no avoiding the fact that most of Kōyō's fiction is mawkish. Even his most mature attempt at realism, *Tajō takon* (1896), is rendered in a tone that is frequently just as sentimental as Kōyō's earlier, heroine-centered works. While Ryūnosuke, the protagonist of the novel, suffers with the same surface expressions of anxiety as the earlier heroines, here Kōyō pays attention to developing his hero inwardly as well, so that the conflicts he must face make his unhappiness seem all the more intense. As long as Ryūnosuke plays the role of a pathetic hero, his prolonged emotionality seems reasonable. But at the moment of climax, when his failure to resolve his conflicts might be expected to culminate in tragedy, the author's untimely restraint dampens the hero's passion like a wet blanket. It is as if Kōyō somehow feared the consequences of his hero's course of thought and suddenly felt compelled to shift direction, even at the expense of credibility. In the end Ryūnosuke is neither joyful nor sad, but merely resigned to what is inevitable from the start. The emotional intensity with which the hero is initially portrayed anticipates a tragic conclusion, ultimately unrealized.

It is easy to condemn sentimentality and exaggerated emotions as inevitable and barely tolerable characteristics of popular fiction, and yet there persists an irrepressible fascination with the more lurid aspects of the fallen heroine. Depiction of untimely death is rare in Kōyō's fiction, but when it does occur, it is developed with care so that the involved reader is likely to be genuinely moved. When Kōyō brings his heroine all the way to the point of death, he succeeds in stimulating the reader's emotions as he does nowhere else. Ofuji in "Oborobune" is the epitome of fragile beauty and purity as, spurned by the man she loves, she succumbs to hysteria and finally dies by starving herself. If such a death reflects the tastes of an emotionally indulgent society, it also represents the author's willingness to deal unhesitatingly with the unpleasant aspects of his environment.

The heroine also dies quite dramatically in "Uzumagawa," an unheralded short story that for all its brevity is probably one of Kōyō's more credible portraits of romantic disappointment. While on a mountain climbing trip, Aoki falls ill at an inn and is cared for by the landlady and her daughter Otsuta, who, providentially, is a ravishing beauty. Aoki and Otsuta soon become attracted to each other, and Aoki manages to find reasons enough to extend his stay. But the day of departure is inevitable, and eventually he leaves the maiden with no intention of seeing her again. In despair Otsuta hurls herself into the Uzuma River and drowns. Despite the lack of extensive character development and the somewhat artificial reassertion of Kōyō's stereotypical view of the faithful woman, Aoki's reluctant but unfeeling rejection of Otsuta and Otsuta's cathartic emotional response evolve naturally from the course of the plot. Forced beyond the limits of emotional constraint to take her own life when her lover leaves her hopeless, Otsuta elicits tears of sympathy reserved for the sentimental heroine.

Kōyō was subsequently to portray few heroines tormented to the point of death until he began *Konjiki yasha* in 1897. Toward the end of its serialization, Kōyō himself learned he was dying. As his health declined, writing became increasingly onerous for him; but what he did write shows an almost obsessive care for the stylistic elegance for which he was so well known. Every aspect of Kōyō's approach to prose literature over the years, from an excess of passion in his characterization to a broad representation of his stylistic idiosyncrasies, gushes forth in *Konjiki yasha*. It is as if Kōyō, unhappy with the lack of popular response to his grand attempt at psychological realism in *Tajō takon*, suddenly abandoned all restraint to reassert the vision of his earlier romantic fantasies.[3] For all its avoidance of the principles of the mainstream realists, the romance of Omiya and Kan'ichi is Kōyō's most impressively vivid creation.

THE TEXT

According to Kōyō's original conception of the plot, *Konjiki yasha* was to be a portrait in two parts of Hazama Kan'ichi, who becomes a ruthless usurer when rejected by his beloved. It was intended that, after accumulating a fortune at his evil trade, he would come to see the futility of his efforts and begin to dispense his money for the benefit of the needy.[4] From very early in his writing, however, Kōyō was apparently unable to keep to the confines of this simple plot, and the characters began to move out of his control toward an uncertain fate. What may be regarded as the principal emotional climax of the novel actually occurs rather early, at the end of part 1, and although Kan'ichi moves toward a second catharsis and reconciliation with Miya in the later chapters, he never achieves it.

The novel appeared in serial form in the *Yomiuri*, in the following sequence:

"Konjiki yasha zenpen"	1 January to 23 February 1897
"Konjiki yasha kōhen"	5 September to 6 November 1897
"Shoku Konjiki yasha"	14 January to 1 April 1898
"Shokushoku Konjiki yasha"	1 January to 8 April 1899
"Shokushoku Konjiki yasha (zokuhen)"	4 December 1900 to 8 April 1901
"Shokushoku Konjiki yasha (zokuhen)"	1 April to 11 May 1902

The last three chapters, published in the *Yomiuri* during April and May 1902, were reprinted in the January, February, and March 1903 editions of the monthly *Shinshōsetsu*[5] under the new title "Shinshoku Konjiki yasha." The increasingly lengthy interruptions after April 1898 are indications both of Kōyō's fickle inspiration and, especially after 1900, of his declining health.

In its present form the novel reflects the slightly different structure of the individual books published by Shun'yōdō. The major divisions are as follows:

"Konjiki yasha zenpen"	(Part 1)	July 1898
"Konjiki yasha chūhen"	(Part 2)	January 1899
"Konjiki yasha kōhen"	(Part 3)	January 1900
"Shoku Konjiki yasha"	(Part 4)	April 1902
"Shokushoku Konjiki yasha"	(Part 5)	June 1903

"Shinshoku Konjiki yasha" (part 6) appears in the seventh Shun'yōdō edition of "Shokushoku" in July 1905, after having already been included in the single volume edition of *Konjiki yasha,* published as volume 6 of the *Kōyō zenshū* (Hakubunkan) in December 1904. In addition, a concluding sequel to Kōyō's unfinished novel, entitled "Konjiki yasha shūhen," was completed by Oguri Fūyō on the basis of Kōyō's notes and published as a separate volume by Shinchōsha in April 1909, but is not included with any current editions of *Konjiki yasha.*

THE STORY OF KAN'ICHI AND MIYA

Konjiki yasha opens with a street scene on New Year's night. Tomiyama Tadatsugu ("Inheritor of Abundance"), parvenu son of a wealthy banker, is on his way to a New Year's party where he will meet and fall in love with Shigisawa Miya. His arrival at the party causes quite a sensation, as a large diamond ring on his finger catches the attention of everyone, including Miya. Kan'ichi, her betrothed, is unimpressed but senses that Miya's curiosity, aroused by the ostentatiousness of Tomiyama's wealth, is more than just a passing fancy.

Kan'ichi is the orphaned son of a dispossessed samurai family. He lives with the family of Shigisawa Ryūzō, who, out of gratitude for some past favor, saw fit on the death of Kan'ichi's father to take responsibility for giving the fifteen-year-old boy an opportunity to complete his education. At first the Shigisawas only felt they were fulfilling an obligation to care for Kan'ichi, but over the years they became increasingly impressed with his diligence and success as a student and gradually came to consider him as a suitable husband for their only daughter, the charming Miya. It is understood, if not formally announced, that Kan'ichi and Miya are to be married upon the completion of his schooling in one year. Ten years have passed between Kan'ichi's arrival at the Shigisawa home and the commencement of the story, and during that time Kan'ichi has come to regard his relationship with Miya as inviolate.

For her part, Miya "did not find Kan'ichi by any means unattractive, but her affection for him was probably no more than half what he felt for her" (70). She is quite conscious of her beauty and occasionally muses about her attractiveness to men whose wealth and status are considerably greater than Kan'ichi's. Yet despite such a lukewarm appraisal of Miya's devotion to her husband-to-be, the expressions of intimacy and tenderness that pass between them suggest that their relationship is deep and far from one-sided. At one encounter in particular, their last before the fatal intrusion of Tomiyama into their lives, the uncertainty and passionate depths of their intimacy are effectively combined in a way that foretells the tragic course of their

love affair. It is late in the evening after the card party, and Kan'ichi
has just returned euphoric from a round of toasts to his anticipated
marriage:

> "Now that all my friends know about it," said Kan'ichi,
> "I'd have no pride as a man if we didn't make a grand hus-
> band and wife."
> "Why, if it's already been decided. . . ." Miya started to
> ask.
> "But it hasn't. These days when I see your mother and
> father, somehow I. . . ."
> "That's just not true! You're too suspicious."
> "Actually, your parents' opinion doesn't matter, it's how
> you feel."
> "My mind is made up."
> "I wonder."
> "'I wonder,' you say! How can you say such a thing!"
> Kan'ichi finally succumbed to the effects of the wine and
> lay down, resting his head in Miya's lap. Miya pressed her
> hands against his burning forehead and cheeks. "Shall I give
> you some water? Oh, have you gone to sleep? Kan'ichi!
> Kan'ichi!"
> How pure love is! In that moment the false desires that
> had soiled Miya's heart were cast adrift. Her beautiful eyes
> gazed on Kan'ichi's sleeping face as if they could see nothing
> else. All thoughts of luxury and wealth melted away under
> the warm weight in her lap. Oblivious to her surroundings,
> she glowed in the dreams of a heavenly sweet dew.
> The sinful thoughts that had crossed her mind now
> faded away as though covered over by the darkness of night.
> Together now, just the two of them in this room, she could
> imagine no one else in the world for her. She was aware of
> something bright, very much like a lamp, shining on the two
> of them alone. (74–75)[6]

Although the description of this tender moment is simplistically
romantic, it succeeds in illustrating the ambivalence that plagues Miya
in her relationship with Kan'ichi. Because he has boarded with them
for many years, she has come to regard him as a member of the
Shigisawa family and to take his affection for granted. Her vanity
naturally makes her vulnerable to the attentions of others, especially
when they are wealthy and of high station. Still, as we see here,

Kan'ichi's faith in her love gives her a deep sense of security and prompts her to return his feelings in kind, at least momentarily.

The extent of her ambivalence is revealed subsequently, when Tomiyama makes his formal proposal. While the Shigisawas are clearly flattered by this proposal from so unexpected a quarter and will not let the opportunity to join such a wealthy family get away from them, they are in a quandary over how to deal with Kan'ichi. Miya's parents are unabashedly moved by the promise of material gain, and their attempts to keep their intentions secret from Kan'ichi stem solely from guilt. But their ultimate decision is unwavering. In compensation for what might be taken as a betrayal, they are prepared to treat Kan'ichi as a son rather than as a son-in-law, by making him their legitimate heir and by affording him the opportunity to continue his education abroad. Miya herself, however, suffers from more than mere guilt. For several days after the proposal she sulks and does her best to avoid having to face Kan'ichi. When Kan'ichi is finally able to corner her and inquire about her strange behavior, his words affect her deeply, and she tries to convince him, as well as herself, that her melancholy is due only to some physical discomfort. For the first time her feelings toward Kan'ichi, which she has always taken for granted, are put to the test, and the torment she now experiences comes from a failure to understand the shallowness of her love.

> She did not dislike Kan'ichi, did she? Naturally it was strange for her to fear seeing this man she had known for so many years. When she did not see him, she longed for his presence in spite of herself. And yet when she was face to face with him, a fear arose within her that left her in a cold sweat. She felt as if she were being rent in two when he spoke comfortingly to her. She was afraid to see how truly tender he was. The tenderness Kan'ichi was showing her now only intensified her depression and brought her to the limits of despair, unable to find solace in thoughts of either life or death. (81–82)

Unable to withstand these conflicting emotions any longer, Miya seeks respite with her mother at the hot-spring resort of Atami. While the two women are away, Ryūzō is to inform Kan'ichi of their plan and to seek his consent.

When Kan'ichi learns from Ryūzō that his worst fears have been realized, he rushes to Atami to hear the truth from Miya herself. At Atami, Tomiyama has appeared in person to lure Miya with sweet words and visions of his wealth. Only too-willing an ally to this seduction, her mother minimizes the effects of their betrayal on Kan'ichi and encourages Miya to stroll along the beach alone with her wealthy suitor. Their efforts are interrupted momentarily as Kan'ichi arrives to confront Miya in a passionate scene that dramatizes the dominant motif of the novel: the conflict between love and money.

The last chapter of part 1 finds Kan'ichi alone with Miya on Atami Beach. The opening lines set the stage for one of the most memorably dramatic scenes of modern Japanese literature:

> As if in a dream, the light of the moon spilled through the
> scattered clouds from the sky above and tinged with white
> the sea that spread as far as the eye could see. The sound of
> the waves, advancing and receding, lulled the senses, and the
> rising breeze intoxicated passers-by. Strolling together along
> the beach were Kan'ichi and Miya. (105)

In translation, the powerful, lulling rhythm of the original language suffers under the weight of the exaggerated metaphors. The portrait of a hazy, moonlit night and gently rolling waves simulates a dreamlike quality that masks a growing tension and anticipates the impending clash between the two lovers. In perspective, the chapter seems almost more appropriate to the stage than to the normally more sedate context of the novel.

The spell is broken when at last Kan'ichi is moved to express what is troubling him. At one point, when Miya begs for his forgiveness, he brusquely asks her if what her father has said truly reflects her own wishes. She is unable to reply. Kan'ichi then launches into a self-righteous declaration of his faith in Miya and what her perfidy means. In his view Miya is already his wife, and her marriage to Tomiyama would make her an adulteress.[7] Despite his gratitude for all the Shigisawas have done for him, he will not be regarded as one who sold his wife for an opportunity to go abroad. He builds himself up to a fit of passion, until, unable to endure his grief any longer, he collapses on the beach, weeping bitterly.

> When he fell, Miya had no time to be startled. As she
> reached out to him, they were both covered with sand. Moon-
> light shone down upon his ashen cheeks, drenched in tears
> that swelled from tightly closed eyes. His breath came in
> great gasps, in time with a terrible pounding in his breast.
> Miya clung tightly to him from behind and swayed gently
> against him. Her voice trembled when she tried to speak.

"Speak to me, Kan'ichi! What's wrong?"

Kan'ichi took Miya's hand listlessly in his. Miya tenderly wiped her lover's tear-stained cheeks.

"Ah, Miya! This is the last night the two of us shall be together. This is the last night you will comfort me, and this is the last night I will say anything to you. The seventeenth of January, Miya, remember it well! Next year, this month, this night, where will I be watching this moon? And this night the year after next, this night ten years from now, I shall not forget this night the rest of my life. Forget? Though I die I shall not forget! Do you hear me, Miya? The seventeenth of January! On this very night next year I will surely cloud the moon with my tears. When the moon, when the moon clouds over, Miya, know that your Kan'ichi hates you and weeps as he does tonight!"

Miya held Kan'ichi with all her strength and sobbed convulsively. (108–9)

Miya, and the audience, cannot but be moved by this vindictive soliloquy. Still unable to reject Kan'ichi directly, she begs him to have patience and speaks of a mysterious plan that she apparently believes will justify Kan'ichi's sacrifice. The nature of this plan is not discussed further, but inevitably it has been seized upon by the critics, who speculate that Miya is probably thinking of funneling some of the Tomiyama fortune Kan'ichi's way or possibly putting some funds aside for a remarriage to Kan'ichi later.[8] But Kan'ichi is unconvinced by her desperate attempts to relieve her own guilty conscience, and he launches into an extended interrogation of her motives for turning away from him. Is it that he is inadequate? Or is it because of Tomiyama's money? Yes, that is the reason—greed. But true love cannot thrive on money alone, and in three years, when Tomiyama has turned to other diversions, he warns, she will regret her decision. He concludes by begging her to reconsider and return to him. There follows a moment of tenderness as the two cling to each other weeping, before the violently climactic break.

As if shielding her from danger, Kan'ichi held Miya tightly. His hot tears flowed down the nape of her neck and he was overwhelmed by her sweet fragrance. He trembled like a withered tree swaying in the breeze. Miya, too, clung to him as though she would never let him go, and as they trembled together, Kan'ichi linked his arm with hers and wept.

"Ah, what should I do?" cried Miya. "If I marry him, tell me, what will you do?"

Like a tree split in two, they broke apart.

"So, you do want to marry him! You haven't listened to a word I've said, have you! You foul woman! You whore!"

With these words, Kan'ichi lifted his leg and kicked Miya squarely on the hip. She fell to the ground with a thud. But she bore her pain silently, weeping on the sand where she fell. Kan'ichi glared menacingly down at her weak and helpless form like a hunter about to kill a wild beast.

"Miya, you, you whore! Because of your fickle heart, this man, Hazama Kan'ichi, will go insane with despair and ruin his life. I'll quit my studies, everything. Out of my resentment of you I shall live on as a demon and prepare to eat the meat of swine like you. Tomiyama's charming wife! Since there will no longer be any occasion for us to meet, won't you raise your eyes and have one last look at me while I'm still normal? It would be proper to meet once more and pay my respects to your father and mother who have shown me so much kindness all these years, but for reasons of my own I shall take my leave of your family here and request that you wish them the best of health for me. And if they ask you what has become of me, tell them that big fool went mad on the seventeenth of January and disappeared from the beach at Atami without a trace!"

Miya suddenly rose and tried to stand but fell again, favoring her injured leg. All she could do was crawl to Kan'ichi and cling to him. Struggling to speak through her tears, she cried out, "Kan'ichi, please wait! Wh–where are you going now?"

In spite of himself, Kan'ichi was startled at the sight of Miya's snow-white knee drenched in blood, quivering through a tear in her kimono.

"Oh, you're hurt."

Miya waved him back as he was about to move closer to her. "It's nothing, really. Where are you going? I have something to tell you, so please come back with me tonight. Please, Kan'ichi, I beg you."

"If you have something to say, I'll listen to you here."

"It's awkward here."

"You have something to tell me—Ha! So, you won't let me go, will you."

"I won't let you go."

"If you continue to be so stubborn, I'll kick you away."

"Go ahead and kick me."

Kan'ichi shook her violently and Miya fell pitifully to the ground. "Kan'ichi!"

Kan'ichi moved swiftly away. Miya struggled with all her strength to get up, and she followed after him, only to be seized by the pain in her leg and fall again.

"Kan'ichi, I won't stop you any longer. Just once more, once more—I have something to say to you."

The fallen Miya lost all strength to rise again and could only depend on her voice to call him. She could see Kan'ichi's already dim form rapidly climbing the hill. Writhing in agony, Miya continued to cry out to him. When she thought she could make out his dark form standing atop the incline looking down at her, she called again at the top of her lungs. From the distance there came a man's voice, "Miya!"

"Ah, ah, ah, Kan'ichi!"

But even as she strained to see him, he disappeared into the darkness. She thought she caught sight of him once more, but it was only a solitary tree. There was just the melancholy sound of the waves crashing on the shore, under the dreary light of the moon on the seventeenth of January.

One last time Miya called out the name of her lover Kan'ichi. (114–17)

Thus concludes perhaps the most famous scene in Meiji fiction. The romantic image of a strong-willed hero forcefully protesting betrayal by his fickle lover represents an appealing contrast to the resignation and depressing subservience to social restrictions that characterize the traditional lover. Kan'ichi's tears, if somewhat detrimental to a sense of his masculinity, are mitigated by his forceful determination to sever all emotional ties to Miya by embracing with a vengeful passion a profession symbolic of the very greed that seduced his betrothed. Moved to sympathize with Kan'ichi's display of righteous indignation, the reader is made to accept his uncompromising self-denial throughout the novel, until Miya's pathetic condition finally begins to weaken Kan'ichi's resolve.

In part 2, Kan'ichi emerges as the efficient, bloodless assistant to the wealthy usurer Wanibuchi Tadayuki. Four years have passed since the scene at Atami, and Kan'ichi's break from the past is complete. Humiliated and embittered by Miya's decision, he has left the Shigisawas and severed all relations with his school friends. His one purpose in life now is to serve the "gold demon" by collecting debts on high-interest loans. He zealously pursues this trade, not out of greed, but out of single-minded vindictiveness.

If there are times when the demands of his profession are too much for a man as sensitive as he once was, his excessive diligence also helps him to resist memories of Miya. When he encounters Miya, now Tomiyama's elegant wife, at the home of a wealthy financier, all the past resentment wells to the surface, and he brushes angrily past her. Except for the moment of the encounter, which triggers Kan'ichi's angry thoughts ("That Miya! That whore! Her bed stinks with the wages of her lust!" [167]), the scene centers mostly on Miya, who, as soon as she is aware of his presence, vainly hopes that a meeting will find Kan'ichi full of forgiveness. When she sees that such is not the case, she is crestfallen and later swoons in the presence of her husband. From this incident we learn that the guilt of her betrayal continues to obsess Miya, and Kan'ichi's behavior only intensifies her despair. For his part, Kan'ichi withstands the shock of the encounter and goes about his business with the same intensity of emotion that drove him from Miya at Atami.

The purpose of part 2 is largely to present a portrait of the changed Kan'ichi. In contrast to the totally internal development of Sumi Ryūnosuke, the protagonist of *Tajō takon,* Kan'ichi is described as he is seen by others. In the opening scene, Arao Jōsuke, a good friend from school days, barely recognizes Kan'ichi when he catches a glimpse of him for the first time in four years from the window of a departing train. Kan'ichi is an unusually diligent and trustworthy assistant to his usurer-employer, Wanibuchi, and to Wanibuchi's wife, Omine. But he is cruel and uncompromising in the eyes of the debtors, especially Yusa Ryōkitsu, in pursuit of whose debt Kan'ichi is zealously persistent. In a dramatic scene at Yusa's home, Kan'ichi is confronted by former classmates, who prevail upon what is left of his good nature to show leniency. His stubborn refusal to listen and his haughty manner confound his friends and provoke them to violence. They quickly restrain themselves but remain indignant and adamant in their refusal to acknowledge the justice of his claim against Yusa. With total enmity established, Kan'ichi is forced to leave empty-handed. Even the letter of surety, the only proof of the debt, is stolen from him. And at the close of part 2, he is set upon by ruffians who beat him senseless in revenge for his cruelty. In contrast to the antagonism shown by his victims, however, there is one who finds him attractive both physically and for the very qualities that make him so repugnant to others. This is the "beautiful usurer" Akagashi Mitsue, who becomes foil to Miya and female companion for the reluctant "demon," Kan'ichi.

By the end of part 2, the plot had grown so complex that Kōyō felt compelled to abandon his original intention and extend the story. With his purpose confused, the plot and characters begin to move beyond his control, and for a time the story loses a clear sense of direction. Part 3 alternates back and forth between Kan'ichi, who is convalescing from the attack, and Miya, who daily grows more estranged from her husband and longs for the youthful and ingenuous Kan'ichi she fondly remembers. While in the hospital, Kan'ichi must tolerate a steady procession of visitors, including Ryūzō, who comes to see if Kan'ichi will not relent for Miya's sake. Ryūzō's attempt at reconciliation comes to naught, however: from Kan'ichi's point of view, no amount of self-pity on the Shigisawas' part will turn back the clock. This section concludes with a sudden, dramatic sequence that marks a recurring structural pattern in the novel: Wanibuchi and his wife are killed and their home destroyed in a fire set by the deranged mother of one of Wanibuchi's victims. In the last scene, Kan'ichi, having left the hospital, is looking over the ruins of his employer's home and business, as Tadamichi, Wanibuchi's staunchly moral son, tries to persuade him to abandon the usurer's trade.

As the original didactic intent of the story is gradually overwhelmed by the complexity of events, the major characters move toward a catharsis that the author himself did not fully understand. Shortly into part 4, it becomes clear that Miya is headed for a reconciliation with Kan'ichi, or will suffer a tragic breakdown if she fails. She is now more disenchanted with her life of leisure, and, as she retreats into her memories of Kan'ichi, her coldness toward her husband intensifies. Tomiyama himself, although still infatuated with Miya's beauty, naturally begins to seek more cheerful attention elsewhere, and their relationship steadily deteriorates.

In spite of his continued efforts to detach himself from an emotional world, Kan'ichi cannot help being impressed by instances of extraordinary personal sacrifice for the sake of love and friendship. He learns from Akagashi Mitsue that his old friend Arao has been forced to abandon a successful law career when he agrees to guarantee a loan for a friend. While waiting for a train, Kan'ichi overhears a conversation between two lovers, in which the young woman promises to be faithful to the young man (coincidentally the same Akura Masayuki who was imprisoned for failing to pay a debt to Wanibuchi and whose mother eventually killed the usurer), despite her parents' opposition.

At first, these examples of uncompromising fidelity cause Kan'ichi to be even more embittered over Miya's betrayal. But at the same time it is apparent that her unhappy situation is intruding more and more on his bewildered consciousness. Arao Jōsuke reenters his life when, in response to Miya's fervent request, he consents to approach Kan'ichi on Miya's behalf. Then Miya herself comes to beg his forgiveness. Later, in the dramatic climax of the section, Kan'ichi dreams that Miya and Mitsue, who has grown particularly aggressive of late, invade his room. Mitsue demands that he kill Miya with a knife that she offers him, in order to prove that he no longer loves the woman who once deserted him. When he fails to respond, she attempts to kill Miya herself. But Miya wishes to be killed only by Kan'ichi, as long as he will not forgive her. In the ensuing struggle, Miya manages to kill Mitsue. Before the dazed Kan'ichi can stop her, she stabs herself but does not die. She flees the house, bleeding profusely. Kan'ichi soon comes to his senses and runs out after her, madly proclaiming that he too will die, so that they will be together in the next world as man and wife. The chase takes them far out into the country until at last he discovers her body floating in a mountain stream. When he awakes, the dream stays in his memory as though it were reality, and he is shocked into realizing that his efforts to forget his love for Miya have failed.

At this point in the story, what happens to Miya becomes the overriding concern, and Kōyō's somewhat naive intention of depicting Kan'ichi's conflict between love and money loses importance to the emotional appeal of Miya's pathetic situation. If Kōyō sought to create a personality that, embittered by betrayal, would turn with vengeance to a life of destroying others for material gain, only to repent in the end, Kan'ichi is hardly the convincing "demon." We are told of his success as a usurer, but this success is expressed only externally through the eyes of his colleagues or victims, and he is never able to escape the pain of losing Miya. Whenever the point of view focuses on Kan'ichi, we find him concentrating, not on all-consuming devotion to his profession, but on how unjustly Miya behaved toward him. Instead of a conflict between the evils of materialistic gain and the beauty of true love, there is simply a conflict between an enduring passion and a stubborn resistance to that passion stemming from the indignity and pain of rejection. Beyond the surface alteration of their appearances, Kan'ichi and Miya never accept their materialistic roles, while the only real transformation they undergo is expressed in terms of a gradual acceptance, or apparent acceptance, of their love for each other. Kan'ichi's dream at the end of part 4 signals the reawakening of his compassion for the unhappy Miya and paves the way for some sort of resolution of her intolerable predicament.

The remainder of the novel as Kōyō left it (72 of 412 pages in the Kadokawa edition) describes a search for that resolution: Will Kan'ichi ever find it in his heart to forgive Miya? Kan'ichi is now obsessed by the temptation to forgive Miya, and in part 5 he sets out for Shiobara Spa in order to find relief from the torrent of his conflicting feelings about her. Although he has not traveled the road before, the countryside is all too familiar to him. Suddenly he realizes he has seen it all before in his dream of Miya's death. To drive home the shock of recognition, he is confronted in his room at the Shiobara inn by the fragrance of a white lily, which, again from his dream, is associated with the image of the dead Miya. These gruesome intimations of death seem to stimulate further Kan'ichi's sympathy for Miya, until he is diverted from his thoughts by the mysterious intrusion into the loneliness at Shiobara of two young lovers, whose predicament contrasts sharply with his own.

The story of this couple, who have come to Shiobara intent upon suicide, arouses Kan'ichi's compassion for their plight and at the same time reminds him of Miya's failings. It turns out that the woman, Oshizu, is a geisha whose attractions have moved none other than Tomiyama Tadatsugu to attempt to make her his mistress. Although such an arrangement would be materially advantageous for Oshizu, she remains steadfastly loyal to her lover, Sayama Motosuke. Since Oshizu and Motosuke do not have the money to redeem her from her professional obligations, they resolve to flee to Shiobara where they will die together. Kan'ichi is much impressed by their exemplary fidelity, and, enviously comparing them to Miya, he decides to give them what they need for Oshizu's release, so that they may live.

Thus, just as Kan'ichi seems to be relenting in his attitude toward Miya, her duplicity is made more poignant for him by contrast to the example of Oshizu and Motosuke. Part 5 comes to a close with Kan'ichi no nearer a solution to his inability to forget her, although he seems to gain some satisfaction from the opportunity to assist the young lovers.

Part 6, which concludes the novel as Kōyō wrote it, also makes no further progress but serves only to contrast Kan'ichi's release from depression, through the companionship of his new friends, with Miya's growing despair. Of the three final chapters, the first and last are letters from Miya expressing her love for the Kan'ichi she once knew, her desire for forgiveness, and finally her view of death as a means of release from the torment she now feels. At this point in the narrative, the strain of his terminal illness seems to have drained Kōyō of motivation to continue. The last installment of *Konjiki yasha* was published in the *Yomiuri* on 11 May 1902; in August of the same year, Kōyō was forced to leave the *Yomiuri* staff, and from then until his death in October 1903, he made no further additions to the novel.

Reference has been made to the attempt in 1909 by Oguri Fūyō, one of Kōyō's more prominent and loyal protégés, to write a concluding sequel to *Konjiki yasha,* entitled *Konjiki yasha shūhen.* Fūyō is especially noted for having written, in 1905, a successful dramatic version of *Konjiki yasha,* which includes a concluding scene entitled "Yasukuni Jinja no ura." This scene is not found in the original story but is derived from Kōyō's own outline notes, which are also the source of the sequel.[9] For the most part, Fūyō's effort represents little more than a patching-up of all the loose ends left by Kōyō. Over the course of the three hundred-page Shinchōsha edition of Fūyō's contribution, all the major and minor characters are accounted for and their lives put into good order.

In Fūyō's version, Miya's mental condition steadily deteriorates, as she determines to obtain a divorce from the now obliviously profligate Tomiyama. She soon goes completely mad, makes several attempts at suicide, and is finally committed to an institution. In the meantime, Kan'ichi's acquaintances, both old and new, prevail on Arao Jōsuke to convince Kan'ichi that he must see Miya and express his forgiveness. As a consequence of his increasingly brighter outlook on life since Oshizu's and Motosuke's coming to live with him, Kan'ichi decides to commit his wealth to good deeds, including the establishment of a scholarship fund for worthy students. Arao's debts are paid off, as are those of other minor debtor-characters. Kan'ichi forgives Miya but is hesitant to see her until Arao informs him that Tomiyama has divorced her. At Arao's urging, Kan'ichi finally goes to see Miya in order to forgive her, but she is too far gone to show much reaction. The pathos of her condition moves the once-embittered Kan'ichi to compassion, and he decides to marry her and take the Shigisawa name. In contrast, Arao, who is at last free of his debts, departs for Europe, leaving Kan'ichi saddled with a demented Miya. In the end Miya's misfortune and Kan'ichi's sacrifice for her are made all the more poignant, as the beautiful Mitsue, once ardent pursuer of Kan'ichi and scourge of Arao's existence, reveals to Kan'ichi as they stroll together on the beach at Atami that she greatly admires Arao and intends to join him in France.

As an interpretation of how the characters were developing when Kōyō left the novel, Fūyō's attempt at a conclusion is intriguing but fails to add anything to the original, and indeed is generally ignored in standard editions and commentaries. Even if the question of what happens to Miya becomes a principal motif toward the last quarter of Kōyō's novel, it is a question that in the end is probably better left unanswered. Aside from the excessive tidiness in accounting for all the characters, the solutions are somehow antithetical to the tone of the original. Though the hero is uncompromising through most of the novel, toward the end he is plagued more and more by doubts, and we can begin to imagine him at last forgiving Miya as she lies dying. In Fūyō's *Shūhen*, Kan'ichi no longer cuts such an interesting figure once he is released from the torment of all his conflicting emotions. And with Miya reduced from a moving, tormented heroine tempted by suicide to a pathetic invalid, the story loses all its dramatic vitality.

It should be evident from this detailed description of the plot that *Konjiki yasha* is a considerably more ambitious work than anything Kōyō had previously written. The longest of his earlier novels, *Tajō takon*, falls short of *Konjiki yasha* by more than two hundred pages in the Hakubunkan edition, while the exhaustive psychological portrait in the earlier novel makes it seem eventless by comparison. Of his other novels, *Sanninzuma* (1892), just half as long, divides its focus among several leading characters, none of whom emerges from the somewhat pedestrian plot long enough to give the novel any semblance of a unifying conception or direction. Similarly inspired by traditional conceptions of prose fiction is the even shorter *Kyaramakura* (1890), which, although devoted to the activities of a single heroine, has a rambling episodic structure and relatively few heightened dramatic moments that might bring the heroine to life. Where dramatic intensity is a major feature in a few of Kōyō's short stories, particularly with respect to the suffering heroines in "Oborobune" or "Kono nushi" (1890), the effect tends to be brief and artificial, and the stories are brought to an abrupt conclusion by unanticipated catastrophe, often in a manner reminiscent of Bunraku or Kabuki.

In contrast, *Konjiki yasha* embodies at once the release of Kōyō's subconscious passions and his sometimes painful struggle to mold those passions into a unified piece of contemporary fiction. The significant events of the story unfold rapidly, establishing the primary themes by the end of the first part, and subsequent developments generally contribute to consistent and purposeful characterization and to a balanced structure for the novel as a whole. The major characters are instilled with genuine, if simplistic, passions that motivate them for the duration of the novel without making them appear too restrained or contrived, as is often the case in Kōyō's didactic novels. For all its obvious appeal to the emotions, *Konjiki yasha* contains characters who begin to embody features common to love themes found in the popular literatures of both Japan and the West and who effectively capture the essence of the modern romance. As the final contribution of a writer who is criticized primarily for his inability to adjust to the demands of the new, Western-derived novel and for his failure to develop contemporary themes, *Konjiki yasha* indicates that Kōyō was beginning to penetrate the superficial application of alien critical theory to a deeper understanding of the integration of motif and characterization.

SOURCES AND INFLUENCES

The search for identifiable models for the characters and themes of a particular novel can be one of the more fruitless exercises in the study of Japanese fiction. Simple reference to a model or source without some attempt to analyze the relationship between the source and the author's creative intention is often misleading, in the sense that analogies may imply that the work in question is nothing more than an imitation of something else, or a mere record of actual experience devoid of imaginative embellishment. Of Kōyō's early novels and stories, many have been compared with Edo generic models, and in general the results have been edifying.[10] Inasmuch as Kōyō was constantly experimenting with new literary forms, reference to models that he may have used can be useful in interpreting the development of his approach to fiction. His early novel *Ninin bikuni irozange*, for example, drew inspiration from the chronicles and confessional genres of the Edo period, and analyses of the influence of Saikaku on Kōyō's style and understanding of realism indicate the magnitude of his debt to Genroku fiction. In later years, as Kōyō worked directly with Western literary forms and "adapted" them into Japanese, he inevitably became familiar with new techniques that were rather alien to the traditional Japanese literary context. A reading of *Konjiki yasha* indicates that by the time he commenced writing his last novel he had assimilated enough of a feeling for his Western models to be able to combine what he learned from them naturally with his own views of romantic fiction into a prototypical mid-Meiji novel.[11]

In their search for actual events that may have inspired the story of Kan'ichi and Miya, scholars have discovered an incident that involved one of Kōyō's Ken'yūsha colleagues,[12] Iwaya Sazanami. It happens that Sazanami knew a pretty waitress named Suma at the Kōyōkan in the Shiba district of Tokyo, who was attracted to the wealthy owner of the Hakubunkan publishing company, Ōhashi Shintarō. When Kōyō heard of this, he precipitously assumed that Suma was abandoning his friend for money, and he went to the Kōyōkan to confront the girl. Seized by the passion of the moment, he dragged her out into the hallway and kicked her in an outburst that must have been inspirational for the scene in which Kan'ichi kicks Miya on the beach at Atami. Kōyō continued to be frustrated by Sazanami's lack of concern for having lost Suma, and indeed *Konjiki yasha* seems to have served as a context for working out these frustrations and setting things right according to his own sense of justice.[13] In the novel, Miya plays the role of a contrite Suma who is made to suffer considerably for her infidelity, and Kan'ichi becomes a more satisfyingly resolute Sazanami, who refuses to tolerate any betrayal of his love. The fate of the unsuspecting villain Ōhashi is provided for in the character of Tomiyama Tadatsugu, who eventually succumbs to debauchery.

More germane to the problem of what inspired Kōyō's fresh dramatic approach to fiction in *Konjiki yasha* are the apparent influences from Western popular literature. Unlike Futabatei's acknowledged debt to Turgenev and other nineteenth-century Russian writers, the immediate sources of Kōyō's literary ideas are unclear, or at least diffuse. A rather arbitrary selection of English, American, French, and Russian authors was generally familiar to him, and documented mention is made of the *Decameron, Arabian Nights,* drama by Shakespeare and Molière, fairy tales by Hans Christian Andersen and the Grimm brothers, and the fiction of Dickens, Irving, Hugo, and Zola, as well as Turgenev, Tolstoy, Gorki and Chekhov.[14] Such for Kōyō were the primary examples of what the leading advocates of the new sophisticated novel were attempting to impress upon contemporary Japanese writers. The increasingly favorable environment for Western literature in Japan notwithstanding, many of the foreign works must have made for difficult reading, and Kōyō's initial attempts to unravel the mysteries of alien technique and theme were painstakingly methodical. When he eventually emerged from his infatuation with Edo generic styles and began paying more attention to contemporary trends, he spent considerable time working on "adaptations," which were for the most part thinly disguised plays and novels of French or English origin. As the new themes became more familiar to him, he grew more proficient in adapting them to his own native vision. Some, like *Iwazu katarazu* (1895), a gloomy tale of infanticide written in an imitation Heian classical style and reputedly drawn from Zola's *Thérèse Raquin,*[15] unfold in a considerably different manner from the European original. With *Konjiki yasha,* Kōyō created a novel with a thoroughly modern Japanese setting in a mode that is disarmingly similar to nineteenth-century French and English popular novels.

Efforts by Japanese critics to draw comparisons between *Konjiki yasha* and Western literature tend to be limited to a search for literary sources. While their observations are imaginative and stimulating, their aim is usually to find the one European novel, or possibly play, that may be cited as a model for Kōyō's novel. What results is an overemphasis on the particular works that Kōyō might have read, at the expense of conclusions that may be drawn about how the works might have contributed to Kōyō's understanding of the principles of the new novel form.

A case in point is the citation of apparent similarities between Kōyō and a popular English writer of sentimental romances of the mid-nineteenth century, Charlotte Monica Braeme (1836–84), who wrote under the name Bertha Clay. The idea that one of Braeme's novels might have spurred Kōyō to write *Konjiki yasha* was first given serious consideration by Kimura Takashi in a 1961 essay, "Bāsa Kurē to Meiji bungaku." Kimura calls attention to a statement by Emi Suiin in *Jiko chūshin Meiji bundanshi* (1927) to the effect that Kōyō was reading something called "Howaito rirī" (White Lily) shortly before he commenced writing *Konjiki yasha*.[16] Another reference by Tokuda Shūsei to Kōyō's fondness for novels by Bertha Clay,[17] and the fact that a translation by Suematsu Kenchō (1855–1920) of one of Braeme's novels, *Dora Thorne*, appeared between 1888 and 1890 under the title *Tanima no himeyuri* (Lily of the Valley) induced Kimura to follow that line of inquiry. *Dora Thorne* is a romantic tale of Dora, daughter of the lodge-keeper at Earlescourt, and Ronald Earle, her father's employer, who fall in love and decide to get married in defiance of social strictures. The tragic suffering that results from such a marriage across class lines is a theme rather common to popular fiction in Victorian England. Unfortunately, except for the specific use of a white lily as an image for Dora (representing her pure heart), which possibly did suggest to Kōyō an identical image for Miya in Kan'ichi's dream, the plot of *Dora* bears little resemblance to *Konjiki yasha*. With this discrepancy in mind, Kimura proposes another novel by Braeme characterized by similar romantic excess, *When the Bell Is Ringing*, in which the hero, rejected by the woman he loves for someone wealthier, flees from the vicinity of the wedding so as not to hear the wedding bells.[18] If not an exact model, this story at least more closely resembles Suiin's brief description of what Kōyō was reading and bears a superficial correspondence to the theme of *Konjiki yasha*.

Efforts to link Kōyō's work with particular novels by this now-forgotten English author can perhaps be overdone, but a random perusal of titles in the Braeme collection reveals at least that we are dealing with the same level of literature. If the plots do not neatly correspond, or if the characters respond somewhat differently in their culturally different environments, the particular divergences are not necessarily consequential in their effect on Kōyō's literary perspective. In fact, a third Braeme novel not mentioned in the commentaries, *Lured Away*, more closely parallels the thematic concerns of *Konjiki yasha*.[19] Here the beautiful young wife of a poor but contented working man is "lured away" by her husband's rich and flamboyant employer. Once she attains wealth and status in her new family, however, she longs for the happiness she felt with her former husband and seeks his forgiveness. The hero meanwhile avenges his loss by turning resolutely from quiet anonymity and raising himself to political prominence. He steadfastly refuses to forgive the repentant heroine, until he is finally softened when she succumbs, like Miya, to melancholia. Yet even as the specific situation in *Lured Away* closely resembles that in *Konjiki yasha*, any one or combination of the Braeme stories might have contributed in the same general way to Kōyō's understanding of romantic themes in Western fiction.

If Kōyō discovered fresh approaches to the technique of telling a story in less-than-sophisticated literature, his crowning contribution to the Meiji novel also reveals aspects that bear comparison to considerably more reputable Western fiction. A number of scholars have noted structural and thematic similarities to Emily Brontë's *Wuthering Heights,* for example. In this instance, the urge to trace inspiration for *Konjiki yasha* to a specific source has led to some difference in opinion. While Oka concludes on the basis of differences in tone and emphasis, as well as from the unavailability of a translation until 1932, that Kōyō was not influenced by *Wuthering Heights,* Ikari notes that Brontë's collected works were at least available in English and equivocates as to whether the similarities in theme and characterization justify the hypothesis that Kōyō was significantly influenced by the Brontë novel.[20] In any case, what one may draw from this comparison is not so much Kōyō's awareness of the English classic as a recognition that *Konjiki yasha* represents a successful adaptation to a contemporary Japanese setting of an archetypal romantic pattern common in nineteenth-century English fiction.

Wuthering Heights is, of course, a much more ambitious novel than *Konjiki yasha*, as the actions of the major characters are interwoven in a more complex and detailed manner and the carefully constructed plot continues a full generation beyond the death of the heroine to encompass the downfall of her entire family. A setting similar to that which serves as the structural focus of *Konjiki yasha* unfolds during the first half of the book and climaxes with the death of Catherine Earnshaw. Like Kan'ichi, Heathcliff is adopted into a modestly wealthy family with an attractive daughter who becomes his close companion. Their relationship is suddenly shattered when Catherine, who is so close to Heathcliff that she does not understand at first the pain her action causes him, decides to marry the wealthy and refined Edgar Linton. Heathcliff is shocked and disappears from the Earnshaw estate. When he eventually returns, it is clear that he is motivated by a wish for revenge, which will somehow be effected by money he has accumulated through suspicious means. Catherine still fails to comprehend Heathcliff's reaction but begins to recall with a passion the simple love they felt for each other as children. On his return she begs for his forgiveness and insists, much as Miya does to Kan'ichi, that she only had his welfare in mind when she married Edgar. And like Kan'ichi, Heathcliff is unyielding in his resentment as he refuses to forgive her, until he is at last aroused to compassion as she lies dying of despair. Despite the awkward plot transitions and sometimes too obvious demonstrations of motivation, the characters of *Konjiki yasha* seem on the surface to have been inspired by an idea of romantic tragedy not unlike Brontë's.

Other possible sources for the incidents and scenes in *Konjiki yasha* have been cited to suggest that Kōyō's ideas for the novel had been a long time in forming. The character Oyae from Kōyō's adaptation of Molière's *L'Avare*, *Natsu kosode* (1892), for example, is seen by Ikari as, like Miya, having a weak resistance to the temptations of wealth.[21] Oyae (Marianne) is the lover of Tokunosuke (Cléante) but has also caught the eye of the miserly usurer Washichi (Valère), and in a moment of weakness when urged by the go-between, an agent of Washichi, she admits to Tokunosuke the appeal of his father's wealth. Although her ingenuous admission hardly becomes a burning issue in this comic plot, for this brief moment at least she seems on the verge of rejecting Tokunosuke for wealth.

Given the nature of this farce (which, except for the omission of certain scenes and characters, follows the original fairly closely), it seems out of place to stress the issue of betrayal.[22] On the other hand, Ikari's suggestion that the play influenced the theatrical quality of the novel deserves some attention. In an analysis by Ikari of the climactic confrontation between Oyae, Okan (the go-between), Goroemon (Harpagon) and Tokunosuke in scene 10 of *Natsu kosode* and the Atami scene in *Konjiki yasha*, the striking similarities in chronology and action seem more than just a coincidence.[23] The application of dramatic techniques gleaned from his adaptation of Molière to the writing of fiction clearly adds to the intensity of the characterization and suggests a basis for the ready adaptation of *Konjiki yasha* to the stage.

The varieties of comparison with all levels of Western fiction and drama testify to the extent of Kōyō's eclecticism as a writer. From the time he began to write for his own satisfaction and for the entertainment of his friends, he took an avid interest in the established forms of prose literature and actively attempted to pattern his own stories after their example. His early stories, including his contributions to the Ken'yūsha journal *Garakuta bunko* (1885–89), reflect his infatuation with the styles and subjects of Edo fiction that were still so familiar to the Meiji townsman. Later, as his tastes broadened and he developed a strong interest in *Genji monogatari* on the one hand and Western themes on the other, he freely drew from wholly different traditions for his inspiration. Regarded by many as representing the end of the Edo tradition rather than the beginning of the new era, Kōyō's works, on the contrary, epitomize the searching, transitional character of the mid-Meiji period. In his final contribution to the legacy of pre-Naturalist novels, the sum of a multitude of impressions drawn from the Western literary context, as well as from his own, coalesce in a burst of romantic creativity that is very much in the spirit of his time.

THE ROMANTIC SETTING

As the culmination of Kōyō's assimilation of Western and Japanese popular literary traditions, the romantic setting in *Konjiki yasha* has a significance that belies the low esteem in which the novel itself is generally held. If the sentimental tale of Kan'ichi and Miya has become a subject of melodramatic caricature and a symbol of Meiji youthful naiveté, the power of its theme to stimulate the romantic fantasies of popular audiences is difficult to ignore. We may now find somewhat excessive his zeal in soliciting the sympathetic tear for his heroines, which began with *Ninin bikuni irozange*. In the case of *Konjiki yasha,* his hero and heroine have perhaps vindicated their creator's passion by surviving as one of the most famous romantic myths of Meiji Japan. The reason for their survival is not simply the Japanese propensity for melodrama, for any number of such stories could take its place. Rather, I would suggest that the passionate portrayal of these two figures, as they strive to discover the meaning of their relationship, gives vivid identity to an archetypal setting that recurs throughout modern Japanese fiction from this period.

Konjiki yasha is set in Tokyo, symbolic of a dynamic new Japan, and centers on the kind of family that perhaps typified the bourgeois experience of the mid-Meiji period. Although the hero of the story is not portrayed as one of the dynamic new breed of Japanese bent on reform, he comes from a background common to many of them and demonstrates the idealism and willfulness that characterized contemporary youth.[24] An orphaned descendant of the samurai class, Kan'ichi comes to Tokyo from the country to live with the Shigisawa family and be provided for by them until he finishes his education. As he becomes an integral part of the family, it seems only natural that he and Miya should marry.

Kan'ichi's place in this perfect circle is suddenly challenged by the intrusion of Tomiyama Tadatsugu, who lures Miya away from her intended path with the glitter of his ostentatious wealth. When Tomiyama replaces Kan'ichi as a more attractive candidate for Miya's hand, Kan'ichi breaks from the family and undergoes a transformation whereby he attempts to replace the love he felt for Miya with avarice, and human warmth with coldness and hate. But Miya and Kan'ichi do not part so easily. Miya's longing for her first love is awakened by the finality of his absence, and as he himself has predicted at Atami, Kan'ichi suffers through the remainder of the novel in a losing battle to erase the image of Miya from his mind.

In an essay on Kōyō, Masamune Hakuchō touches on the issue of Miya's—as well as Mitsue's—love for Kan'ichi as an aspect of the hero's masculine appeal. According to Hakuchō, Kan'ichi is a Meiji *iro otoko* (gallant) succeeding to a literary heritage that can be traced back through Saikaku's Yonosuke to Hikaru Genji.[25] This view is rather tenuously derived from the fact that, in effect, Kan'ichi is in the enviable position of having to fend off two beautiful women, Miya and Akagashi Mitsue, who are both madly in love with him.[26] That Kan'ichi is never "captured" by either of these women, says Hakuchō, is Kōyō's way of tantalizing his audience and stimulating their more prurient interests.

Although Hakuchō is not wrong to suggest that the appeal of the novel lies partly in the strength of Kan'ichi's masculinity, this "pleasure quarter" image of the hero, which is influenced perhaps by an Edo literary perspective, ignores the contemporary bourgeois moral restraints that characterize the special relationship between Kan'ichi and Miya. Far from being the conqueror of many women in the manner of Genji or Yonosuke, Kan'ichi is in fact attracted to one woman only, and is inextricably bound to her by the protective, familial context within which Kōyō sets their romance.

The familial context for the Kan'ichi-Miya romance, which provides the controlling framework of character development in the novel, can be described generically as the "student (*shosei*) setting." As

a term of reference for students of the Meiji period, the student pro-
totype in the modern novel appeared in Tsubouchi Shōyō's *Tōsei shosei
katagi* (1885–86) and described students of rural samurai heritage
brought up in an environment of Confucian and martial ethics.[27]
Since such students generally came from the provinces to study in
Tokyo, the characteristic of the *shosei* as a boarder, either in a dormi-
tory or with a family, came to be associated with the term. In the
fictional context, the student's role as boarder is significant, for it is
this position that serves as a catalyst for a romantic fantasy in which
the hero is conveniently provided with a lover from within the confines of his surrogate family.

In Kan'ichi's case, as we have seen, the boarder comes to be regarded as son and heir to the Shigisawa household, but by virtue of his
status as an "outsider," he is also an ideal mate for the Shigisawa
daughter. When the harmony is upset as Miya deserts Kan'ichi for
Tomiyama, Kan'ichi resolves to sever all ties with the family. But even
after he leaves the family and struggles to forget Miya, the pattern
described by the family circle continues to determine the course of his
thoughts and action. At the peak of his attempts to immerse himself in
the usurer's trade, his thoughts return to the meaning of his love for
Miya:

> Cast adrift in the world at an early age, Kan'ichi would never
> again know the warmth of his parents' love that was denied
> him by their death. He was alone, like a rolling stone on a
> spreading, lifeless plain. While he lived with the Shigisawas,
> he loved Miya, whose sweet voice, tender caresses, and pure
> heart gave him so much satisfaction that he seemed oblivious
> to all other pleasure. He might have made this woman his
> wife and experienced true happiness the rest of his life. In
> the one body that was Miya he saw a whole happy family: to
> him she was part mother, part younger sister, even part fa-
> ther and part older brother. In truth his love was not merely
> something that titillated young men in their dreams of ideal
> beauty, it was purer than words can express. (204)

Thus, Kan'ichi admits, even as he is driven by feelings of bitter-
ness, that his love for Miya transcended the simple love of a man for a
woman and embodied the concept of an inviolate family ideal. It is the
strength of this ideal that interferes with a convincing portrait of
Kan'ichi as the cruel, money-mad "demon." At the end of the novel as
Kōyō left it, the ambivalence implicit in Kan'ichi's attempt to break

away from the familial setting comes to the surface, as his dreams and wavering intentions point toward a reconciliation with Miya.

The significance of the student setting in Meiji fiction becomes evident in comparisons of this somewhat ingenuous but definitive example of the pattern with its occurrence in works of the period commonly given more serious attention. In stories by such diverse writers as Futabatei Shimei and Mori Ōgai, for example, the pattern emerges to tell us something about motivation in the romantic hero. That it does so suggests the archetypal proportions of the setting and its importance to an understanding of the portrayal of relations between men and women in the modern Japanese novel.

In what is generally considered to be Japan's first modern novel, *Ukigumo* (1887–89) by Futabatei, we find an earlier example of the romantic hero in a setting strikingly similar to that in *Konjiki yasha*. Like Kan'ichi, Bunzō belongs to a provincial samurai family that has found adjustment to the new social order difficult but believes that its redemption lies in education and government service. Though not an orphan, Bunzō has left a dependent mother in the country and has come to live in Tokyo with his uncle's family, who take responsibility for seeing him through school.

It is perhaps no coincidence that Kan'ichi and Bunzō both join foster families at the impressionable age of fifteen and stay with them for approximately the same length of time before the events in the novels begin. Bunzō also finds his romantic partner, Osei, provided for him from within the family context, and marriage is at first considered a matter of course. Romantic conflict arises as Osei, who like Miya is ambivalent about her feelings toward her foster brother-suitor, looks for more interesting prospects elsewhere. Unable to be forceful one way or the other with Osei, Bunzō lingers on in the family, driven by the illusion that he is somehow responsible for her welfare. The novel ends with Bunzō undecided whether he should leave the family or stay on in the vain hope that Osei will eventually be his. Futabatei's hero is perhaps a truer portrait of the unhappy man than Kan'ichi, and yet it is through a comparison with the unrestrainedly sentimental environment of *Konjiki yasha* that we come to understand Bunzō's universal bond with the frustrated lover in Meiji fiction.

While Futabatei's Bunzō is a disappointing lover whose failure occurs in a conventional domestic environment, the dynamic hero of Mori Ōgai's short story "Maihime" (1890) lends a new perspective to the student setting that illustrates both its pervasiveness and its limitations. Here the familiar domestic setting is transplanted to far-off

Germany, mecca to the youthful elite of Meiji Japan. Placing his hero in an alien environment enables Ōgai to portray him with a degree of individuality and frankness that would seem out of place on native ground. Europeanized like Ōgai himself, the protagonist, Ōta Toyotarō, contrasts sharply with the restrained and insular hero of Futabatei's novel. The familial student setting is established when Toyotarō comes to live as a student in the household of a German girl, Elise, to whom he is romantically drawn, but there the similarities stop. Instead of being provided with his romantic partner from within the familiar context, Toyotarō chooses his lover before joining his foster family. Rather than the young hero struggling against a subconscious bond he cannot understand, Toyotarō is the enviable creator of his own family environment. Yet in the end, he too must lose his sister-lover and accept the inevitable tragic separation that is the fate of the student hero.

The example of Ōgai's Toyotarō, despite the contrasting situation, reaffirms the ultimately unhappy consequences of the student setting for the Meiji hero and heroine. If *Konjiki yasha* was an accurate and popularly successful re-creation of the pattern, Kōyō was certainly slow to realize its full potential as a structural element directing the fate of his characters. For most of the novel he found it difficult to maintain the thematic conflict between love and money and often was at a loss as to where to lead his characters next. He made various attempts to escape from his predicament, and when he finally did stop writing, he appeared on the verge of letting the student romance take its natural course. Had he been moved to finish the story before his death, it seems likely that the force of the characterization would have brought him naturally to a more decisive resolution of Miya's fate.

In *Konjiki yasha*, Kōyō brought to the Meiji novel his vision of uncompromising fidelity and an image of the sentimental heroine that finds close parallels in nineteenth-century Western romances. For the first time in Kōyō's stories there appear a hero and heroine who together capture and define the romantic imagination of the age. Though bewildered by his ambivalent feelings, Kan'ichi is far from vacillating. In contrast to a Bunzō or a Ryūnosuke, he is unencumbered by an oppressive self-consciousness and yet is sensitive enough to feel compassion for the tormented lover who betrayed him. Miya, for her part, combines an independence of spirit (which Kōyō found to be an abrasive feature in the modern Japanese woman)[28] with a devotion to her intended lover so passionate that she is willing to sacrifice her life for his forgiveness. So often in Kōyō's earlier fiction the women either are models of passive subservience, enjoying euphoric nuptial relationships, or (with the exceptions of Ofuji in "Oborobune" and Otsuta in "Uzumagawa") are unhappy and yet not forced to suffer too long before they are able to find some contrived solace. Miya's virtuous suffering in the face of Kan'ichi's intransigence overshadows the sin of her betrayal, thus intensifying our sympathy. Her slow but steady decline toward death completes the image of a sentimental heroine whose universality is affirmed by the continued response of contemporary audiences. Melodramatic and unsophisticated though the novel may seem, in its overstatement *Konjiki yasha* provides a key to an understanding of the romantic consciousness of modern Japanese fiction.

NOTES

1. The Kōyōsai (Kōyō festival) is observed in Atami each year on the seventeenth of January to commemorate Kan'ichi's dramatic parting from Miya at the climax of part 1 of the novel. January is also the occasion for television dramatizations and other productions, both serious and satirical, performed throughout the country.
2. From the preface to *Ninin bikuni irozange* in Fukuda Kiyoto, ed., *Ozaki Kōyō shū*, in *Meiji bungaku zenshū* 18 (Tokyo: Chikuma Shobō, 1965), 3. All translations are mine unless otherwise noted.
3. Tayama Katai, "Ozaki Kōyō to sono sakubutsu," in *Gendai Nihon bungaku taikei* 3: *Ozaki Kōyō, Hirotsu Ryūrō, Uchida Roan, Saitō Ryokuu shū* (Tokyo: Chikuma Shobō, 1970), 383.
4. Oka, note 1 to *Konjiki yasha*, in Oka Yasuo et al., eds., *Ozaki Kōyō shū*, NKDBT 5, 504. Additional references to this edition will be noted in the text.
5. Ibid., 43.
6. The "sweet dew" (*kanro*) alludes to a particular expression of divine grace shown in response to beneficent rule, according to Chinese tradition. A less explicit interpretation than that suggested by a literal translation might be, "she dozed in the warmth of his love." The last paragraph is particularly elliptical and difficult to translate. Arthur Lloyd, who is responsible for the only English translation of *Konjiki yasha*, avoids the problem altogether in the following imaginative "adaptation" of the same passage:

> "Kwanichi could restrain himself no longer. He seized the girl in his arms, pressed his burning cheeks against hers, and poured forth his love in that universal language which is common to every nation and which needs no word to express it. In a few moments Miya tore herself from his embrace and left the room. The pair had been for a brief second in Paradise, and as the girl slipped out and closed the *shōji* behind her she knew that come what might her heart was wholly Kwanichi's." Reprinted from Arthur and Mary Lloyd, trans., *The Gold Demon* (Tokyo: Seibundō, 1905), 41.

7. The way Kan'ichi expresses the nature of their relationship has supplied fuel for overdrawn arguments that Kan'ichi and Miya have already had sexual relations. Because this possibility never becomes an issue in the story, emphasis on the credibility of the fact itself seems to be misplaced. (A summary of the major

opinions on the problem is presented by Oka, *Ozaki Kōyō shū (NKDBT* 5), 508–9 n. 41.) What is more important is the presumptive manner of the reference, which tends to indicate how intricate and binding Kan'ichi regards their relationship even before the occurrence of any formal ceremony.

8. Ibid., 109–10 and 509 n. 43. Katsumoto Seiichirō examines the problem on the basis of Kōyō's cursory knowledge of the legal issues involved. Katsumoto, *"Natsu kosode ni tsuite," Meiji-Taishō bungaku kenkyū* 9 (December 1952): 16. In a later response, Ikari Akira goes to some length to refute the suggestion of a later marriage and its legal implications, in *"Natsu kosode no kōsei to Konjiki yasha," Kokugo to kokubungaku* 47 (July 1969): 49–50.

9. Oka, note 83 to *Konjiki yasha, Ozaki Kōyō shū (NKDBT* 5), 516.

10. See especially Peter F. Kornicki, *The Novels of Ozaki Kōyō: A Study of Selected Works with Special Reference to the Relationship between the Fiction of the Tokugawa and Early Meiji Periods* (D. Phil. dissertation, Oxford University, 1978); and Kornicki, *The Reform of Fiction in Meiji Japan,* Oriental Monographs 3 (London: Ithaca Press, 1982).

11. Shinoda Hajime, for one, feels that Kōyō's later writings, which include several adaptations of Western fiction, indicate a more thorough grasp of Western techniques of the novel than might be expected of a writer regarded as regressive. From a dialogue with Miyoshi Yukio, "Kōyō, Rohan, Kyōka: Kindai bungakushi no mō hitotsu no kijiku," *Kokubungaku: Kaishaku to kyōzai no kenkyū* 19 (March 1974): 15.

12. Established by Kōyō, Yamada Bimyō, Ishibashi Shian, and Maruoka Kyūka in 1885, when Kōyō was a student at the Tokyo University Preparatory School, the Ken'yūsha was an association of writers that dominated the literary scene in Japan throughout the late 1880s and 1890s. Although it served during this period as a useful forum for the exchange of literary ideas and held an important social function, it is not characterized by any particular style of writing.

13. Iwaya Daishi, *Ozaki Kōyō* (Tokyo: Jinbutsu Ōraisha, 1966), 93–94. Also, Oka, note 11 to *Konjiki yasha,* in *Ozaki Kōyō shū (NKDBT* 5), 505.

14. Oka, "Kōyō to gaikoku bungaku," in *Shōgai to bungaku* (Tokyo: Meiji Shoin, 1968), 44–55. Kōyō read widely in English, while his familiarity with the Russian and European authors was based on translations into English as well as into Japanese.

15. Ikari, "Ozaki Kōyō to Moriēru [Molière] oyobi E. Buronte [Emily Brontë]," *NKB,* 130.

16. The two articles, "Hon'yaku bungaku zakkō," *Waseda bungaku: Meiji bungaku gō* (July 1925), and "Bāsa Kurē to Meiji bungaku—watashi no omoide o tōshite," in Shimada Kenji Kyōju Kanreki Kinenkai, ed., *Hikaku bungaku hikaku bunka* (Tokyo: Kōbundō, 1961), are cited by Ikari in "Ozaki Kōyō to Moriēru oyobi E. Buronte," *NKB,* 143.

17. *Nihon bungaku kōza, Meiji jidai,* vol. 2: *Ozaki Kōyō kenkyū* (Tokyo: Shinchōsha, 1932). Cited by Kimura, "Bāsa Kurē to Meiji bungaku," 402.

18. No such title appears in the *National Union Catalogue.* Oka fails to give any further specific information about this novel but presumably found it or reference to it in the *Bertha M. Clay Library,* an anthology of dime novels available in the British Museum. Oka, "Konjiki yasha—kōsō no genkyo," 110 and 123–24.

19. Charlotte M. Braeme, *Lured Away; or the Story of a Wedding Ring* (New York: George Munro, 1889). Other suggestive titles cited in the *National Union Catalogue* include *Fair as a Lily; or The Pride of His Heart* and *Set in Diamonds.*

20. Oka, "Konjiki yasha—kōsō no genkyo," 116; Ikari, "Ozaki Kōyō to Moriēru oyobi E. Buronte," *NKB,* 142–46.

21. Ikari calls attention to the point in three separate articles: "*Natsu kosode* no kōsei to *Konjiki yasha*," 43; "Ozaki Kōyō to Moriēru oyobi E. Buronte," *NKB*, 134–39; and "Kōyō no onna—Kōyō no josei kan," *Kokubungaku: Kaishaku to kyōzai no kenkyū* 19 (March 1974): 46.

22. One discrepancy noted by Ikari that bears on an issue troubling critics of *Konjiki yasha* is the inescapable implication in Kōyō's adaptation that Tokunosuke and Oyae have had sexual relations. By making the ties between the lovers equivalent to the inviolate connubial bond, Kōyō means to suggest the greater seriousness of Oyae's supposed perfidy. That womankind is fully capable of such frailty is, according to Ikari, entirely consistent with Kōyō's low regard for feminine nature. "Ozaki Kōyō to Moriēru oyobi E. Buronte," *NKB*, 137–38.

23. Ibid., 140–41.

24. For a detailed description of the spirit that moved the more politically and socially conscious youth of this period, see Kenneth B. Pyle, *The New Generation in Meiji Japan: Problems in Cultural Identity, 1885–1895* (Stanford: Stanford University Press, 1969).

25. "Ozaki Kōyō ni tsuite," in vol. 8 of *Masamune Hakuchō zenshū* (Tokyo: Shinchōsha, 1968), 150.

26. It is interesting to note here another parallel with *Wuthering Heights*, in which the grasping and vengeful Heathcliff stimulates the passions of the otherwise frail Isabella Linton. Brontë's creation is much more complex, however, as Isabella's attraction to Heathcliff is irrational and self-destructive, while Mitsue is moved not only by Kan'ichi's physical appeal but also by what she believes to be a common bond in their profession.

27. Another, somewhat different treatment of students is found in the *shosei shibai* (or *sōshi shibai*), dramatic plays about students and activists popular during the late 1880s and 1890s.

28. Kōyō generally held the modern Meiji woman in low regard. These women, he thought, had turned their backs on traditional morality and tended to sacrifice considerations of *giri* and *ninjō* for the satisfaction of their material desires. Ikari, "Kōyō no onna," *NKB*, 46.

"The Secret"
by Tanizaki Jun'ichirō

TRANSLATED BY ANTHONY HOOD CHAMBERS

TRANSLATOR'S INTRODUCTION

Tanizaki Jun'ichirō (1886–1965) is best remembered for his masterpieces set in western Japan—*Some Prefer Nettles, The Makioka Sisters,* "A Portrait of Shunkin," and others—but he was an Edokko, a native of the plebeian lowlands of Tokyo, and Tokyo is the setting for most of his early works (which is to say, those written before the earthquake of 1923).

One of the best of these is the 1911 story "Himitsu," translated here as "The Secret." The story takes place in and near Asakusa, the premier entertainment district of the time and the subject of many pages in Edward Seidensticker's history of Tokyo from 1867 to 1923, *Low City, High City.* Nowhere is Tanizaki's love of *shitamachi* Tokyo clearer than in "The Secret"; nowhere does he better evoke late-Meiji Tokyo as he saw it.

"The Secret" is also representative of Tanizaki's early mystery stories—some of the first examples of the genre by a Japanese writer—in which the element of mystery invests Tanizaki's "commonplace Tokyo" with a certain exoticism. "The Secret" combines mystery and exoticism explicitly by referring to Kuroiwa Ruikō (1862–1920, the pioneer translator of Western mystery stories) and Arthur Conan Doyle. Western words printed in Roman letters ("obscure," "sexuology," "arrested at last," "love adventure," "labyrinth") and Sinified Sanskrit Buddhist terms (*arhat, bhiksu, bhiksuni, upāsa, upāsikā*) add to the exoticism. Most important, the narrator works hard at making Tokyo seem exotic, both to himself and to the reader. It is no coincidence that he loses interest near Kakihama Bridge and the Dōryō Gongen Temple: these places may sound exotic to the reader, but they are only a few steps from the narrator's birthplace in Ningyōchō.

157

Readers who know Tanizaki's later fiction will spot several familiar themes in "The Secret." One is a fascination with secrecy itself. Another is the related theme of blindness, induced here by a blindfold, and in later works by other means. Finally, the narrator's attitude toward "T" is echoed by many Tanizaki men: initially assuming a submissive role, he allows himself to be dominated by her, but the object of his submission is to gain mastery. Once he has accomplished this, he abandons her.

It appears that one of the germs of "The Secret" was Oscar Wilde's story "The Sphinx Without a Secret."[1] There are obvious similarities between the two stories, but Tanizaki made fundamental changes. "The Secret" is longer and more complex; the transposition from London to Tokyo is complete; and the narrator's transvestism, self-conscious degeneracy, and amorality are original with Tanizaki.[2]

The translation is based on the text in *Tanizaki Jun'ichirō zenshū*, 28 vols. (Tokyo: Chūō Kōronsha, 1966–68), vol. 1, 249–70.

THE SECRET

On a whim I withdrew from the lively atmosphere around me, slipped away from the circle of men and women with whom I had maintained a variety of relationships, and finally, after searching for an appropriate hideaway, found a Shingon-sect monastery in the Matsubachō district of Asakusa, where I rented a room in the priests' quarters.

The monastery was in an obscure, labyrinthine neighborhood in the shadow of the Twelve-Story Tower, reached by following the Shinbori Canal in a straight line from the Kikuya Bridge and behind the Honganji Temple. The slum spread over the district like an overturned trash bin, and along one edge stretched the orange earthen wall that surrounded the monastery. The enclosure gave an impression of great calm, gravity, and solitude.

Rather than secluding myself in a suburb like Shibuya or Ōkubo, I thought from the outset that somewhere in the central city I could surely find a mysterious, timeworn place, unnoticed by anyone else. Just as stagnant pools form here and there in a swift mountain stream, secluded pockets must lie between the bustling streets in the heart of the city—quiet sections through which most people would never have occasion to pass.

There were other considerations as well.

An enthusiastic traveler, I had been to Kyoto and Sendai and from Hokkaido in the north to Kyushu in the south, but right here in Tokyo—where I had lived for twenty years since my birth in Ningyōchō—there were probably streets on which I'd never set foot. Indeed, there must have been many.

In the honeycomb of countless streets, wide and narrow, at the heart of this huge city, I could no longer be certain which were more numerous—those I had traversed, or those I had not.

I must have been eleven or twelve when I went with my father to the Hachiman Shrine in Fukagawa.

"Now we'll take the ferry and I'll treat you to the famous noodles at Komeichi in Fuyugi," he said, leading me around behind the shrine buildings. The narrow, brimming, low-banked river, so unlike the canals at Koamichō or Kobunachō, pushed its languid way between the eaves of houses packed together on either side. Weaving its way between the barges and lighters that floated parallel to the banks and looked longer than the river was wide, the little ferry boat crossed back and forth with only two or three strokes of the pole against the bottom.

I had often visited the Hachiman Shrine before, but I never gave any thought to what might lie behind the compound. I always paid my respects to the main building from the direction of the *torii* gate in front, and so I suppose I simply thought of it as a flat, dead-end view, all front and no back, like a panoramic picture. Now as I gazed at the river and the ferry and the land stretching forever beyond them, the mysterious scene reminded me of the worlds one often encounters in dreams, far more remote from Tokyo than either Kyoto or Osaka.

I tried to picture the streets behind the Kannon Hall at Asakusa, but nothing came to mind except the tile roof of the massive red building itself, seen from the line of shops leading up to it. As I grew older and my contacts expanded, I felt as though I'd explored every corner of Tokyo in the course of visiting friends, viewing cherry blossoms, and other outings, but often I would stumble upon mysterious, separate worlds, like those I had experienced as a child.

I searched high and low, thinking that just such a separate world would be the ideal place to hide, and the more I explored, the more neighborhoods I found through which I'd never passed before. I had crossed Asakusa Bridge and Izumi Bridge many times, but I'd never set foot on Saemon Bridge, which lies between the others. Going to the Ichimuraza Theater in Nichōchō, I would always turn at the corner by the noodle shop, from the avenue where the streetcar runs; but I couldn't recall ever having walked the two or three blocks beyond the theater, toward the Ryūseiza. What was the east bank like to the left of the old Eitai Bridge? I couldn't be sure. The neighborhoods around Echizenbori, Shamisenbori, and San'yabori were also unfamiliar to me.

The monastery at Matsubachō was in the strangest neighborhood of all. Just around the corner and down the alley from the Rokku amusement district and the Yoshiwara licensed quarter, this lonely, forgotten section delighted me. It was great fun to leave my dearest friend behind—that "gaudy, extravagant, commonplace Tokyo"— and be able to watch the commotion quietly from my hiding place.

I did not go into seclusion to study. My nerves in those days were worn smooth, like an old file, and responded only to the most vivid, cloying stimuli. I could no longer enjoy first-rate art or cuisine that required a delicate sensibility. My heart was too jaded to respond to the ordinary urban pleasures, to appreciate a chef in the gay quarters—the embodiment of smart, downtown style—or to admire the skill of Kabuki actors from western Japan, like Nizaemon and Ganjirō. The dull life of indolence that I had been leading from force of habit, day after day, was now more than I could bear. I wanted to try an unconventional, fanciful, artificial mode of life.

Was there nothing weird and mysterious enough to make my jaded nerves shudder with excitement? Would it be impossible to dwell in a barbaric, fantastical, dreamlike atmosphere, far removed from reality? With this in mind, I wandered through the worlds of ancient Babylonian and Assyrian legends, recalled the detective stories of Conan Doyle and Ruikō, longed for the burnt land and green fields of the tropics, where the sun's rays are so intense, and looked back fondly on the eccentric mischief of my naughty childhood.

I thought that dropping out of sight and needlessly keeping my activities secret would be enough to provide my life with a certain mysterious, romantic hue. I had savored the pleasures of secrets since childhood. The pleasure of games like hide-and-seek, treasure-hunt, and blindman's buff—especially on a dark evening, in a dimly lit storeroom, or before the double-leafed storehouse doors—came primarily from the mysterious aura of secrecy that lurks in them.

It was from a desire to experience once again the sensations I had as a child playing hide-and-seek that I hid myself downtown in an obscure, unnoticed spot. Also, the monastery's affiliation with the esoteric Shingon sect, intimately associated with secrets, charms, maledictions, and the like, was well suited to drawing my curiosity and fostering my daydreams. My room was in a newly enlarged section of the residence building. It faced south, and the eight floor mats had been slightly discolored by the sun, imparting a rather peaceful, warm feeling to the room. In the afternoon, when the gentle autumn sun blazed red like a magic lantern against the *shōji* at the veranda, the room was as bright as a paper-covered lamp stand.

Shelving the documents on philosophy and art that had been my companions until then, I littered the room with books rich in weird tales and illustrations—detective novels, books on magic, hypnotism, chemistry, and anatomy, which I'd take up at random and immerse myself in as I lay sprawled on the mats. Among them were Conan Doyle's *The Sign of Four,* De Quincey's *Murder, Considered as One of the Fine Arts,* tales like *The Arabian Nights,* and even a strange French book on *sexuology.*

I pleaded with the head priest to lend me old Buddhist paintings of Hell and Paradise, Mount Sumeru, and the recumbent Buddha from his secret collection. These I hung haphazardly on the walls of my room, like maps on the walls of the teachers' room at school. A steady thread of purple smoke rose calmly from the incense burner in the alcove and filled the bright, warm room with its fragrance. Now and then I'd go to a shop beside the Kikuya Bridge and buy sandalwood or aloes to put in the burner.

The room presented a thrilling spectacle on clear days, when the dazzling rays of the noontime sun struck the *shōji* in full force. From the old paintings that covered the surrounding walls, brilliantly colored Buddhas, *arhats, bhiksu, bhiksuni, upāsa, upāsikā,* elephants, lions, and unicorns swam forth into the abundant light. A multitude of marionettes from the countless books thrown open on the floor— carnage, anesthesia, narcotics, enchantresses, religion—merged with the incense smoke and loomed over me dimly as I lay on a small, scarlet rug, gazing with the glassy eyes of a savage, conjuring up hallucinations, day after day.

At about nine o'clock in the evening, after the other residents of the monastery were fast asleep, I'd get drunk by gulping down some whisky from a square bottle. Then I'd slide open the wooden shutters at the veranda, climb over the graveyard hedge, and set out for a walk. Changing my costume every night so as not to be noticed, I plunged into the crowd in Asakusa Park or picked through the shop-front displays of antique dealers and secondhand bookstores. One night I'd tie a scarf over my head, don a short cotton coat with vertical stripes, apply red polish to the nails of my carefully scrubbed bare feet, and slip on leather-soled sandals. Another night I might go out wearing gold-rimmed dark glasses and an Inverness with the collar turned up.

I enjoyed using a false beard, a mole, or a birthmark to alter my features. But one night, at a secondhand clothing shop in Shamisen-bori, I saw a woman's lined kimono with a delicate check pattern against a blue ground, and was seized with a desire to try it on.

When it came to clothing and fabric, I felt a deep, keen affection that went beyond simple admiration for a good color combination or a stylish design. And it was not only women's garments that attracted me. Whenever I saw or touched a beautiful piece of silk, I wanted to wrap my body in it. Often my pleasure would rise to its highest crest, just as when one gazes at the texture of his lover's skin. Sometimes I even felt jealous of women, whose lot permitted them to wear, without embarrassment and whenever they wanted, the silk crepes I loved so much.

That fine-patterned crepe kimono, languid and fresh in the sec-ondhand clothing shop—the delicious sensation of that soft, heavy, cool fabric clinging to my flesh made my body tremble when I imag-ined it. I want to put on that kimono, I told myself. I want to walk the streets dressed as a woman. Without a second thought, I decided to buy it. I even bought a long, Yūzen underkimono and a black crepe jacket to go with it.

The kimono must have been worn by a large woman, because it was just right for a small man like me. As the night darkened and silence fell over the big, empty monastery, I took my place stealthily before the mirror and began to apply my makeup. The effect was a bit grotesque at first, when I smeared some white paste on the yellow skin at the bridge of my nose; but when I used my palms to extend the thick, white liquid to every part of my face, it spread surprisingly well, and my skin rejoiced at the sweetly fragrant, cool dew seeping into its pores. When I applied rouge and polishing powder, I was delighted at the transformation of my alabaster-white face into the face of a fresh, animated woman. I realized that the techniques of makeup, tested every day by actors, geisha, and ordinary women on their own bodies, are far more interesting than the arts of the painter or the man of letters.

Long underkimono, detachable collar, underskirt, rustling sleeves lined in red silk—my flesh was granted the same sensations that are tasted by the skin of every woman. I whitened my wrists and the nape of my neck, donned a wig in the gingko-leaf style, covered my head and mouth with a hood, and ventured out into the streets of the night.

It was a dark evening and the sky looked like rain. I wandered for a while in the lonely streets of Senzokuchō, Kiyosumichō, and Ryū-senjichō, all laced with canals, but neither the policemen on beat nor passersby seemed to notice me. When the night wind coolly stroked me, my face felt dry, as though an extra layer of skin had been stretched over it. The hood over my mouth grew warm and moist from my breath, and with every step the hems of my long crepe underskirt entangled themselves playfully in my legs. Thanks to the waistband binding my pelvis and the one-piece sash wrapped tightly from the pit of my stomach to my ribs, I felt as though feminine blood had naturally begun to flow in my veins, and masculine feelings and postures gradually disappeared.

When I extended my white-painted hands from the shadows of my Yūzen sleeves, their sharp, sturdy lines faded in the darkness, and they floated there softly, white and plump. I was enchanted by the beauty of my own hands. I envied women for having beautiful hands like these. What fun it would be to dress like this and commit all sorts of crimes, like Benten Kozō on the stage! Experiencing something close to the "secrecy" and "suspicions" that constantly delight readers of detective novels and crime stories, I gradually turned my steps toward the crowded Rokku section of the Park. I was able to think of myself as someone who had committed a particularly brutal crime, perhaps murder, or robbery.

When I went from the Twelve-Story Tower to the bank of the pond, and then to the intersection by the Opera House, decorative lighting and arc lamps glittered on my heavily made-up face and brought out the colors and stripes on my kimono. Arriving in front of the Tokiwaza Theater, I saw myself reflected in a giant mirror at the entrance to a photographer's studio, splendidly transformed into a woman among the bustling throng.

Under my thick white makeup, the secret called "man" was hidden completely—my eyes and mouth moved like a woman's and seemed on the point of smiling like a woman's. The many women who passed me in the crowd, giving off the sweet smell of camphor and gentle murmurs from their rustling silk kimonos, never doubted that I was one of their own species. Among them were some who looked enviously at the elegance with I had made up my face, and at my old-style clothing.

Everything about the familiar nighttime commotion in the Park looked new to my secret-bearing eyes. Everywhere I went, everything I saw was as rare and curious as something encountered for the first time. Ordinary reality seemed to be endowed with a dreamlike mystery when I viewed it from behind a veil of secrecy, deceiving human eyes and electric lights and concealing myself beneath voluptuous cosmetics and crepe garments.

Continuing this masquerade almost every night thereafter, I grew confident enough to mingle in the gallery of the Miyatoza Theater and in motion-picture houses. It was near midnight when I returned to the monastery, but as soon as I went inside I would light the oil lamp, sprawl on the rug without loosening the clothing on my tired body, and gaze with lingering regret at the colors of my gorgeous kimono as I waved the sleeves back and forth. When I faced the mirror, the white powder had begun to wear thin but was still clinging to the coarse skin on my sagging cheeks. As I stared at the image, a degenerate pleasure, like the intoxication of old wine, stirred my soul. With the paintings of Hell and Paradise behind me, I would sometimes recline languidly on my quilts like a courtesan, still wearing my showy long underkimono, and flip through the pages of weird volumes until dawn. As I grew more daring and more skilled in disguise, I'd slip a dagger or an opiate into the folds of my sash before I went out, the better to excite fanciful associations. Without committing any crime, I wanted fully to inhale the beautiful, romantic fragrance attendant on crime.

Then, one evening about a week later, thanks to a strange affinity, I stumbled upon the beginnings of an even weirder, more fanciful, and more mysterious affair.

That evening, having quaffed a good deal more whisky than usual, I went up to the seats reserved for dignitaries on the second floor of the San'yūkan movie house. It must have been close to ten o'clock. The packed theater was laden with thick, foggy air, and the smell of humanity rose warmly from the silent, squirming crowd below to float about me, threatening to spoil my makeup. With each sharp squeak of the projector in the darkness, and each ray of light piercing my eyes from the dizzily unfolding movie, my drunken head hurt as if it would split. Now and then the movie would stop and the electric lights would go on suddenly, and I'd look around from the deep shadow of my hood, through the tobacco smoke that floated over the heads of the crowd downstairs like clouds rising from a valley floor, at the faces of the people who overflowed the theater. I took secret pride in the fact that many men were peeping curiously at my old-fashioned hood, and many women stealing covetous glances at the smart hues of my clothing. In novelty of attire, seductiveness, and beauty, none of the women in the audience was as conspicuous as I.

At first no one was sitting next to me. I don't know exactly when the seats came to be occupied, but when the electric lights went on for the second or third time, I realized that a man and a woman were sitting just to my left.

The woman looked twenty-two or -three, but in fact was probably four or five years older than that. Her hair was done smartly in the *mitsuwa* style, and her entire body was wrapped in an azure, silk-crepe manteau; only her lovely face, glowing with health, was clearly and ostentatiously exposed. Something about her made it difficult to know whether she was a geisha or an unmarried young lady, but it was apparent from the attitude of the gentleman with her that she was not a respectable married woman.

". . . Arrested at last. . . ." In a low voice she read an English title that appeared on the screen. Blowing richly fragrant smoke from an M. C. C. Turkish cigarette into my face, she threw me a sparkling glance with her big eyes, eyes that gleamed more sharply in the dark than the jewel on her finger.

It was a husky voice, like that of a professional balladeer, out of keeping with her charming figure—unmistakably the voice of T, a woman with whom I'd formed a casual, shipboard relationship when I traveled to Shanghai two or three years before.

In those days, too, I recalled, I couldn't tell from her deportment and attire whether she was a professional woman or a respectable lady. The man who accompanied her on the ship and the man with her tonight differed completely in bearing and features; but no doubt there were countless men running like a chain through the woman's past, linking the gap between these two men. In any case, she was clearly the sort of woman who constantly flits like a butterfly from man to man. When we'd met on board ship two years earlier, we reached Shanghai without having exchanged our real names or any informa-tion about ourselves. Once there, I casually betrayed the woman who loved me, and slipped out of sight. I'd thought of her simply as a woman in a dream on the Pacific Ocean; I never expected to see her in a place like this. She'd been a little plump before, but now she was sublimely slender and sleek, and her round, moist eyes, with their long eyelashes, were perfectly limpid and imperious enough to make a man doubt that he was a man. Only her lips—so fresh that one would think they might leave a crimson bloodstain on whatever they touched—and the length of the hair on her temples were unchanged. Her nose appeared to be higher and sharper than before.

Had she noticed me? I couldn't be certain. When the lights went on, I guessed from the way she was flirting in whispers with her companion that she'd dismissed me as an ordinary woman and was paying me no particular attention. In truth, sitting next to the wo-man, I couldn't help but despise the costume I'd been so proud of. Overawed by the charm of this animated, vital enchantress, I felt like a hideous monster in the makeup and clothing I'd taken so much trouble with. Unable to compete with her in femininity or in beauty, I faded away like a star before the moon.

How charming her supple, fluttering hand, swimming like a fish from the shadow of her manteau, clearly defined in the filthy air that hung so densely in the theater. Even as she was speaking with the man, she'd raise her eyes dreamily and look at the ceiling, knit her brows and look down at the crowd, or show her white teeth as she laughed, and her face would brim with a different expression each time. Her large, black eyes, capable of expressing any meaning at all, were studied like jewels, even from the furthest recesses of the ground floor. The instruments of her face were too suggestive to be mere organs for seeing, smelling, hearing, or speaking; her face was less the face of a human being than sugary bait for seducing a man's heart.

None of the gazes was directed at me now. Like a fool, I began to feel jealousy and rage over the beauty of the woman who had usurped my popularity. It was mortifying to be slighted, to have my own light extinguished by the charming features of a woman I'd toyed with and abandoned. Perhaps she had recognized me after all and was taking her ironic revenge.

I sensed my jealousy for her beauty change gradually to longing. Defeated as a woman, I wanted to conquer her again as a man, and to revel in my victory. I was seized by an irrepressible desire to clutch her supple body violently and shake it.

> Do you know who I am? Seeing you tonight after all this time, I am falling in love with you again. Would you like to join hands with me one more time? Would you like to come and wait for me at these seats again tomorrow evening? I do not wish to let anyone know my address, and so I beseech you to come here tomorrow at this hour and wait for me.

Under cover of darkness I took a piece of Japanese paper and a pencil from my sash, dashed off this note, and slipped it into her sleeve; and then I observed her carefully.

She watched the movie calmly until it ended at around eleven o'clock. Taking advantage of the confusion when the audience rose and began noisily to disperse, she whispered again in my ear, ". . . Arrested at last. . . ." She gazed at my face for a moment with even more confidence and daring than before, and finally disappeared with her companion into the crowd.

". . . Arrested at last. . . ."

She had recognized me. The thought made me shudder with fear.

But would she come obediently the following night? She seemed far more experienced than before. Had I miscalculated her powers and given her the advantage? Seized by anxiety and trepidation, I returned to the monastery.

I began as always to remove my outer garments, so that I would be dressed only in my long underkimono, when a small piece of Western paper, folded into a square, fell from inside my hood.

"Mr. S. K." The ink inscription shined like silk when I held it up to the light. It was unmistakably her handwriting. She had stepped out once or twice during the film—in the interval she must have penned an answer quickly and slipped it into my collar without anyone noticing.

I never dreamed to see you here of all places. You may have changed your clothing, but how could I fail to recognize the face I have never forgotten these three years, even in my dreams? I knew from the beginning that the woman in the hood was you. It is amusing, by the way, that your whimsical tastes have not changed. It makes me uneasy to think that you may simply be indulging these tastes when you say that you want to meet me, but my happiness makes good judgment impossible, and so I shall do as you say and wait for you tomorrow night without fail. I have my own reasons and ideas, however, and so I wonder if you would not be good enough to go to the Thunder Gate between nine and nine-thirty. A rickshaw man whom I shall send to meet you will recognize you and guide you to my house. Just as you conceal your address, I, too, prefer that you not know where I live, and so I shall arrange for the man to bring you to me blindfolded. I hope that you will agree to this one condition, because if you do not, I shall never be able to see you again, and nothing could be sadder than that.

As I read this letter, I felt that I'd become a character in a detective novel. Curiosity and terror swirled in my head. Perhaps the woman had grasped my own proclivities, I thought, and was acting like this deliberately.

There was a torrential rain the next evening. Changing my costume completely, I donned a man's silk kimono and a mackintosh and went splashing into the night. The rain pounded on my silk umbrella

like a waterfall. The Shinbori Canal had overflowed into the surrounding streets, and so I tucked my *tabi* socks into the breast of my
kimono and walked on my clogs barefoot. My feet glistened in the
lamplight that spilled from the houses along the street. Everything
was negated in the din of the driving rain; most of the shutters were
closed on the usually bustling avenues, and two or three men with
their skirts tucked up ran off like routed soldiers. Aside from an
occasional streetcar spraying puddles of water from the rails as it
passed, there were only the occasional lamps placed above utility-pole
advertisements, dimly illuminating the hazy, rain-filled air.

When I finally reached the Thunder Gate, my mackintosh, my
wrists, and even my elbows were soaking wet. Standing dejectedly in
the rain, I looked around in the light from the arc lamps, but no one
was in sight. Perhaps someone was hiding in a dark corner and keeping an eye on me. I stood there for a time with this thought in mind,
until finally, in the darkness toward the Azuma Bridge, I saw a red
lantern begin to move, and an old-fashioned, two-passenger rickshaw
rattled swiftly across the paving stones by the trolley tracks and came
to a stop before me.

The rickshaw man was wearing a large, round wicker hat and a
rain cape. "Please get in, sir." As his voice melted in the echo of the
downpour, he moved quickly around behind me, wrapped a length of
fine silk twice around my eyes, and pulled it so tight that it pinched the
skin at my temples.

"Here, please get in." The man grasped me with his rough hands
and lifted me into the rickshaw.

The rain beat against the musty canvas hood. Clearly, a woman
was riding beside me. Inside the hood, the air was stuffy with body
heat and the smell of white makeup.

Lifting the rickshaw's shaft, the man spun us around several times
in the same spot to mask the direction in which he finally started off.
Before long he turned right, then left. It felt as though we were
wandering in a labyrinth. Now and then we entered a street with a
trolley line or crossed a little bridge.

We were rocked by the rickshaw for a long time. The woman
beside me must of course have been T, but she sat there without
speaking or moving. No doubt she was riding with me to make sure
that I kept my blindfold on. Even without her supervision, though,
I would have had no desire to remove the blindfold. The dreamlike
woman I had met at sea, the interior of a rickshaw on a rainy evening, the secrets of the city at night, blindness, silence—all these elements had merged to plunge me into the haze of a perfectly balanced
mystery.

Presently the woman parted my tight lips and put a cigarette in my mouth. Striking a match, she lit it for me.

After about an hour, the rickshaw finally stopped. Taking hold of me again with his rough hands, the man guided me fifteen or twenty feet down what seemed to be a narrow alley, opened something that must have been a back door, and led me into a house.

Left in a room with my eyes still covered, I sat alone for a while. Before long I heard the sound of a sliding door being opened. Without saying a word, the woman snuggled up to me, her body as limp and fluid as a mermaid's. She lay back on my lap, put her arms around my neck, and untied my blindfold.

The room was about eight mats in size, or twelve feet by twelve. The construction and furnishings were excellent and the wood well chosen, but just as the woman's status was unclear, I couldn't tell whether it was an assignation house, a kept-woman's house, or a respectable, upper-class residence. Beyond the veranda was some thick shrubbery, enclosed by a wooden fence. Given only this range of vision, I couldn't begin to guess what part of Tokyo the house might be in.

"I'm so glad you came," the woman said, leaning against a square, rosewood table in the center of the room and letting her white arms creep languidly on its surface like two living creatures. I was astonished by the tremendous change in her appearance from the night before—she was wearing an austere, striped kimono with a removable collar and a lined sash, and her hair was done in the everyday, ginkgo-leaf style.

"You must think it odd that I'm dressed like this tonight. But the only way to keep others from knowing your circumstances is to alter your appearance every day." As she spoke, she lifted a cup from the table and poured wine into it. Her manner was more gentle and subdued than I remembered.

"I'm glad you haven't forgotten me. Since we parted in Shanghai, I've known all sorts of men and suffered as a result, but, strangely, I couldn't forget you. Please, do not abandon me this time. Keep on meeting me forever, as a dream woman whose position and circumstances you do not know."

Every word and phrase reverberated in my breast with a sorrowful tone, like a melody from some distant land. How could the flashy, spirited, intelligent woman of the night before present such a melancholy, admirable figure tonight? It was as if she had discarded everything and was throwing her soul before me.

"Woman in a dream," "secret woman"—savoring this hazy *love adventure,* in which there was no distinction between reality and illusion, I went to the woman's house almost every night and enjoyed myself until two o'clock in the morning. Then I'd be blindfolded again and escorted back to the Thunder Gate. We met for a month, then two months, without knowing each other's address or name. I had no desire to investigate her circumstances or seek out her residence, but as the days passed, I was moved by a strange curiosity—to what part of Tokyo was the rickshaw carrying us? How did we get from Asakusa to here, the neighborhood I'm passing through now with my eyes covered? I was determined to know this much. Maybe the woman's house, where the rickshaw finally came to rest after thirty minutes, an hour, sometimes an hour and a half of rattling through the city streets, was surprisingly close to the Thunder Gate. As I was rocked every night in the rickshaw, I couldn't prevent myself from speculating secretly about our location.

One night I could stand it no longer. "Take off this blindfold, won't you?" I pleaded with the woman while we were in the rickshaw. "Just for a moment."

"No, no, you mustn't!" She gripped my hands in panic and pressed her face against them. "Please, don't say such a selfish thing. This route is my secret. You might abandon me if you discover my secret."

"Why would I do that?"

"Because I'd no longer be a 'woman in a dream.' You love a woman in a dream more than you love me."

I tried everything I could to persuade her, but she wouldn't listen.

"I have no choice, then," she finally said with a sigh. "I'll let you see . . . but only for a moment." Dejectedly, she removed my blindfold. "Can you tell where we are now?" She looked uneasy.

Against a strangely black sky the stars were twinkling everywhere in the wonderfully clear air, and the white mist of the milky way flowed from one horizon to the other. The narrow street, lined with shops on both sides, was gaily illuminated by lamplight. The lane was a lively one, but oddly enough I had no idea where it was. The rickshaw ran on down the street until the name "Seibidō," written in large letters on a seal-maker's shop sign, came into view at the end of the street, a block or two ahead.

When I peered from the rickshaw at the small, distant lettering at the edge of the sign where the shop's address was written, the woman seemed suddenly to notice. "Oh, no," she said, and covered my eyes again.

A busy little street with many shops and a seal-maker's sign at the end—I concluded that it must be a street I'd never traveled before.

Once again I felt the allure of the world of riddles, such as I'd experienced as a child.

"Could you make out the letters on that sign?"

"No, I couldn't. I have no idea where we are. And I know nothing about your life, except what happened three years ago on the waves of the Pacific. I feel as though I've been seduced by you and led to a phantom land, far beyond the sea."

Hearing my reply, the woman said in a poignant, sad voice, "I wish you'd always feel that way. Think of me as a woman in a dream who lives in a phantom land. Please, never say the selfish things you've said tonight."

I guessed that tears were streaming from her eyes.

For some time after that, I couldn't forget the mysterious street scene I'd been allowed to glimpse that evening. The seal-maker's sign at the end of that busy, brightly lit lane was etched sharply in my mind. I racked my brains trying to think of a way to find that street, until finally I worked out a plan.

In the course of those long days and months when we were being pulled around together nearly every night, the number of revolutions the rickshaw made in front of the Thunder Gate and the number of right and left turns settled into a routine, and before I knew it, I'd memorized the pattern. One morning I stood on the corner before the Thunder Gate and, with my eyes closed, turned myself around two or three times. When I thought I had it about right, I trotted off at the same pace as a rickshaw. My only method was to calculate the intervals as best I could and turn into side streets here and there. Sure enough, there was a bridge, and there was a street with trolley rails, just where they should be; and so I thought I must be on the right track.

The route, beginning at the Thunder Gate, skirted the edge of the Park to Senzokuchō and followed a narrow lane through Ryūsen-jichō toward Ueno. At Kurumazaka-shita it bore to the left and, after following the Okachimachi street for seven or eight blocks, once again turned to the left. Here I ran smack into the narrow street I'd seen that night.

There was the seal-maker's sign, right in front of me.

Keeping my eyes on the sign, I advanced straight forward, as though I were probing the inner depths of a secret cavern. When I reached the end of the street and looked at the cross street, I was surprised to see that it was a continuation of the Shitaya Takechō avenue, where a bazaar is held every evening. Just a few yards away, I could see the secondhand clothing shop where I bought that fine-patterned crepe kimono. The mysterious lane connected Shamisen-bori and the Naka-Okachimachi street, but I couldn't recall ever having passed through it before. I stood for a while in front of the Seibidō sign that had puzzled me for so long. The houses lining the street had been crowned that night by a sky full of dazzling stars, wrapped in a dreamlike, mysterious air, and brimming with red lamps; but now they looked like wretched shacks, withering under the hot rays of the autumn sun. Immediately I was disappointed, and my interest flagged.

Spurred by an irrepressible curiosity, I guessed at the direction and ran on, like a dog that returns to his home, following a scent on the road.

When I entered Asakusa Ward again, the route advanced to the right from Kojimachō, crossed a street with a trolley line near Suga Bridge, followed the Daichi Riverbank toward Yanagi Bridge, and emerged at the avenue leading to Ryōgoku. I could see what a round-about way the woman had taken to make me lose my bearings. I passed Yagenbori, Hisamatsuchō, Hamachō, and crossed Kakihama Bridge—and suddenly I didn't know which way to go.

I was sure that the woman's house was in an alley nearby. I spent an hour going in and out of narrow side streets in the neighborhood.

Directly across from the Dōryō Gongen temple, in a narrow space between the eaves of the tightly packed houses, I found a humble, narrow, nearly invisible alley. Intuitively I knew that the woman's house lay concealed down that alley. I went in. The second or third house on the right was enclosed by a handsome wooden fence that had been treated to bring out the grain, and from the railing of a second-floor window, through a screen of pine needles, the woman was staring down at me with an ashen face.

Unconsciously raising my sardonic eyes, I looked up to the second floor, but the woman gazed at me expressionlessly, as though she were feigning ignorance and pretending to be someone else. Indeed, she might as well have been disguised as someone else, so different was her appearance now from the impression she'd given at night. She had agreed, just once, to a man's request to loosen his blindfold, but that had been enough for her secret to be exposed. The consequent remorse and despair showed fleetingly on her face, and then, without a sound, she disappeared behind the *shōji*.

Her name was Yoshino. She was a widow, and wealthy for that neighborhood. As with the seal-maker's sign, all her riddles had been solved. I abandoned her at once.

Two or three days later I left the monastery and moved to Tabata. My heart could no longer be satisfied with the bland, pallid pleasures of "secrets." I tended now to seek more vivid, gory delights.

NOTES

1. Tanizaki read and wrote English well. There is much evidence for his familiarity with Wilde, including his 1919 translation of *Lady Windemere's Fan*.
2. See Yoshida Seiichi, ed., *Tanizaki Jun'ichirō*, vol. 9 of *Kindai bungaku kanshō kōza* (Tokyo: Kadokawa Shoten, 1959), 278; and especially Paul Francis McCarthy, "The Early Life and Works of Tanizaki Jun'ichirō" (Ph. D. dissertation, Harvard University, 1975), 82–88, for more on the relationship between the stories.

"Literature of the Lost Home" by Kobayashi Hideo

TRANSLATED BY PAUL ANDERER

TRANSLATOR'S INTRODUCTION

"Kokyō o ushinatta bungaku" (Literature of the Lost Home) was published in May 1933 in the widely circulated monthly *Bungei shunjū*. Kobayashi had been carrying on a vigorous discussion of contemporary Japanese writing over several years in such literary and cultural magazines. In so doing he brought respectability to the critical review (*bungei jihyō*), a genre that Kobayashi himself regarded with constant vigilance and suspicion. At a time when government authorities were moving with force against proletarian and other forms of allegedly subversive literature, Kobayashi argued persistently for the place of ideas, as distinguished from ideology, in writing. And he called on writers to work at longer fiction that could better convey a sense of intellectual texture and sophistication, along with the conditions of Japanese society, while retaining the personal, stylistic intensity of the ubiquitous short story. Still, in the brooding tone of "Literature of the Lost Home," Kobayashi signals his predicament: that of a critic looking for live ideas and historical connections within an unsettled, immature, fashion-conscious youth culture. The essay also anticipates the direction much of his later writing would take, toward a rediscovery of the Japanese classics.

The translation was made from *Kobayashi Hideo zenshū*, vol. 3 (Tokyo: Shinchōsha, 1978), 29–37.

LITERATURE OF THE LOST HOME

It might be said that in Japan today a literature read by adults or by old people scarcely exists. Our politicians are taken to task for their lack of literary sophistication, or for being oblivious to what is happening in the literary world, but does the blame not lie with the literati themselves?

People are not necessarily cool or indifferent to literary matters. . . . Still, it is true that adult taste runs mostly toward the Chinese classics, or else toward certain Japanese classics, though certainly not toward modern writing. Modern Japanese literature, especially what is known as "pure literature," is read by young people, that is, by a certain "literary youth" between the ages of eighteen and thirty, or, to stretch the point, by writers only, or else by aspiring writers. . . . Our so-called literary world is in fact a special world populated almost entirely by like-minded youth, and this situation has not changed since the days of Naturalism. Although a proletarian writer might be expected to have an interest in political institutions or in social conditions, once he becomes a member of the literary world, and becomes absorbed in writing monthly review columns, his readership narrows to that limited sphere that is the focus of pure literature itself. Few can claim avid readers scattered widely throughout the population, among the farming and the working classes. Among the arts of Japan, literature alone is trapped inside this narrow and cramped universe. Of course, it is well known that Japanese music and painting, not to mention the theater, have always maintained a broad-based and devoted patronage. Popular literature, too, as if in compensation for having been exiled from the monthly reviews of the literati, seems to attract a circle of readers drawn from every sector of the society. Yet even here, the overwhelming majority of its fans are doubtless men and women under thirty. I am approaching fifty, and I can feel only sadness knowing that the likely readers of my work will be youth. And putting myself in the position of the adult reader, who claims there is nothing he can bear to read beyond the classics, I must acknowledge that our modern literature is somehow defective. For only that writing which one has leisurely pursued by the hearth, which has offered consolation and a lifetime of untiring companionship—only such writing can be called true literature.

As I was reading Tanizaki Jun'ichirō's essay "On Art" (in the April issue of *Kaizō*), I encountered the above passage, and fell to brooding about it. I did not brood with any thought to refute Tanizaki, or with any sense that I could resolve his dilemma. Mine was the artless brooding of a man, in Tanizaki's words, "trapped inside a narrow and cramped universe," and my feelings turned heavy and gloomy.

Reading over both parts of the "On Art" series, it occurred to me that although Tanizaki's style was measured, the author's conviction was intense. If in formal terms the writing seemed obscure, what the author wanted to say was nevertheless unmistakably clear. Such intense conviction and unequivocal opinion, were we to look for a counterpart, might be found in an address given at Kudan Nōgaku Hall by George Bernard Shaw, whom Tanizaki dubbed the "boyish grandpa": "Ladies and gentlemen, humanity is hopeless! Many of those who are artists, however bad, declare that they cultivate art for the sake of humanity. This is not so. Let us leave to the Philistines of the outside world the pretense that everything they do for us is for the good of humanity."

Shaw's words in themselves are of no special interest. In our time it is not at all strange that a writer's passion would seem perverted in some way. Yet in the power and integrity of the sentiments Tanizaki himself expresses, which are founded on that author's lifelong experience, something else is at work, something hard to fathom, which provokes in us as readers a heavy, gloomy feeling. Tanizaki concludes his essay by remarking that "young people who laugh at my perversity will perhaps one day come around to my way of thinking when they reach my age." Although at my present age I have yet to "come around," I wonder—has Tanizaki said anything to invite my ridicule?

Whenever someone refers to me as an Edokko, I grimace. This is because a rather considerable distance separates what others mean by this expression and what I take it to mean. Most people of my generation who were born in Tokyo know very well how bizarre a birthplace it is. Recourse to an expression like Edokko is wholly unsuitable. People like myself feel their situation will not be understood by outsiders. Even among one's Tokyo friends, there is a feeling that with maturity and passing time it will only become more difficult to express one's feelings on the matter.

Neither have I thought of myself as an Edokko, nor do I possess what are known as "Edo tastes," although perhaps unconsciously I harbor traces of an Edokko temperament. This is fine with me. I have never lamented the situation. Indeed, my feelings about the city, which have always been strange, are part of my being. "Born in

Tokyo"—I cannot comprehend what that fully means. Mine is an unsettled feeling that I have no home. It should be recognized that this is not in the least a romantic feeling, although it may be harder to see that it is to no small degree real and actual.

Once I was traveling from Kyoto with Takii Kōsaku. As our train emerged from one tunnel, the mountain roads suddenly flashing into view, he gazed up and heaved a deep sigh. I was startled. Listening to him then describe the fullness of his heart, how a stream of memories of a childhood spent gazing upon just such mountain roads welled up within him, I felt strongly that I do not know the "country." It is not so much that I do not know the country as I do not understand the notion of a "birthplace" or a "first home," or of a "second home"—indeed, what "home" of any kind in fact is. Where there is no memory, there is no home. If a person does not possess powerful memories, created from an accumulation of hard and fast images that a hard and fast environment provides, he will not know that sense of well-being that brims over in the word *kokyō*. No matter where I search for such a home, I do not find it. Looking back, I see that from an early age my feelings were distorted by an endless series of changes occurring too fast. Never was there sufficient time to nurture the sources of a powerful and enduring memory, attached to the concrete and the particular. I had memories, but they possessed no actuality, no substance. I even felt they were somehow unreal.

Putting aside this rather extended example, we all on occasion recall something our mother might have told us about her own childhood. Just a simple story, nothing special or inspiring, and yet for that very reason a strong and unwavering sentiment courses through it. A story of such commonplace memories contains the precondition for fiction. And so I am envious, because no matter how I try there are some things I am unable to recollect. Without embellishment, or, if that sounds too crass, without a device allowing a subjective response—a point of view or a critical perspective—I feel my memories would have no unifying structure, even as I realize that no matter what the necessity, the use of such devices is somehow unnatural.

Once it occurred to me that mine was a spirit without a home, I found evidence for it everywhere. It is especially instructive to record certain unusual experiences. I enjoy walking, and often go off to the mountains, being someone who takes pleasure in remote, even dangerous places. Of late I have come to realize a particular oddity about such behavior. To go off for inspiration to the beauty of Nature may seem to be a perfectly natural activity, but on reflection we must admit that it is just another manifestation of our quotidian intellectual unease. It is not at all a matter as straightforward and reasonable and innocent as "loving nature." I have grown increasingly skeptical about the existence of anything concrete and actual behind my being moved by the beauty of Nature. Looking closer, I see much in common between one's intoxication by the beauty of a mountain, and one's intoxication by the beauty of an abstract idea. Consequently, I am not heartened by the recent craze for mountain climbing. And I feel all the more uneasy as the number of afflicted climbers rises each year.

On reflection, I know that my life has been lacking in concrete substance. I do not easily recognize around me people whose feet are planted firmly on the ground, or who have the features of social beings. I can more easily recognize the face of that abstraction called the "city person," who might have been born anywhere, than a Tokyoite born in the city of Tokyo. No doubt a meditation on the various components of this abstraction may produce a certain type of literature, although it will be deficient in real substance. The spirit in exhaustion takes flight from society and is moved by the curiously abstract longing to commingle with Nature. It may well be that a world of actual substance is to be found in the beauty of Nature isolated from society, yet there is no reason to believe any real writing will come of it.

In his essay, Mr. Tanizaki referred to a "literature that will find a home for the spirit." Of course for me this is not a mere literary issue, since it is not at all clear that I have any real and actual home.

The other day, rereading Dostoevsky's *Raw Youth* in the translation of Yonekawa Masao, I was struck by several things that had not occurred to me when I first read this book. In particular I sensed the importance of the title chosen by the author. Illuminating the world seen by a single youth through the language of a single youth, the author revealed all the attributes of youth in general: its beauty and ugliness, its hypersensitivity and insensibility, its madness and passion and absurdity; in short, its authentic shape. I was left with an almost unbearably strong feeling that it is incorrect to call young people "youth." They are rather a species of animal that must be called by some other name. It struck me too that Dostoevsky's youth is no stranger—a youth whose mind is in turmoil because of Western ideas and who in the midst of this intellectual agitation has utterly lost his home. How very closely he resembles us. Indeed, I repeatedly ran into scenes that made me feel the author was describing me, that he had me firmly in his grasp.

"Our so-called literary world is in fact a special world populated almost entirely by like-minded youth," Tanizaki writes, "and this situation has not changed since the days of Naturalism." However, the role of youth in literature, I feel, has grown steadily more blatant. In the days of Naturalism, issues of social order or social chaos were not so clearly pressing as they are now. As a consequence, we are today overwhelmed and prone to sacrifice: our reflective spirit for the sake of dreams about the future, our ideas for the sake of action, our feelings for the sake of ideas, facts for the sake of theories, the ordinary for the sake of adventure. In short, we might say that as society has assumed a youthful character, it has cheapened the value of a mature spirit. It is then perfectly natural that the literary world too should become increasingly a special world of youth, although this is not reason enough to question the value of the literature it produces. Still, I believe that literature formerly brought as many benefits to society as it allowed evil in. Given our situation today, I can only feel that the evil, by degrees, is spreading.

It cannot be claimed that mature adults necessarily have no interest in writing about youth. For example, *The Sorrows of Young Werther* is a type of "youth writing," yet it has been able to attract great numbers of people. It is not then simply a matter of recent Japanese literature being literature by and for youth. Rather, ours is a youth literature that has lost its youth. And whatever its intentions may have been, in practice is it not the distinctive trait of such literature to be fundamentally conceptual and abstract and, at least since turn-of-the-century Naturalism, to come more and more to lack a taste for reality? Of course, we should not always overlook literary motives or intentions and regard only practice or results. But quite apart from those current social and economic issues that are being so vigorously debated, it is in the practice of such "youth writing" that we are able to read the peculiar context and inevitable fate of the literary youth of our nation who are in the sway of the precipitous influence of Western models and have lost a sense of tradition.

Popular writers have emerged recently to attack the narrowness of "artful" literary fiction, proclaiming its demise. However, these popular novels too exhibit a spectacle unique to our country. The readership of our literary fiction may be young, but it takes a certain literary sophistication to understand such work, and there are a number of very fine books that could not be fully appreciated were they to be read by adults, sophisticated only in worldly affairs. Of course I cannot imagine mature adults reading the alternative— modern popular fiction. Adults are not about to read a story, however interestingly written, about what they already know, and which reveals no further discoveries. And so they turn to historical romances, *mage mono*. Surely it is not so elsewhere, but in our country conditions are such that most popular writing relies not on contemporary incidents but on historical tales for its contact with an audience of adult readers.

This becomes all the more clear if we turn to film. From the outset our film masterpieces were done in the old style, on historical themes. The fine actors and directors all tended in that direction. In comparison to literature, film is a far more immediate artistic medium, and so one need hardly argue the point that the average fan would likely wish his masterpieces to be based on contemporary events. In Japan a contrary situation exists, although perhaps we might admit that, if not for Japanese films, we would not recognize so clearly the true strangeness of our cultural condition.

Historical romances and samurai—*chanbara*—movies exert a profound influence over the masses. Although this peculiar phenomenon may not be long-lived, it cannot be argued that it will easily pass away. Its roots are quite strong. Some suggest that in a period of social collapse, when no definite or stabilizing ideas are in force, people have a renewed desire for sensual stimulation or excitement. Still, I do not feel this alone can explain the popularity of such fare. If that were the only reason, these popular entertainments would have no hope of such success. Far-fetched ideas and convoluted theories alone would not stimulate the interest of the masses, no matter how culturally naive they may be. I believe that the hearts of the masses are captured almost involuntarily along a slower but surer path, at the crossroads of the marvelous and the commonplace, amid an unfathomable and incomprehensible stream of real emotions. This stream flows through our *chanbara* movies, though not through our movies about modern life—*gendai mono*.

I often go to the movies with my mother. Of course her preference is the period film, as she finds nothing of interest in *gendai mono*. Once I took her to see the Western film *Morocco*. It occurred to me that this was quite futile, but to my surprise she was greatly moved by it. She has since cultivated a taste for Western movies.

Even my old mother, then, has been overwhelmed by the complications and confusions of our modern Japanese art forms and has turned away.

Morocco has been called a modern masterpiece, but its content is in fact quite shallow, and in this respect there are a number of our *gendai mono* that address more serious concerns. However, *Morocco* has a certain style that our films about modern life cannot match. It is a wholly captivating charm that leaves no room for discussion about the plot meaning this or that. And what is most lacking in our *gendai mono,* as well as in our current popular fiction, is just this inexplicable style. Were we to inquire why such entertainment, utterly lacking in this charm, nevertheless had fans to see it or to read it, we might find it is because the majority of the fans are satisfied merely with the plot. Being young, of an age when the world is seen through movies and life is known through fiction, this audience does not question whether a given work lets flow a stream of real emotions so compelling as to overpower a mere plot. Only when such youth reach maturity will the plot seem silly to them, and all but unconsciously will they begin to look for the kind of style that might conceal the silliness.

In film, this demand is presently met by period pieces or by Western movies; in literature, by popular renditions of historical adventure. The manners and mores that appear in *chanbara* movies and in *mage mono* fiction already seem as distant and removed from us as the manners and mores depicted in Western films. Still, the psychology and emotional temperament expressed in such works seem perfectly in harmony with the social scenery of that time. And the expression of such human feelings, free of contradiction, possesses an unimaginably powerful charm and fascination. This style elicits a sense of intimacy, so that we feel closer to the Moroccan desert we have never seen than to the landscape of Ginza before our eyes.

Some speak of the modern world as one beset by a common, universal social crisis, although I can only feel that contemporary Japanese society is collapsing in a quite distinctive way. Obviously, our modern literature (for all practical purposes we might substitute "Western" for "modern") would never have emerged without the influence of the West. But what is crucial is that we have grown so susceptible to this Western influence that we can no longer distinguish what is under the sway of this influence from what is not. Can we possibly imagine the profound emotion and wonder that Futabatei's *Ukigumo* or Ōgai's *Sokkyō shijin* aroused in the youth of their day, we who came of literary age when translations were so numerous that they could not all be read? Can we fear that anything remains to be taken away, we who have lost a feel for what is characteristic of the country of our birth, who have lost our cultural singularity? Is it any consolation to know that those writers of a preceding generation, for whom the struggle between East and West figured crucially in their artistic activity, still possessed what we have since lost?

It is a fact that ours is a literature of the lost home, that we are young people who have lost our youthful innocence. Yet we have something to redeem our loss. We have finally become able, without prejudice or distortion, to understand what is at the core of Western writing. With us Western literature has begun to be presented fairly and accurately. At this juncture, it is indeed pointless to call out for the "Japanese spirit" or the "Eastern spirit." Look wherever we might, such things will not be found. Not existing, they are hardly worth the search. And so Mr. Tanizaki's notion that we must "return to the classics" will not readily be embraced and passed on. It speaks simply to the fact that Tanizaki himself has chosen a certain path and matured in a certain direction. History seems always and inexorably to destroy tradition. And individuals, as they mature, seem always and inexorably to move toward its true discovery.

"The Puppet Maker" by Uno Chiyo

TRANSLATED BY REBECCA L. COPELAND

TRANSLATOR'S INTRODUCTION

Uno Chiyo (b. 1897) is a respected member of Japanese society and a highly regarded writer. She was not always so. By the time she was seventeen, she had been ostracized from Iwakuni, her small home town in southwestern Japan, because of a scandalous love affair. She fled to the anonymity and freedom of Tokyo, where she soon made a name as a writer and as a femme fatale. Although the former has won her lasting recognition, it was the latter that brought her immediate attention. Married three times and ever eager to embark on a new romance, Uno Chiyo easily earned notoriety in prewar Japan. She wrote of her romances, or, more correctly, her failed romances, with equanimity and nonchalance. In 1935, for a change of pace, she portrayed the various affairs that one of her lovers had enjoyed before he met and subsequently left her. *Irozange* (Confessions of Love) was hailed as the finest romance to appear in prewar Japan. It was followed in 1942 by *Ningyōshi Tenguya Kyūkichi* (The Puppet Maker), a sensitive narration of the life and work of an old puppet carver—a surprising departure for an author heretofore enthralled by romance.

By the time Uno reached her sixties, her attention to her own love life had begun to wane. She concentrated instead on fiction and on kimono design, an art she had cultivated since the late 1930s. It was at this time that Uno began to produce her finest works: *Ohan* (1957), *Kaze no oto* (The Sound of the Wind, 1969), and *Kōfuku* (Happiness, 1970). Uno received the Noma Prize for Literature in 1957 and the Women Writers' Award in 1958, both for *Ohan*. She received the latter award again in 1971 for *Kōfuku*.

Uno Chiyo enjoyed a resurgence of popularity in the 1980s. Her bestselling autobiography, *Ikite yuku watashi* (I Will Go on Living, 1983), was dramatized for television and the stage. *Ohan* was filmed

under the direction of Ichikawa Kon. Uno herself appeared on countless talk shows, where she entertained young viewers with anecdotes
of her life of passion.

Now well into her nineties, Uno continues to write memoirs, essays, and occasional short stories. She is said to be working on a sequel
to her autobiography. When she is not writing, she busies herself with
the kimono store she operates in Minami Aoyama, a fashionable district of Tokyo. She still maintains her old Iwakuni house, renovated in
1974. Today there is a sign in front of the house designating it "Uno
Chiyo's birthplace." With the famous Kintai Bridge, Uno has become
one of Iwakuni's favorite attractions.

When Uno Chiyo first met the puppet maker Tenguya Kyūkichi
(1858–1943), she was known primarily for her scandalous love life
and for the stories she had written to celebrate it. With the outbreak of
the Pacific War, she was forced to temper her tales of love. The mili-
tary authorities had demonstrated all too well that excesses of passion
had no place in a state of emergency. Uno would have to find a new
subject for her fiction if she were to continue writing. Curiously, she
found this new subject in the form of a Bunraku puppet.

One spring afternoon in 1942, Uno visited the home of Shimanaka Yūsaku, editor of the magazine *Chūō kōron,* where she noticed a
puppet on display in the alcove. Shimanaka's wife manipulated the
puppet for Uno, turning its head and opening its eyes. Uno was struck
by the intensity of emotion expressed by the puppet. "The depth of
sorrow visible in her eyes, closed into a thread, could never be expressed in the closed eyes of a living woman."[1] Uno decided, with
typical impulsiveness, to visit the man who had carved the puppet.
Shimanaka told her to contact Kume Sōshichi, a Shikoku journalist
who had written an article about the puppet maker for *Chūō kōron.*
Uno sent him a letter describing her "burning desire" to meet Kyūkichi. Kume offered to arrange an interview; Uno was off to Shikoku
on the next boat.

Tenguya Kyūkichi lived in the village of Wada, on the outskirts of
Tokushima. He was the same puppet maker Tanizaki Jun'ichirō had
referred to as Tengu-Hisa in chapter 11 of *Tade kuu mushi* (1928–29;
translated by Edward Seidensticker as *Some Prefer Nettles*).[2] The puppet maker was already an old man in Tanizaki's work. By the time Uno
met him, he was eighty-six years old, but still applying himself diligently to his art. Uno was profoundly moved by the old man's dedication and by the simplicity of his life. He had sat on the same cushion,

facing the same dusty road, doing the same work, for over sixty years. For a woman who could hardly stay with the same man, let alone live in the same house, for more than five years, this was an incredible feat.

Uno visited Kyūkichi regularly during her month's stay in Shikoku—she had little else to do, it seems. Her third and last husband, Kitahara Takeo (1907–73), had been dispatched to Southeast Asia as a member of the government propaganda corps, and she had no idea when he would return. Life in Tokyo was dismal, but the war had not quite reached Shikoku. Uno spent her days rummaging through secondhand shops and sitting with the old puppet maker. While he entertained her with tea and stories of the past, she jotted down his words. When she returned to Tokyo, she used both notes and memory to compile the story of his life. She serialized the result, *Ningyōshi Tenguya Kyūkichi,* in two installments for the November and December, 1942, issues of *Chūō kōron.*

The work was a singular achievement, for it revealed Uno's ability to create a world removed from her own. "The Puppet Maker" provides insights not only into the career of a master craftsman, but also into life in rural Shikoku, changes brought by the Meiji Restoration, the history of performing arts in Japan, and especially the theater tradition for which Kyūkichi provided puppets—the Bunraku theater of Osaka. (Of the many works available in English on this most impressive and sophisticated of puppet theaters, one of the first was Edward Seidensticker's introduction to *Some Prefer Nettles.*) The work also demonstrates Uno's keen ear for dialect: Kyūkichi's speech is rendered in the rich, colorful Tokushima dialect. Unfortunately, overtones arising from the juxtaposition of Kyūkichi's speech—at once rustic, elegant, and courteous—with the narrator's straightforward Tokyo Japanese cannot be completely captured in translation.

Appearing at a time when little but propagandistic drivel was being published, Uno's story invited notice. Commentators have struggled to categorize the work in relation to the war. Some contend that it obliquely supports the war; others disagree. Although Uno denies any interest in the war, it did affect her art. In a world stripped of the garish Western colors she had so admired, Uno was forced to consider the beauty and simplicity of the past. Soon after her encounter with Kyūkichi, she began attending puppet plays as frequently as possible, though she admits, "I felt just like a foreigner going to see Bunraku for the first time."[3] Her experience with Kyūkichi also taught her to value her own art. She has written that, shortly after interviewing him, she gathered her pencils and papers about her and sat down at her writing desk determined to give to her writing the same devotion Kyūkichi gave to his puppets. It is this persistence and patience that led to her masterpiece *Ohan,* a work that took more than ten years to complete, and which is said to echo with the cadences of the old *jōruri.*

Tenguya Kyūkichi died on December 20, 1943. Uno erected a stone monument to him in Tokushima on the twelfth anniversary of his death. Kyūkichi's business passed to his grandson Osamu, but when Osamu died the Tenguya shop was closed. Uno believes that the Oyumi puppet she possesses, sent by Kyūkichi after the interviews, is the last one he made. The puppet now stands in Uno's alcove, a constant reminder of Kyūkichi's legacy.

Even now, Uno likes to remind others of Kyūkichi's determination to work until death. This has become her own motto. She did not stop living once she reached an advanced age—she did not stop writing, exploring, or loving, but has continued to work, to strive for that final masterpiece. She paraphrases Kyūkichi: "I want what I write today to be better than what I wrote yesterday. I'll do what I can to go on living, and while I'm alive I'll work with all my might. Death will be the final stop."[4]

The translation is based on the text in Uno Chiyo, *Uno Chiyo zenshū,* vol. 5 (Tokyo: Chūō Kōronsha, 1977), 5–56. It is reprinted, with permission by the publisher, from my *The Sound of the Wind: The Life and Works of Uno Chiyo,* © 1992 by University of Hawaii Press.

THE PUPPET MAKER

I first saw one of his puppets last spring when I was visiting a friend. It was an Oyumi puppet from the play *Awa no Naruto.*[5] She was dressed in a simple kimono of coarsely woven, striped cloth, yet I found the sorrow in her face compelling. My friend's wife took the puppet in her arms and, slipping her hand up the sash, began to move her for me. Being a female puppet, her eyes were the only movable features on her face, and they should have opened when the appropriate toggles were pulled. But for some reason, this puppet's eyes remained tightly shut. I heard myself gasp. In the puppet's eyes, eyes that refused to open, I could sense an emotion so profound it could never be expressed in the face of a living woman.

The puppet I saw that day was not one of his better works, and yet those eyes, held shut as they were for some unknown reason, startled me. Perhaps that is why I gasped, and perhaps that is why, days later, I still could not forget the beautiful sorrow that had been etched so deeply in her face. To tell the truth, I know very little of the old arts, of *jōruri* and the like, and knowing nothing of the play that features the character Oyumi, I did not understand why she should be so sad. Yet as I gazed at the puppet I felt implicit in her face the very depths of a woman's sorrow, and I grew curious about the person who had carved her.

After some inquiry I learned that the puppet maker lives in Tokushima of Awa in the neighborhood of Wada. His name is Yoshioka Kyūkichi, though he is more popularly known as Tenguya Kyūkichi; and very often this is abbreviated to Tengu Kyū. He is in his eighty-sixth year. I rather impulsively decided that I would pay him a visit. Even I was surprised at myself. After all, we are in this state of emergency, and it hardly seemed appropriate for me to be dashing off to Shikoku to meet a man for no better reason than that his puppet impressed me.

1

"Well, come on in and make yourself at home. If I'm to tell you my story I can't be thinking of you as some guest come down from Tokyo.

"I was born eighty-five years ago, the Fifth Year of Ansei,[6] in Nakamura of Myōdōgōri, little over half a mile west of here. When I was a boy, folks in a village like ours didn't have such a thing as a surname, but being of samurai stock my family bore the name Kasai. I was born the third son of Kasai Iwazō. My mother died when I was three.

"My father made his living as an indigo pattern-dyer. Nowadays they're just called 'dyers.' They made pictures with their dyes, too, called 'dye-shop prints.' I expect you've seen the banners set up at a boy's first Boy's Day celebration in May. Some'll be of the great Benkei surrendering to the young Ushiwakamaru, or sometimes they'll have Yoichi of Nasu piercing the fan target with his arrow. Well, those were the sort of pictures my father made.

"My father raised me single-handedly. He was a pattern-dyer, but even so didn't have a workshop of his own. He and my brothers worked at the master-dyer's place and weren't often home. I was left to run wild until, at the age of seven, they put me in the local temple school.

"I went to school there for eight years. Now that might not sound like much to you, but in a country town like ours it was something of a long time. Back in those days about all we did in school was work in our primer, the *Teikin Ōrai*,[7] reading and copying. We had none of the high-minded learning children have today!

"Now as I look back on it, I can see that I enjoyed working with my hands even as a boy. I was clever at it too, if I do say so myself. I wasn't much when it came to writing out my lessons, but I did like to paint. Perhaps I was thinking of following in my father's footsteps. I'm not too clear on it now. But then I began making puppets. Some I fashioned from paper stiff with mud, and others I whittled out of paulownia wood. I had a friend at the temple school named Fujimoto Benkichi. He was a bit touched when it came to making puppets. Around here we call folks 'touched' when they carry on about something with such fever they seem near crazy. Well, Benkichi was touched on puppets. He'd make them out of balled up paper, right there at school. We'd stretch a cloth over the little desk where we studied, as our curtain, you see, and then one of us would crouch down low and move the puppets about while the other one watched from across the way.

"Oh, now let me think . . . would have been back when Tokushima was under the rule of the Hachisuka family. Puppet shows were allowed within three leagues of their castle lands, but only puppet shows, mind you. Kabuki and the like were strictly forbidden. And so, you see, the puppet shows caught on like wild fire. Why, traveling troupes would come out as far as this village nearly every day. Folks took to calling them 'box puppeteers' on account of they kept their puppets in the box they carried along with them. Usually had around six—a youth and a maiden, a mother and child, an everyday man and a buffoon. With six puppets they were able to put on a decent enough show. They'd carry their boxes strapped to their backs, and then, sounding the wooden clappers 'ka-chi! ka-chi!' would march right in the front gate of some estate. They operated their puppets themselves, you see, reciting the story as they went along. Sometimes there'd be one among them to play the *shamisen*.

"Well, Benkichi and I couldn't think of anything more exciting than pretending to be box puppeteers. Every chance we got we played our puppet game under the school desk. But now if the school master caught us at it, he'd have us stand at attention atop the desk for half an hour, sometimes a whole hour.

"So, you see, even as a child I gave myself over to this sort of tomfoolery. I never lifted a finger around the house. When it came time to weed the back field I wouldn't so much as pluck a stalk. I was in school from dawn to dusk, and when I got home there usually wasn't anyone around to tell me what to do, so I'd set in to playing my puppet game again all by myself. Oh, I didn't need much to make my puppets, but if I ever found myself wanting a piece of cloth or such, there was always someone in the neighborhood kind enough to give me an old scrap or two. I'd sew costumes—kimonos and undergarments and such—and then I'd dress my puppets up and set about playing theater. Now I expect this'll sound strange, but do you know there were some who'd come along to see my plays, even though the only puppets I had were those childish paper-made ones? I had my share of patrons, too. Yes, back in those days you had to have 'patronage,' as they called it, to get along in the theater world. Well, I counted as my patrons the young wife next door and her daughter and all the other children in the neighborhood. They were all likely to bring me something, a cloth for a curtain, say; or something I could use in my plays.

"Around that time, I believe it was, there was a man named Abe Kamekichi who ran a sword dōjō on the grounds of the Hachiman shrine back in Nakamura. Times being changeable though, before long sword practice fell out of fashion, and Mr. Abe began teaching the Chinese classics there instead. My father was in charge of helping with the school. I don't quite know what you'd call his position nowadays, but he was responsible for opening the school and locking up afterward and for preparing tea and such. But as my father was generally too busy with pattern dyeing to see to his tasks, he passed the job along to me when I turned thirteen. You can't really say I got much of an education there, but in my spare time I was able to ask questions about this and that. I couldn't read the whole of *The Four Classics*, mind you, but I did manage to get through *The Great Learning* and *The Analects of Confucius*. Yes, I suppose you could say I was left to grow up wild. But I wonder now if that wasn't the way my father intended it."

2

"Back then there were about three men in the region known as puppet makers. There was Deko-Chū, Tsunezō of Ōe, and then there was Tomigorō, sometimes known as Deko-Tomi, the man who would later become my master. I often wonder why I took it into my head to become a puppet maker. I was just a boy of fifteen or sixteen, after all, still wet behind the ears. How could I have been so certain I was to follow the puppet trade?

"Well, let me tell you . . . off in the countryside around here there was such a thing as the cotton exchange. In Akui, the town just down the road, there were quite a few cotton dealers. They'd store up cotton brought in from Sanuki, and the womenfolk here would go to town, buy up some of that cotton and cart it home where they'd run it through a gin to remove the seeds. Oh, I expect a city person like yourself hasn't had occasion to see such a contraption, nor a spinning wheel for that matter, but the woman would spin the cotton into thread on a spinning wheel. Oh my, they'd make those wheels whir. And when they were through they'd lash the thread onto a loom and weave out bolts of cloth. It doesn't take much time at all when you consider how it's done now, but back then, well, it took a long while. Once they'd finished a bolt of cloth they'd take it back to the same store and trade it in for more cotton. From the profit they turned, they were able to make a little extra for their purses. Most of the women-folk in my village gave themselves over to this sort of sidework. The young wife next door was no different. That woman, I tell you, all she had to do was see my face and she was off telling me to learn puppet making. Oh yes, every time she saw me that's just what she said.

"Truth be told, the theater was thriving right about then. By theater, now, I mean the puppet theater. When autumn rolled around, what with the festivals and such, there'd be a good many puppeteers out on the road. One day they'd set up a performance in Wada, and the next they'd come around to Nakamura. Yes, they traveled round all the villages in the area, from the hundred-family villages to those of a hundred and fifty or so. The young fellows would hire on a master chanter and practice *jōruri* chanting. There wasn't a man or woman around who hadn't had at least a taste of *jōruri*. My, things were different then, no denying it. Nowadays folks won't take part in anything, no matter what, unless you first hand them a nice sum of money. But back then, you did work because you enjoyed it, and that was pay enough. Far as meals were concerned, there'd always be someone to feed you. In a sense, yes, it was like playing, but it was one way to set yourself up in an occupation. And, when the puppet theater was in its heyday, there were more than thirty theaters in Awa alone. About all the villages around here had the kind of theaters farmers operated in their spare time—not a proper building, mind you, but just one in the fields. They'd spread straw matting down along the ground and put up a roof of thatch. Long as the weather lasted, that was good enough. But sometimes the local squire would stage plays on his property—for three days running.

"As a boy I was sickly, coughing and wheezing all the time. Folks said I had asthma. Seeing as how I was so weak, everyone thought it best for me to find a job that would have me seated most of the day.

The young wife next door came out and told my father what she'd been saying all along, that I ought to become a puppet maker, and so he finally took me to see Master Tomigorō. I was sixteen. I don't recall if it was spring or summer. Anyhow, folks had been after me so long to learn the trade, I soon found myself believing it was the job for me. If anyone asked me, 'Will you become a puppet maker, boy?' I answered right away, 'Yes, I will!' And so, you see, I didn't feel any regrets being sent off to an apprenticeship.

"My master was a tight-lipped man, and somewhat of a stickler for details. When you're to serve a master—and I suppose it'd be the same no matter what kind of trade you're in—you've got to prove yourself worthy before you can set about learning your master's craft. You do this by giving yourself over to his demands. Well now, I was an ornery boy by nature, but I soon found myself answering to disciplines I'd never had at home. I got up at five o'clock every morning, and I worked until ten at night. That's right, I had night duties to see to until ten o'clock. But as soon as they were done, I'd head out for my nightly entertainment. What's that? Oh heavens no, by nightly entertainment I mean the sumō matches held on the grounds of the nearby shrine. That's right, there were matches there every night, and I'd go to wrestle a bout or two. I suppose you couldn't expect someone as slight as me to be much at sumō, and let me tell you there were more than a few who had a laugh at my expense. 'Look there!' they'd holler, 'He can't be but four foot tall! Little fellow like you got no business wrestling!' And then they'd break into great guffaws of laughter.

"Yes, that's right. I did receive a salary, but can't say I'd know how much it would be at today's count. I suppose it was around twenty sen. As I recall, I was paid on Obon and New Year's Day. But other than that I can't remember ever receiving anything else from my master— be it money or praise. It wasn't like it is now. Why, the master might say something like, 'You're a hard worker, boy!' But that was as close as you'd ever get to a compliment. He'd never praise the puppet you'd carved, or tell you you'd done a good job. But now I guess that was just the master's way of disciplining his students. Yes, I believe it was as much as three years after I'd become an apprentice before someone came upon me at my work and praised me for it, saying I looked like I'd turn into a fine puppet maker someday.

"I've told this story to any number of folks, but there was a time in my life that I knew I'd be heading down the wrong path if I didn't watch my step. Back then, on the north side of the village, there was a man by the name of Tamaki Toyosō who was touched on kendō. He wanted a sword partner. Oh, not that he was interested in teaching swordsmanship. He was a wealthy man, you see, and didn't need to be teaching; he just wanted someone to spar with. Anyone would do, so long as he liked the sword. Well, being a boy, I figured a little kendō practice would help me with my wrestling, so as soon as the hour struck ten I was off to Mr. Tamaki's for lessons. He was kind enough to wait up for me. Yes, I went every night—never missed a night—and I soon found that I was throwing myself into my lessons, heart and soul. Even Mr. Tamaki said to me, 'Boy, you show real promise. You ought to devote yourself to the sword.'

"All the while my master knew none of this. But then one day a customer, one who'd come to place an order for a puppet, mentioned on his way out, 'I hear you do fine work with the sword.' I guess someone had told him of my kendō lessons.

"About three years or so passed, and I saw a customer who used to come to our shop earlier, one who always had a word of praise for me before he left. But this time as he was leaving he looked down at me and said, 'Your carving hasn't improved one bit, now has it?' His remark cut into my heart. Man can't give himself but to one occupation. I'd already promised myself to the puppet master for ten years. Didn't matter how long I studied the sword, I'd never be able to feed myself by it. I realized what I was doing was wrong. Well, I continued to go off to my lessons every night just as I'd been doing; after all, Mr. Tamaki was a wealthy man, and he wanted a partner. Wouldn't do for a boy like me to anger him. I continued to go, though I did so with only half a heart, and before long I had Mr. Tamaki telling me that my kendō skills weren't getting one bit better. But now as a consequence my carving had improved. I suppose it makes a difference when you put your heart into what you do. I gave myself over to carving puppets. The sword was nothing more to me than a hobby. Oh, I was so devoted to my puppets now that I was improved five years' worth in a single year. When that customer came around again, he took one look at my work and said with a sigh, 'Well, well, next time I come with an order, I'll place it with you instead of the master.' I don't mean to boast now, I'm just telling you what he said. But, I guess if you give yourself over to your work, really put your heart into it, then folks are bound to notice.

"Yes, when I think back on how it was to be young, on how I poured myself into my work, well, I guess you could say I'm somewhat jealous of my youth. If only I could work that way now.

"I stayed on at the master's place for nearly ten years. Let's see . . . yes, I was twenty-six when he finally released me. Guess it doesn't sound right for me to be judging my master; after all, he was kind enough to see to my training. But I must say he was keen on perfecting the smallest detail of a puppet's inner mechanisms. Yes, he was a real stickler for details, he was. And, as a consequence, he was known far and wide for making puppets that never fouled up during a performance. Why, you could ask any puppeteer, in any theater, and he'd tell you Tomigorō's puppets were the easiest to handle. Tomigorō poured everything he had into making certain the puppet's inner workings were done just right—just the way they'd been done for centuries. But you see, no matter how close his puppets kept to tradition, no matter how smoothly they turned even the trickiest of stunts—when it came to the power in the puppet's face, well, I'd say his weren't any better than ordinary. And, I suppose that's why folks often said his puppets failed to come to life on stage. Now here I am talking in a big way like this—but it's because I've only just come to understand it myself, now that I've reached this old age of mine.

"You see, art is tradition. It's the same for carving puppets, too. If you're going to carve Lord Hangan,[8] you carve him the way tradition tells you he's got to look. And, if you're going to carve the hero Yuranosuke,[9] you carve him in keeping with the Yuranosuke tradition, the way he's been carved for centuries. But what happens to art when it's done the same way over and over for hundreds of years? Back in the old days folks did things a certain way because it seemed natural to them. But now we've reached the point where we're just copying the way things were done long ago without really understanding why, and so long as we're just copying, it doesn't have much meaning for us. Years ago folks lived with one goal in mind, and once they reached that goal, well, they were ready to die. But now, if you don't set your sights higher and higher and aim to get beyond whatever goal's been set, you might as well go ahead and die, and you sure don't have any business talking about art. But, you see, I didn't come to figure this out till four or five years ago—and it dawned on me when I finally noticed folks weren't coming to the puppet plays much anymore. They were turning up their noses at it. How I wish I'd realized this sooner!"

3

"If this story were a play, then I suppose you could say we've come to the third act. If we do the third act today, the rest of the play won't last another week.

"Won't you have a cigarette?

"Yes, I suppose about all I ever did was work. No, that's not exactly it either. All I ever did was carve. Puppet heads, that is. This may be the third act—but let me tell you a thing or two about art.

There're folks who set their sights on one level in art—and once they've reached that level, they figure they're finished for life. Then we've got craftsmen like Hidari Jingorō[10] who keep right on perfecting their skills until the day they die. You see, there are those who always push for better, who are always struggling and trying so long as they've got breath in their bodies. And, I wonder if this isn't where art is said to live. Once you've decided that you've gone far enough—you can't do better—well, then that'll be the end for you. I don't know how much longer I'll live. Maybe two more years, maybe three, but this that I'm telling you is what is closest to my heart.

"That's right, I was twenty-six when I was let go from my apprenticeship to the master. I don't remember exactly how it was I got my release. But Heaven must have been looking out for me. I was adopted by the noodle-seller Yoshioka Utarō to be a husband to his daughter, and before long we had a daughter of our own. We moved into a house not but a stone's throw from the master's place. That's right, this very house. Oh, I was young then. I don't quite remember if she fell for me, or maybe I was the one to fall for her. Her name was Oryō. I'm not sure how old she was then, just can't remember unless I sit here and count up the years; it was so long ago. She was a girl from these parts, of course. And she was able to eke out a living on the cotton exchange I spoke of earlier. That's right. I've lived in this house ever since I left the master's place. Now it's such a tattered old place, all black with soot. When I moved in, it had a heavy thatched roof, but we replaced that a while back with this tile roof here. That's about the only change we ever made on the house, though. Otherwise it's just as it was when we moved in.

"Well then, to make a long story short, soon after we married my wife had the child. I still had two, maybe three months to serve on my contract, but the master let me go anyway. I got to take the chisel I had used over the years and a few tools—but that was all I was given. I was a craftsman, after all. When my term was up I didn't need to be hauling about bundles of belongings like some hired servant. Instead, I carried off a few of my master's customers. But that's the way things were done back then—it didn't anger the master.

"No, he never uttered one word of praise for anyone, and he didn't criticize either. That was just his way. When I think back on it now, I was a busy fellow in my youth. You might find this hard to believe, seeing as how my calling in life was to make puppets, but do you know I couldn't recite one line from a puppet play? That's right. Not one line. I didn't have time to be learning lines. That's just the way it was when you had to serve a master!

"What's that you say? The puppets? Well now, when you look at a puppet here, right up under your nose like this, and when you look at that very same puppet up there on the stage, you'd think they were two different puppets. Here's what I find most interesting about carving. If you compare the eyes, nose, and mouth on a puppet's face to those on a person's face, you'll find the puppet's much larger in scale, too large, really. But, if they weren't, you'd never be able to see them up there on the stage. The puppet you see living and breathing up there, and the one I see here in my hands while I'm carving, are different puppets in different worlds. I had to learn to focus my mind on how the puppet would look on stage. I had to learn that if I carved one way, it'd show up well, but if I did it another way, it wouldn't. No, I never got to feeling satisfied with myself for a puppet well made. But now and then I'd see one up there on the stage and I'd think to myself, 'My, doesn't it show up nice!'

"Everyone's said to do some things better than they do others—and the same holds true for carving. Now, you'll find some who'd rather carve female puppets, while others are better at males. Me, I can't force myself to choose between the two. But I do prefer to carve main character puppets, male or female. If I carve a minor character, say a scoundrel like Bannai,[11] folks'll look at my work and say I've done a fine job. But when I carve a character like Yuranosuke, I want people to look at that puppet and feel right down to their bones that this indeed is Yuranosuke and that he couldn't be carved any other way. Now that's no easy task, let me tell you.

"The difference between carving a male and female puppet, I think, is that a woman's face seems easier to carve. It's smooth, you see, and mostly blank. But a man's face has to have clear-cut features, and character. You know how it ought to look before you set to carving. So, you cut out the mouth, and, as you commence to fasten the toggles to the eyes and brows, you realize that the puppet you've carved looks nothing like the one you had in mind before you got started. That's why they say it's so much more difficult to carve a male puppet. But, when you get right down to it—whether you're carving a male or a female—it doesn't matter how well you've made the toggles. No, whether they work all that well doesn't have much to do with the success of the puppet. It's the spirit in the face that matters, and that is decided the moment you take up the block of wood and make your first cut.

"Well now, just a minute. This's the strange part about it. I said that the toggles don't have much to do with the success of the head; but, now, I guess that's not exactly true. You see, it just won't do to have somebody else make the toggles for you. I don't understand it quite myself, but for some reason you've got to make those toggles yourself. Otherwise, well, it just wouldn't be right. So, I guess when all is said and done those toggles really do have something to do with bringing out the spirit in the puppet.

"There are a lot of things about my work that I understand with my heart but can't put into words. Yes, there're a lot of things I can't explain. Now, say you've got two puppets here: one's a nice-looking fellow and the other looks mean. Both of them are forty years old, and both are highborn. But there's something that sets them apart from one another, you see, something about their spirit. And that difference is made, that spirit flows into them, the minute you take up the block of wood and make the first cut.

"Or now take a farmer. All his life he's worked the fields. But one day he up and travels to the city. He stays just a month doing business with the townfolk there, and all of a sudden he's a different man. Doesn't even look like a farmer any more. That's how it is with all the classes, don't you see. Men are born a samurai, a farmer, a craftsman, or a merchant, and they ought to be going about the work they were born to do. But there're always those who'd rather try their hand at something not theirs by birth. That's the way it is with the world, and it makes it hard to carve. To confound it further, there's a shadow to every ray of light, a backside to every front. Man may seem hard and cold on the outside, but if he's like that at home—well, he's going to have a hard time getting himself a son, let me tell you!"

The old puppet maker is in his eighty-sixth year. He's been in the puppet-making business for close to seventy years, from the time he first began his apprenticeship at the age of sixteen to the present. As I listened to him describe how he spent these years devoting himself to his puppets, I was moved beyond words. During the course of those seventy years he has been sick but once. He had, in his words, a touch of stomach catarrh (paratyphoid fever, actually) and the illness forced him to stay in bed for twenty-seven days. But other than that he has not missed a day of work. "During those twenty-seven days," he said, "I lay my head down." I am not certain exactly what he meant by "lay my head down." He may have meant that, since he was ill, he stayed in bed with his head on the pillow. But for someone like the old man, who has worked continuously his whole life through, the words "lay my head down" must have a special resonance.

Whenever I saw the old man at his work he was always in the same position—almost as if he were a statue—his hands frozen in motion.

What must he be thinking, I wondered, as he plied his chisel back and forth, pouring heart and soul into his work—the very same work he has been doing for seventy years! Just trying to imagine it left me struck by an emotion I could not describe.

The old man married when he was twenty-six. Almost sixty years have passed since then, and over those sixty years he has lived in the same house. Well, that might be common enough here in the country. But the old man has sat on the same tatami mat, surrounded by the same weather-beaten *shōji* screens, facing the same old road. Yet the world outside, the people who have passed along that road, have changed more than I could ever imagine.

I had never thought anyone could actually sit in the same place for sixty or seventy years doing the same thing day in and day out. If the person were performing a religious austerity, like those who practice *zazen,* perhaps I could understand it. And yet here was this old man, doing just what I had thought impossible.

"I don't know how it looks to others," he told me, "but I've a reason for sitting right here all day long, never going out. You see, if someone came on business while I was away—well, wouldn't be anybody else here who'd know what to do. No, I decided it was for the best if I stayed in as much as possible. Look, I've got my tools and things all laid out around me so I can sit right where I am with everything at hand's reach."

The sort of life the old man has led may not seem all that strange in a country town like this. No, he has lived just as a tree or flower might live, completely natural. When I looked around, I noticed the house across the road, and wondered if, in the old days, it hadn't been a gathering place for the young women in the cotton exchange. Out front there was a sign that read "Paper-Rope Factory," and every now and then, when the reed screens hanging down over the storefront swayed, I caught a glimpse of the young girls inside busily at work. I could hear the whir of wheels and the high, clear voices of the girls singing "China Nights," "Oh Woman Your Fickle Heart," and other ballads. Their voices were so close I couldn't believe they were being wafted across the road by an errant wind. No, it seemed the girls were sitting right beside me. I wondered if the old man heard them, too.

"You know what I think?" he said. "I think the puppet theater has seen its last days."

Indeed, the old man believes that it is now only a matter of time before the puppet theater perishes completely. And yet he continues to devote himself all the more to this dying art. If those in my line of work ever heard that the alphabet we use—that is, the alphabet I am using now—was shortly to go out of existence, I doubt they would continue to write, hoping against hope that by doing so they could perpetuate their art. No, we would give up immediately, and that is why I sense in the old man an extraordinary depth of passion.

"That's right. When I was young I wanted to carve puppets just as fast as I could. But now I don't much care about the money. If I can just make a good puppet, I'll be satisfied. You see, when you're carving a puppet, if you're worried about all kinds of things, you'll end up making one that's not at all like the one you would've made if you'd just gone about your business with a peaceful state of mind. I like thinking over my work as I go along. I'll say to myself, 'Now if I'm to cut here I'll get a wise face, but here'll give me a cantankerous one. And then again, if I was to do it this way, why I'd get a sorrow-stricken face.' Sometimes I'll be so caught up in my thoughts—wondering how the face'll turn out—I can't sleep at night. I don't know the words to describe the way you ought to carve a puppet. I don't know how to tell you that if you cut this way it'll make for a wise face, but if you cut here the puppet'll come out looking mean. All I can say is, while I'm sitting here carving, my hands know just what to do. Oh now, I'm not the only puppet maker around with hands that can carve and chisel. I expect it's the same for all of us.

"I've been making puppets for a long time now and passing them along to other people. Even so, I don't recollect feeling they were especially good. And, if I was to make a particularly good puppet, I certainly wouldn't regret parting with it. No, every time I finish a puppet I'll always be thinking to myself that the next'll be even better. That's right. 'You can do better,' I'll tell myself. I guess death'll be my first and final stopping place—can't very well be making anything better after that, now can I? Even Hida no Takumi[12] and Hidari Jingorō didn't go and say, 'Yes, this's my masterpiece, now I can die.' No, they kept on working, and if they'd lived any longer there's no telling how many great works they'd have been able to make. But death is, after all, the final stop. It puts an end to your art."

4

"You say you want to know how I came about the professional name 'Tenguya'? My master Tomigorō was known as 'Wakamatsuya.' He had a Tengu[13] mask painted on the *shōji* screen out in front of his shop, you see, and when it came time for me to leave him and start up a shop of my own, well, I decided I'd go and name my place 'Tenguya.' I could have taken over his shop name 'Wakamatsuya,' but I thought 'Tenguya' would be a bit more interesting. Now when folks pass by my sign they'll say, 'You can wager that fellow's a braggart!' But I suppose there's not a soul works with *jōruri*—reciting and such—who isn't something of a braggart!

"What's that you say? Oh, about the 'Best in the World' that's written on the sign out front. I imagine there are those who'll tell you it's an exaggeration, but I figure if you're going to write anything at all you might as well exaggerate. Now, some'll swear there never was any such thing as a Tengu—not even in the old days. Most will tell you a Tengu is just someone who talks nonsense and goes about proud and puffed up telling lies. But then when they look at my shop, you see, they say, 'Well now that Tengu's a real serious sort.' Least that's what I've heard. Yes, they say there isn't a lot of sense to my name, because I'm too honest to be a Tengu. Then they're all the time going by and calling me a 'master artist.' Oh yes, 'master artist' is what they say. Now I may put on like a mighty artist, but of all the things to be saying! I'm no master. I'm just the only puppet maker around! But if folks are going to have to remark on my talent—well, I guess there's just not much I can do to stop them.

"Yes yes. Folks call this little patch behind the house the 'Tengu Garden.' I don't remember when it was they gave it the name. I take real pleasure in growing chrysanthemums, you see, and before I even knew what had happened, why my garden here was overrun with the flowers. I doubt you'll find anyone else who'd grow such a common old flower on the same patch of earth for forty or fifty years on end.

"But listen, my heart was never divided. No, I was devoted to my puppet carving just the same, and I didn't go about my gardening with the same spirit I gave to my puppets—I didn't ever try to either. But whenever folks saw me tending my flowers, why they'd say I was completely given over to gardening. That's just the way I am. Once I set my mind to something, I'll chase at it with a fever. Let's say I'm to go net fishing down by the river. I'll be likely to fish there until my net breaks, and if that should happen, I'll run off to have it mended so I can fish some more, and, if the net breaks again, well then I'll go have it mended again. You see, I'm just the kind of person to get carried away over any old thing.

"But my whims and my carving are two separate things, completely separate. Back when I was young, I had an interest in wrestling and swordsmanship, but I never ran off to practice my sports until well after ten o'clock at night, and up till that time I was hard at work in the master's house. Even after I got my own place and set myself up in business . . . well, I suppose I would allow myself to step out into the garden now and again after I'd finished up my work. But that's about all. Never a day went by that I was too busy in the garden to work on my puppets.

"No, I might take a liking to just about anything I chance to see, but I never once thought I'd turn my full attention to any trade but carving. I'm just the sort of fellow who can do 'most anything he sets his mind to, that's all. I suppose I might have thought once or twice about taking up the sword—getting me a group of students and teaching them the skill. Oh, I suppose there was a time I was even half serious—I was just that taken with the sport. But, now listen, times weren't like they are now. I wasn't of the right kind of family to be teaching the sword, and it wasn't long before I gave up the idea.

"My wife, you say? Well now, once we got married she took to helping me with my work. Why yes, she made puppets too, of a sort. I mean, after I carved a puppet she'd cover it with paper and paint it and such. She was my assistant with the puppets, and she also made papier mâché dolls for children. Yes, she did all sorts of things. She died seven or eight years ago. When was it now? Well, I won't know unless I look it up. The month and day are written out on her Buddhist name tablet, you see. Her age'll be there, too. She was a year older than me. Or now maybe it was a year younger. Well, to make a long story short, she didn't die of any illness—seems it was just old age that took her. We lived together in this very house for years and years. It's sad, yes. But, after all, old age being what it is—you've just got to learn to live with loss.

"Once people leave this world they don't come back. Being left behind, well . . . it's not the best thing that could happen to you. She was such a help to me all those years. Yes, I'd have to say 'Old Grandma' took care of me best. I tell you, my old wife and me, we went through some hard times together—mighty hard times. But I don't want to burden you with all that now. Let me just say that when you surmount your sorrows, you'll find joy on the other side. It's the same for everyone, I expect.

"Now as a rule I don't like bawling others out. I make it a point never to get angry with anyone no matter what, and I don't recall ever getting into a fight. There are some who are always thumping others on the head, but I just wonder what good it does to be hitting people on the head? Now when you get to the relations between husband and wife, they're the same for everyone, in all walks of life. Difference lies only in the depth of feeling between the couple. Well, I don't know how it looked to others, but I don't believe anyone could say that the feelings between my wife and me were shallow. No, I tell you—if anyone with eyes in his head came into this house, he'd see right away

that that old wife of mine was the one who ruled the roost. Goodness!
I was always getting into trouble with that woman! She'd fume over
something and then there I'd be bowing and scraping and doing my
best to beg her pardon. But no matter what I say now, she certainly
did help me with my work. Why, if I'd ever step out back and lose
track of time tinkering in the garden, she'd be there railing at me. I
suppose you could say she was something of a nag!

"Well now let me see . . . What was it she'd do for me that I
appreciated most of all? Sometimes I'd work late into the night, you
see, and when I did she'd always wait up so she could lay my bed out
for me. Well now I suppose just about anyone would have done the
same. Laying out bedding is no great task. But once I'd crawled into
bed and started off to sleep, I'd sometimes feel my old wife go around
behind me and pat the quilt down soft around my shoulders. That's
all. But no one else would have done it.

"When she died I was grief stricken. Oh, I suppose anyone would
have felt the same. But now quite a few men'll take a second wife. I
suppose their feelings for the second'll be different than those for the
first. When my wife died I couldn't forget her right away. And I found
it hard to mention my pain to others. Reciting the sutras was one way
to find release. But if someone asked me just what kind of pain I felt,
well, I could go on and exaggerate, but now how was I to describe the
fine threads of feeling in my heart?"

Except for the vivid recollections of his boyhood, the old man's
memories came back to him in hazy wisps. He was not even certain
when his wife died—the woman who shared his life for more than
fifty years. "My children were all girls," he told me. "There're three:
Shigeri, Yoshie, and . . . well now, there's one more. What is her
name? Looks like I've clean forgot." Then after a pause he added, "It's
Katsuno," and having finally recalled his daughter's name he continued with his story.

From what the old man told me, I found it hard to imagine him as
a youth, riding the angry waves of the floating world and making his
name as a new master craftsman. But that is to be expected, I suppose.
He is such an old man now. In fact, it seemed to me that the Tenguya
Kyūkichi I saw before me had left far behind him the young Tenguya
Kyūkichi of his stories. And this was not simply because the old man's
memories had grown dim. Rather, there was something about him
now, something in his presence and spirit that reminded me of a
stately old tree stripped of leaves. And he was more reluctant than

most (even among the typically reticent country people) to talk about his past. He meant to speak of art.

"There's one thing that sets me apart from others," he told me. "Most folks'll guard their trade secrets, won't tell them to another for the world. They figure that if they can keep them to themselves they can profit. But not me. As soon as I learn something new I'm eager to share it. I'll tell one or two fellows and before I know it five or six have heard. Yes, others are much better at keeping secrets—and turning them to their advantage. And I suppose that is where we differ most."

5

"Looking back on it now I'd say the puppet theater peaked around 1880 or 1890 and has been going downhill ever since. Yes, that would mean the theater was at its height when I was in my thirtieth or fortieth year.

"There were theaters in Kyoto and Osaka, all through the Central Region and on down toward Kyushu—always livelier in the west than up toward Tokyo—and all of it born right here in Shikoku. Not but twenty leagues from Tokushima is the birthplace of those first traveling box puppeteers. Four villages claim the honor—Hiruma-machi, Ikeda, Kamomura, and Nakanoshō. Among the four they always had about a hundred puppeteers out on the road. The area around here is mountainous, as you see, not enough flat land to go around. Not everyone could make his way as a farmer, planting fields and such. That's why, I imagine, so many fellows set out with their boxes. Well now, nothing's changed the land since then. This place is still all mountains, but you hardly see a traveling puppeteer anymore. Why, they've become such a rare sight along these roads that when one was spotted the other day there was a newspaper man right behind him asking to take pictures. But, you know, the puppeteer begged him not to do it and said, 'If you take my picture and run it in that paper of yours, even if folks mightn't recognize my face, they're bound to recognize the puppets I've got here in my hand, and if they do, then before long the whole village'll know that I'm back on the road.' That's just what he said. Now in the old days you'd never hear of it, but nowadays when a fellow sets out on the road he's ashamed of it and the fact he's got to make his living traveling about from place to place. Well, they can say what they will, but I tell you, the only reason they head out there in the first place is because they like it. They liked doing it back in the old days, and they like doing it now. Wouldn't be out there otherwise.

"Now, when was it? There came a time when my wife and I and our oldest girl Shigeri—yes, the one who lives with me now—went off to Osaka to make those life-size puppets, the kind they use in those old sideshows. You know the ones, don't you? 'Have a Glimpse at Heaven— Have a Peek at Hell.' But, just saying we had to go all the way to Osaka to make them ought to tell you how the world had changed. At the time life was full of hardship. The war with the Russians had just drawn to a close and my wife and I set out alone for Iyo, where we worked for nearly half a year. The theater in Yawatahama had burnt down, you see. They'd built a brand new one right after the war and were using real gunpowder for stage effects when one day they didn't mix the shot just right and it exploded in a raging fire. Burnt the place to the ground with not so much as a puppet saved. That's why someone came around asking me to go there and help out.

"After Yawatahama we went back around by Sanuki. Goodness! If I'd known I was to talk about all this someday I would have kept a record of dates and such. Yes, when I was a youngster folks said my memory was keen. But now they're saying I'm downright forgetful. I suppose being able to forget is something of a blessing though. When I look back on those days—no matter how painful they were at the time—they're just like a dream to me now.

"I was busy with the shop here, so my wife and daughter went off to work with a traveling puppet-show troupe. They went as far as Sakushū, as I recall. Well, you see, when you're starting out to make a puppet head—starting out clean with just a block of wood—we say that you're 'chopping out' a new puppet. And now a woman just isn't up to a task like that. They're good at repainting the faces and repairing the wigs for the puppets—and that's just what my wife and daughter did when they worked for that traveling theater. And now listen here, in the old days the theaters would set their stage down along the dry riverbeds, and that's where they'd hold their shows. But sometimes it would rain while they were there and would keep right on pouring, and nobody'd be able to eat. That's where the saying 'No food when it rains' comes from. Now, if you had yourself an easygoing, generous sort of patron, you could expect a little money even when the rains forced you to close your shows. But if your luck ran out, well, wasn't long before you'd pawned off nearly all your puppets for your daily fare. Oh, admission fees would have been around two sen for adults, I believe, and one for children.

"Well, once things took a turn for the worse, everything started going wrong. I'll be damned if I could figure it out—everywhere I turned there'd be a new problem. Speaking for myself, I suppose it wasn't so bad. I had my work, and if I'd only had myself to worry about it wouldn't have been much trouble at all. But soon after the war all manner of new amusements came flooding into the area. There were the *naniwabushi* ballads, the reformed plays, and the new-style drama. Of course, the movie pictures hadn't made it out this far yet, but even so, the puppet plays were being squeezed so bad you hardly chanced to see them anymore. Since I was living in my old hometown, we didn't need to worry about going hungry, and I'm grateful for that. But the years were lean, and we had children to raise, old folks to tend, and rice to buy. That's right, we had to buy rice, and it went for about one yen a bushel, if I recall. I lived in the country, that much is true, but I didn't own one patch of rice land. Had to buy my own rice.

"My goodness, if that's all I'd done in times like those I doubt I would've lived to see this day. There came a time when I set out with the traveling troupes myself. Now I just told you theater folks don't eat on days of rain, but I was different. I was the puppet carver and I got paid right away, show or not. Sometimes I'd even get paid before my work was finished. So I guess you could say I had it a good bit better than the chanters and the puppeteers. Anyway, no matter how difficult life became, I always told myself that I'd never do anything but carve puppets.

"Over my long life I've seen lean years and rich years. During those lean years though, I can't honestly say I never wished for a different sort of occupation. But then I figured if a fellow fails to make a living at one kind of job, he isn't likely to succeed at another. When times were bad it often happened that I'd be commissioned to make a puppet, and then the person who'd placed the order wouldn't show up when the job was done. Oh, I'd try to sell the puppet off, but I'd have a time finding someone to buy it. It's not like selling food or such that anybody'd want. Then, just when I was about to give up, why times would change and someone would come along with the money for the puppet.

"Strange, isn't it—the ways of the world. I'd be thinking as much as I went about my work. I decided that whether I made fistfuls of money, whether it rained or shined, I was going to keep on working. I figured that was the only way to keep from suffering when times got rough. Now there were days when I didn't get any work from the theaters. But I never sat idle. If I wasn't carving *jōruri* puppets, I'd make masks, ornamental dolls, or children's toy dolls, and somehow or another I'd make enough for a day's wage. Oh, I wasn't disappointed with the kind of life I led, but I don't know how I looked to others. My eldest grandson works for the Osaka Railroad. Once I remember saying to him, 'Boy, you ought to take over the puppet trade.' He's the heir to the family business, after all. Well, times were rough then and he looked at me and said, 'Grandpa, how much you make a day?' 'Oh,' I told him, 'I make as much as fifty to sixty sen.' I suppose that's what decided him. As soon as he graduated middle school he signed on with the railroad. Well, since that time I've become this famous puppet maker folks are always talking about. I wonder what he thinks of me now? No way for me to know, of course. I haven't seen the boy in twenty, thirty years. But I have to say, I'm quite proud of that grandson of mine. The way I see it, once you've made up your mind to do something, you ought to give yourself over to it body and soul. I've heard that over these last twenty or thirty years my grandson has been at his work without taking off a single day, not a single day. Yes, the boy turned to me and said, 'How much you make a day?' all worried about money. But for that very reason, see, I think he's a fine fellow. He has my praise.

"'Do whatever you want,' I always tell the young folk around here. 'Just don't quit halfway.'"

6

"My religion? Well, what would you say it is? Three days out of the month I go to the family shrine to pray. That'll be on the first, the fifteenth, and the twenty-eighth. Even so I couldn't point to any one thing and say this is what I believe. And yet, as I'm making my puppets, I feel as if I'm praying to the gods. Don't you see, where my skill stops—when it doesn't go any further—that's where you'll find the gods. Yes, they're there just beyond human understanding.

"If you hurt somewhere you call in a doctor, and you're probably grateful for his services, but I imagine you'll be looking to some power even higher than the doctor, praying and making all kinds of promises. Now I'm not saying that's what I'm about when I'm carving puppets. But let me just say that if you don't reach out to the gods first—make some kind of effort—then they sure aren't going to go out of their way to help you. If I was to tell you what I thought about the gods and the buddhas, then I'd have to explain it like this: Before I start to carve a puppet I have it all clear in my mind how that puppet ought to look. But there's always one part I just can't get no matter how I try—yes, there's always something missing, and it's in that part, that missing part, where the gods reside.

"What's difficult about carving a *jōruri* puppet is first of all making one that'll come to life on the stage, and second of all making one that'll be in keeping with the story of the play. Puppet makers always have to keep these two facts in mind. Well now, I've lived a long life, and I've been at this business quite some time, so I can say a thing or two about it, and I'll tell you right now that most of the puppets I've seen in my day are just ordinary.

"They say that when you're fixing to carve a young girl puppet you should make your heart like a young girl's—all meek and mild. But when you're to carve a samurai you should pull yourself up proud and proper. Now it'll sometimes happen that when I set out fully intending to carve a manly looking fellow like a samurai, by some accident I end up with a puppet that looks downright mean. This's the mystery.

"To make a long story short, before you start to carve you should make yourself humble, the way you are when you pray to the gods. When I'm to carve Yuranosuke, I try to imagine what he must have felt. There he was a masterless samurai, yet he was bent on slaying the man who wronged his lord. While I'm thinking on it I start to carve, and while I carve I think about which way I ought to cut to bring out the face I want.

"In a puppet play they'll sometimes use a different puppet head for the same character, depending on the scene. Take the play featuring the warrior Kumagai,[14] for instance. The Kumagai head they use in the second act won't do at all for the third. In the third act his face has got to be full of the sorrow he feels as he trudges back to camp after slaying the handsome young Atsumori. A Yuranosuke puppet looks a good deal like the third-act Kumagai, and that's why the same head is used for each character. But I suppose Kumagai looks more courageous. He's a bit fierce, truth be told. You see, in the puppet theater there are two types of chief retainers. There are the Great Retainers and there are the Yuranosuke Retainers. In the old days, those who were puppet connoisseurs would tell you which type they wanted when they placed an order.

"After you've set yourself up as a full-fledged puppet maker you can't have any difference in the spirits of the puppets you made early on in your career and the ones you made later. Yuranosuke is Yuranosuke, and there's no reason to ever stray from tradition in carving him. You carve your puppets according to the type of role they're to perform and you cut each one differently to account for their spirit, their age, and whether they're male or female. Now you can carve a houseboy and a lord out of the same block of wood, but they'll still come out different because the way you cut the wood determines the puppet's age, rank, and even the way the puppet seems to feel. I don't really know how to explain it. I suppose most anyone could carve a rough outline of a puppet's face. Most anyone could do it, but now if you don't carve each puppet differently according to age and rank and such, and if you don't follow the traditions for carving that've been passed down over the ages—well, nobody's going to buy your puppet.

"The way to carve's been determined long ago. If a fellow comes up to me and remarks that a puppet's spirit differs with the mood of the puppet maker when he sits down to carve, then I'd have to say that man's a liar.

"You see, not too long ago one of those moving picture fellows came around and asked to make a movie of my work. He filmed me making a new puppet—got me making the first cut in the wood. Well, months passed and I finally finished the puppet about the time the Gennojō, one of the puppet theater troupes still left in these parts, came to town. The moving picture man said he wanted to film my new puppet on the stage in a real drama. He talked it over with the theater folks, and they said it'd be no problem filming them with my puppet, no problem at all except they didn't want to use the brand new puppet—said they'd much prefer to use the puppet I'd made some twenty years ago. It was the same puppet as the one I'd just carved. Now you might already know this, but once a puppeteer's been using a puppet for a number of years he becomes attached to it, and he's going to find it difficult to all of a sudden start using a different one. Anyway, they explained all this to the fellow, but he said no, said it had to be the new one. He wanted to show how I'd taken a block of wood and turned it into a puppet that could hold its own on stage. He went on about it, real insistent fellow, until finally the theater folks pulled out the Kumagai puppet I had made some twenty years ago and stood him up alongside the one I'd just made. 'Take a look at this,' they told him, and sure enough there wasn't one splinter of difference between the two, not one splinter of difference. I can tell you that fellow sure was surprised.

"It's a fact. The puppets I carved over twenty years ago and the ones I make today are exactly the same. They're exactly the same and yet there's a difference. How are they different? They're different in my heart, that's all. There's nothing you can see with your eye, but I know there's a difference. I just don't know quite how to explain it. Guess it's something only the gods can know.

"Now, as I told you earlier, the way a puppet's to be carved was decided long, long ago, and no puppet maker, no matter how famous he may be, ought to break with tradition. Not only does a puppet maker have to follow tradition, he has to be sure that his heart accords with it too, and that his puppets come to life. You can turn puppets out clean and even, as if you were stamping them out with a mold, but they'll never draw a single breath. I don't know how to tell you to give life to a puppet, and even if I was to take up a block of wood right here and carve it for you, I doubt that I could show you what it is that gives a puppet life. But I suppose that's just the way it is with any art.

"I can't even say that I understand puppets that well myself, but what I don't know with my mind I feel with my heart. It's like judo. In judo you want to throw your opponent but you can't do it with your own strength alone. You have to wait until you sense your partner getting ready to make his move and then, when he comes at you, you twist him down. Or, if you've got a timid partner you wait until you feel him draw back and then you sweep him down. It's all a matter of reading the other's mind.

"Mr. Tamaki, the man I took sword lessons from when I was a boy, only used frontal attacks when he sparred with me. He wanted me to learn to face my opponents so I could see into their hearts.

"Now I imagine this won't seem to have much to do with what I've been saying, but when I meet people, I always study their faces to see what kind of puppets they resemble. Most of the time I don't even realize I'm doing it. 'Are they the flirty type?' I ask myself. 'Or grimly serious?' I try to figure out what kind of people they'll be by examining their faces. You could say it's stood me in good stead with my puppet carving. At one point I went so far as to study fortune-telling, the kind that's based on the reading of a person's face. But like they say, a fortune-teller can't tell his own fortune. If he was to seek his customers only among the wealthy—because they're the ones likely to pay the most—then what kind of fortune-teller would he be?

"Well now, I'd say it's the ears that hold the key to a puppet maker's style. You see, when you come across a stranger, you can't tell just by looking at his ears whether he's good or bad—and the same holds true for puppets. There's no set pattern for carving ears. We don't carve them one way for a righteous man like Yuranosuke and then another for the wily scamp Gonta.[15] No . . . whether old or young, man or woman . . . whether the puppet's role is big or small or his character good or bad . . . the ears are always going to be the same. And, because they are, I'd say here is where a puppet maker's own character shines through. Yes, it's all in the touch of the fine-bladed knife and, mind you, the difference is slight, indeed!"

7

"That's right, I had three children, each one of them a girl. The oldest, Shigeri, lives with me here. We adopted the son of the rice dealer across the way as her husband and the heir to my name. My father was an adopted heir, I was too, and then my daughter's husband came to us the same way. That's three generations of adoptions, you know.

"Katsuno's still living. The second girl, Yoshie, she was the best of the three, I thought, but she died young. From the outside I guess it must have seemed that I'd done all right by my girls. Shigeri had her husband, and I had my heir. Yoshie was the type who could do just fine for herself, so we sent her out to marry. And then Katsuno took off some place, I don't recall where.

"Kaname was my adopted son. His family ran a rice shop and worked the fields and such. Oh, now, I'd have to ask Shigeri when it was he came into our family. She'd know. I'd planned to train him in the ways of puppet carving myself, and did manage to set him up as a full-fledged puppet maker. Took the name Tengu Kaname. But wouldn't you know, just around that time we were so tied up with orders to repair old puppets that he never did have a chance to test his mettle. He died before he could make a puppet worthy of his name. It broke my heart to lose him. He wasn't just a son-in-law, he was my heir.

"Whenever I get set to teach someone a thing or two about carving, I tell him right from the start that I'm not going to sit there and explain every little thing. I show him one of the puppet heads I've carved and tell him to try and carve one like it. Then, as he goes along, I tell him 'that looks fine,' or 'that's no good.' But what I can't ever tell him is how he should make the final strokes, the finishing touches. For a long time I'll ponder over those finishing touches myself. I think on them so hard I become completely swallowed up in my thoughts, and then I proceed to carve. But even if I can't come right out and explain to my students all they should do, I show them with my hands. I guess it amounts to the same thing. When I do try to tell them a thing or two about their carving, I usually end up saying more than they want to hear. Someone's feelings get hurt, and I wish I'd never said a thing. Yes, I tell you, when you're trying to teach students to carve, best thing to do is say nothing at all, least that's what I believe . . . and yet it's hard to know exactly what to do. Every master's going to find something he doesn't like about his student's work. There'll be something. But what good does it do blurting it out? No, my father told me long ago, he said, 'Don't ever say anything to anyone about their work,' and he lived to be ninety-three. I suppose it was this advice of his that kept him alive so long.

"Well now, let me see, the only apprentices I ever had were Kaname and my nephew Benkichi. Owing to certain reasons, Benkichi and I don't speak anymore. A while ago it was decided that Kaname's boy Osamu would follow in the puppet trade. Now there's a story here I'd like to tell, though I do feel a bit sheepish mentioning it since it concerns His Imperial Highness the Prince. Oh, now when was it? Prince Nashimoto paid a visit to our city of Tokushima. I was asked to call on him at his lodgings, on account of him wanting to see a puppet. So I went to him with one of my puppets. Not one that had been used yet, but one I'd just made—a Kusunoki Masatsura puppet.[16] He seemed rather taken with it. 'How splendid,' he said. Yes, that's what he said, and he beckoned me to come close so I could show him how the puppet moved. Now can you just imagine it? There I was a humble old puppet maker, yet I was being treated better than the governor himself, who had to watch it all from a distance. I sat right up beside His Imperial Highness and showed him what my puppet could do. I was up there with him for some time, too. Yes, it was the honor of a lifetime!

"When I was summoned to the prince's lodgings I went along with the governor, now let's see, that would've been a gentleman by the name of Kanamori Tarō. When he saw how pleased the prince was with my puppet, he remarked, 'It'd be a real shame if the art ends with you. Hurry up and name an heir!' As soon as Osamu got wind of that he began to work at puppet carving for all he was worth! Yes, up to then I'd just about given up. I figured I'd die and take my art with me; and Osamu, for his part, hadn't much felt like carrying on the business.

"Nowadays the only other puppet maker in these parts is that Benkichi I mentioned earlier. Used to be there was Deko-Chū of the Fukuya Shop and Deko-Tsune to the west; we knew him as Tsune-han. He had a boy named Junjirō. They're all dead now. What with all the other fellows dying off you'd think my life would be that much easier. I guess folks believed we were all rivals, seeing as how we were in the same line of work. But that wasn't the case. Each of us worked for a different theater and didn't need to bother about the others. And since we all carved puppets—which take quite some time to finish— we couldn't exactly be competing over the numbers turned out. But, of course, in our heart of hearts each one of us wanted to be the best.

"Now when was it Deko-Chū passed on? I don't remember just now. His work was well known in these parts, and there was a reason for it. You see, his father got himself in some kind of trouble. Nowadays I doubt his crime would have seemed that bad, but at the time it was serious and he was exiled on account of it. Had to go to Osakagoe [the boundary between Awa and Sanuki]. Once his sentence was up, he came on back to his old home, but having been branded a criminal, he wasn't allowed to use his own name anymore. Well, since he couldn't use his own name, he used his son's. Every time he made a puppet he signed it 'Chū,' or 'Made by Chū.' Bequeathed everything to that boy, even though he wasn't but an infant at the time. And so, you see, ever since Chū was just a little fellow his name'd been spread far and wide.

"Now Umanose Komazō was a puppet maker years and years ago. There's never been another who could carve brave and dignified puppets as well as he—least not so far as I can tell. He was best at main character puppets. His female puppets were said to be sweetly girlish, but I don't suppose they were his strongest point."

While the old man and I sat and talked, people stopped by from time to time to see him—all sorts of people. Some would come on business and others just to sit at the doorway and gossip. Occasionally they would come inside for a cup of tea. The old man never went out of his way to receive his guests. He simply went on with his work—a tranquil look on his face.

Next to the old man there was an ancient-looking brazier with a pot of glue on top of it lightly simmering. The old man always had a teakettle there, too, warming over the coals. Now and then he would stop long enough to pour himself a cup of tea. When guests stopped by he would offer them a cup and would drink along with them. In fact, the old man drank constantly. "Now you be sure to write this down," he told me with a laugh. "Some say tea is poison, but that just isn't so. If it were, do you suppose I'd have lived as long as I have drinking the way I do? And then there're those who never drink tea and still die young! Oh, I don't touch liquor; never smoke. But I couldn't very well just drink water, now could I?" Yes, the old man certainly is fond of his tea. He uses high-quality leaves and brews his tea until it is as strong as possible.

The old man is not particularly fond of socializing. Perhaps it would be more accurate to say he is somewhat withdrawn. And yet there is something about him that puts others at ease. I guess someone who has lived as long as he has does not worry over little things the way others do. For instance, once while I was there someone called to the old man from the road out front and asked if they might cut a few of the chrysanthemums that were blooming behind the house in his garden. The old man glanced up long enough to call out in a loud voice, "Go help yourself!" But then he was back hard at work.

Kyūkichi always wears a smile when he is talking with one of his guests. Well, it is not a smile actually, but he makes one feel that he is smiling. His face is gentle and kind. He told me that he had made up his mind long ago never to get angry with anyone no matter what happened, and that is why his expression is always quiet. But when he was engrossed in his work his face took on an entirely different cast. He began to look irritated, adamant, as if his features were set in stone. This face of his is neither young nor old; it is timeless and beautiful. I imagine when he was young he was very handsome. Once, while we were talking, he did happen to mention something of the sort. "Years back I was a good-looking fellow," he told me. "They say that pine trees have their prime, and all living things their bloom. Well, human beings, too, have their moment to flower. Now when I look back on when I was young, I'm struck by the truth of it. Oh yes, there was a time when I was right handsome, falling in love with the girls and breaking a few hearts, too."

8

"Oh, it puts me in a bad mood, let me tell you. And when I'm angry I can't do a bit of work. Well, to make a long story short, sometimes my wife would come and tell me, 'I'm off to such-and-such a place.' Now I'd tell her that on account of me being so busy that day she'd have to put it off, go some other time. But then she'd set in to telling me why she had to be going that very minute, and before I knew it she was gone, and I was fuming. Oh, the madder I was the madder I'd get at myself for being all fired up over something as piddling as that. I suppose it's my own fault. I'm just not the sort to argue. Well, let me tell you, I do the best I can to steer clear of that sort of business.

"No, I can't exactly say I do it for my health, but around noontime I'll walk about a half mile down the road and then turn around and walk back. Never once had a massage, but it's become my habit to stretch out all the joints in my body—once in the morning and once at night—just to be sure they're in good working order. Yes, while I'm still lying in my bed in the morning I do these exercises before getting up. I stretch my arms out over my head as high as they'll go, and then I lift them up and down, up and down—just to see how well they move. Do the same thing at night after I crawl in bed. Sometimes I'll be so stiff I can hardly lift a finger. Happens more frequently now that I'm getting on in years. But I'll keep trying to lift my arm, and as I'm working on it these old muscles'll finally loosen up and let me move. I guess you could call this a lazy man's sport, seeing as how I do it in bed. But my father used to do the same thing, and I can remember watching him when I was a boy. He'd say, 'Oh it hurts me here today—

when I go like this. Looks like I won't be able to move at all.' Now I know just what he meant by it.

"My father was fit as a fiddle up until the day he died at ninety-three. He'd walk over here from Nakamura and then walk back the same day. He only worked at the dye shop till he was sixty or so, but he always had his wits about him. Age didn't muddle his mind. What's most precious to me now is the fact that I was able to be with him when he died. I walked into the room where he was and said, 'How you doing, Pa?' I guess he'd been waiting for me because he looked up at me and said, 'I'm so glad you came.' Two hours later he died. I was fifty-two or fifty-three at the time. When it suddenly came to me that a father could love his child that much, well, my heart was filled with joy. So this is what it means for parent and child to part? . . . My father was ninety-three, after all, yet he could still answer clearly when spoken to."

I was startled to find that the old man was crying. We had talked about all kinds of things and he had hardly registered any emotion. But now here he was in tears. Old people, it is said, are easily reduced to tears, but there was only one other time that I chanced to see Kyūkichi cry. His tears poured down his cheeks in a torrent too swift to wipe away.

"The other day I heard Kōtsubo-han[17] on the radio reciting the *Chūshingura*. If I ever were to meet him face-to-face I'd certainly like to congratulate him on the fine job he did. He came to the part where Lord Hangan cries out in despair, 'Has Yuranosuke still not come?' Oh, I can hear those words even now, just like they were inside my ears. I'll never forget them. Yes, and then of course Lord Hangan must thrust the sword into his belly and kill himself even though he's not said good-bye to his beloved retainer." As he spoke the old man's eyes filled with tears that spilt down over his face. I watched silently, overwhelmed.

From time to time Kyūkichi would receive distinguished guests. While I was with him a banker from Tokyo stopped in, and on another occasion the school inspector came by from the prefectural office. I do not know what they thought of the old puppet maker, but they asked him all sorts of questions. "Whom do you admire most?" for example, or, "What was the most interesting moment in your life?" To these questions the old man answered:

"Person most admired? Well, let me think. Folks in my line of work don't know anything other than their trade. But I'd say I admire those who set their mind to something and are always striving to do better. Whether a carpenter or a farmer makes no difference, so long as they spend their life questing after knowledge. Yes, I think that sort of person's worthy to be admired.

"Now about that most interesting moment. . . . I guess it'd have to be back when I was fifteen years old or so. That was right when the age of the Daimyō was giving way to the Meiji Restoration, you know, and everyone was up and celebrating the changes taking place. Men and women, grandpas and grandmas . . . didn't matter who . . . everyone was up and shouting 'Well, why not! Anything goes!' They'd burst into a stranger's house shouting and carrying on—didn't much care if the owner cursed them or laughed at them. Some of the merrymakers hid their faces behind masks and some painted theirs up, but others just went with the face they were born with. They'd eat all the rice cakes they could lay their hands on, and they'd drink their fill of liquor, too. But as soon as they'd be full, why someone'd shout 'Let's dance a bit till we're hungry again!' and they'd all set in to dancing. 'Well, why not! Anything goes!'[18]

"A group of fellows set out like that, dressed only in their loincloths. Didn't have a penny to their name, but they made it all the way to Ise Shrine feasting and dancing. I wasn't but a little fellow at the time so I could only follow after them as far as the neighboring village. Oh my, it was some celebration—the likes of which I've never seen. Yes, I'd have to say that was the most interesting moment in my life.

"Now I suppose there was a reason for it all, but seeing as how it happened when I was just a boy, well, I didn't really understand it. It's just that everything was undergoing changes. The next-door neighbors'd be at their spring cleaning—when along would come a gust of wind and carry off their prized paper charm. It'd land down the road aways, and then someone'd come along and pick it up. The next thing you know, he'd be carrying on like it was a blessing from heaven. Yes indeed, thought that charm had just fallen out of the sky! Why even when folks came across an old Daikoku[19] charm lying in the road, they'd set into dancing, shouting all the while, 'Look! Oh look! A blessing from Heaven!' Happened so often the little dance they did came to be known as the 'Blessing from Heaven Jig.' Oh, I suppose a blessing from heaven was reason enough to celebrate, because soon the whole household'd be up and dancing. 'Well, why not! Anything goes!' they'd holler, and they'd dance on down to their neighbor's house, shouting and carrying on. And when they were done there, they'd march right on to the next house. 'Well, why not! Anything goes!' It got to be that for a whole half a year or so no one could do a lick of work. And then the Fushimi Battle[20] put an end to it all."

The old man had a faraway look in his eyes as he described the past. It seemed that these events of long ago—events we could not truly understand—were still very much alive in his memory.

Once when I came to visit the old man and called to him where he sat at his work, he did not answer. After a minute he raised his head slightly, but he still did not say anything to greet me. Instead I overheard him mutter to himself, "Not worth a damn today." Someone came and led him off to bed. I sat by myself in the old man's workshop for close to an hour wondering what would become of him. Was this the way he would die? Other members of the family, though, told me that he was put to bed like that from time to time. But they added that after he had slept nearly half the day he would return to work refreshed. As I waited for him to awaken, I found myself caught in a tangle of feelings.

Before long the old man returned, wearing his usual gentle smile. He looked straight at me, greeted me politely, and then began to talk as he always did, as though nothing had happened. He soon settled in to telling me the following account. Now I am not certain that I learned this story that day, perhaps it was the next. At any rate, he spoke clearly and buoyantly, and this is what he said:

"When I pause to think, I realize that all people, no matter who they are or what they do, ought to work with all their might up to the moment they die so as to leave behind something worthy. For myself, you see, I hope to leave something that folks'll praise, instead of something that'll make them laugh. I'll be working on it up to the day I die. Don't you see, if you can leave behind something that you've poured all your energy into, well, you won't mind dying much. Now, I've outlived the span of life allotted to most folks, and I don't know how I'll have to suffer come my time to die, but I do know that whatever falls my way I want to be able to face it. Twice now I've had these fainting spells where I've blacked out, and I've worried that my time might come while I'm in the midst of one. Now that would be just too easy, don't you think?—slipping away like that unawares. There are those who'll say that a fellow like me'll have an easy death, seeing as how I've lived so long. Oh, I suppose my time to go is drawing near, but I figure I'll hold out for another year or so.

"Well, years back I'd hear folks remark on 'heaven and hell.' I'm not sure there are such places. Long time ago there was a song that went 'You can say there's a heaven, but no one really knows. The path there is long, and no one's yet come back. Even Shaka and Miroku are still on their way.' [By that the old man means that the path is so long the buddhas still have not reached heaven.] I expect it's true. I'm figuring I ought to go ahead and set out on that road, see what it looks like up there. If it looks good, I'll holler back down to my girl here and tell her to hurry up. But now I just wonder if my message'll get through! Yes, that's the way things stand with me."

9

The day before I was to return to Tokyo I went to visit Kyūkichi again. It just so happened that the Gennojō Puppet Troupe had come to town that day, and I thought I should see one of their plays before I left. I also thought it would be nice if the old man would accompany me, and that is why I paid him this last visit.

"A play, you see, used to be an event everyone enjoyed—something to look forward to, and you wouldn't find anyone complaining of being tired after a day at the theater. It was something of a treat back then. Yes, that's the way it was, but, truth be told, I don't much want to go these days. The theater has changed—why, it's changed more than you could imagine.

"Now, in the old days when you went to see a play, the theater was always full of young people. There'd be ground-blessing celebrations in the autumn, you know, time to give thanks to the gods of the earth for their bountiful gift of rice. Oh, now I suppose it's not just the earth that produced that rice, but anyway, that's the sort of celebrations there'd be. Folks would use the occasion to stage plays and such. The chanters and puppeteers would all be young, and the only thing the old folks did was go and watch. Lots of young girls would come around, too.

"But look here, now you've got these moving picture shows that everybody's so crazy about. All you've got to do at a movie is sit back and watch the screen, and you can follow the story without much trouble. Young girls nowadays are so used to the movies, they have a real time trying to make sense of the old-fashioned language used in the puppet plays.

"Was it summer before last? Yes, I believe it was then that I had occasion to go and see a play. But if I was to go to the theater now, I expect I'd find that the folks I knew in the old days, old folks like myself, are all dead and buried. And, if one or two of them are still living, well, I don't imagine they get out much. Yes, you see, once you've lived to be seventy or so—well, that's just about as far as you can go. You'll find only a sprinkling as old as that at the theater. Isn't that right, Shigeri? Wouldn't you say Old Man Ino and his wife are about the only ones left who still go? That old Mrs. Ino, she must be close to ninety, maybe even ninety-one, but she certainly does love the theater. She still gets out to the plays.

"No, I don't really recognize the puppets they're using nowadays. In this region there're still a number of theater troupes but none any better than the Gennojō and the Rokunojō. Both of them mostly use the puppets I made. Now when I see my own puppets up on stage, I don't start into grumbling to myself like I used to about how I ought to have carved them—wishing I'd cut a little more here or made the face rounder there. Folks know that puppets are my life, and I imagine when they see me at the theater they think I'm going to be criticizing every little slipup there on stage. But I'm not that way anymore. I just go to the theater and watch the play like any other fellow. I don't pay attention to any one thing. Most of the puppets there are mine. But I guess that's just the way it should be, and I don't think much of it.

"In the old days they'd stage plays in a field somewhere. They'd start around seven o'clock in the morning and would go till nightfall. Once the sun went down they'd take split logs and pile them up one on top of the other to make a bonfire. Oftentimes the faces of the puppeteers would turn black with soot because of it. And, oh my, the village girls would scamper noisily over the meadow paths with groups of young men on their way to see the play."

That was the last I heard of the old man's stories. Exactly ten days had passed since I had paid my first visit. As I bade him farewell, the old man stopped what he was doing and turned to me. "You and I . . . there's more difference in our ages than I can even figure. But every day we've shared tea and stories just like two old friends. Well, I don't know that we'll ever meet again."

I went to the village play by myself, unable to convince Kyūkichi to join me. And yet, I felt that he was there beside me just the same. The theater was a typical country one. When I went inside I found it very quaint. The old man had told me what to expect, and yet I was still surprised to see that almost all the people sitting there on the floor watching the play were old. There was even an old nun among them, and several old gentlemen who seemed to be retired town officials. But most of the audience was composed of simple men and women from the neighboring villages. They had come dressed in kimonos of homespun cloth. Alongside them were oil-paper umbrellas, stacks of lunch boxes, and other bundles. The people were interested in the drama, of course, but instead of sitting quietly and watching the events on stage they talked to one another, ate, and seemed truly to enjoy themselves. Perhaps, being as old as they were, they knew the plays so well they could talk and carry on like that and still follow what was happening on stage. I suppose all they had to do was sit there.

"Do you like it?" I overheard an old man ask the woman beside him.

"Oh, yes, whenever I hear the *jōruri* ballads I feel all calm inside."

"Certainly was a wealth of passion in the words of old!"

The puppets I knew so little about were performing on a darkened stage. They were large, and the puppeteers, I could see, had to put a great deal of energy into the roles their puppets performed. At first I was at a loss as to what I should feel, but before long I ceased to notice the puppeteers, and at that point I was pulled into the drama. We came to the scene where Kumagai, having captured Atsumori, looks down to see that his foe is a handsome boy. I found that I was in tears when the chanter sang the line, "He brandishes his sword. But behold, beneath the armor a jewel-like face." What power must this art possess, I thought, if it can move to tears even someone like myself, someone who knows so little of its secrets.

It was raining. In the country they call this sort of day "a rain holiday," as there is nothing left to do once the fields have been planted. The countryfolk set out for the theater early in the morning, holding aloft their oil-paper umbrellas and hoisting their big picnic bundles upon their backs. They brought rice balls with them stuffed with pickled plums, and loquats, which they peeled before eating. They brought tea, too, in old bottles. When I first entered the theater, all the munching I heard reminded me of silkworms chewing away at their mulberry leaves. I was enveloped in a nameless mood. As I sat there amidst it all, I felt that I was beholding the death of the puppet theater. This was the way it would go, would it not? It would simply fade away. I felt all about me an undercurrent of sorrow. The other spectators, unaware of the fate awaiting their beloved theater, were talking among themselves in loud, cheerful voices. I wondered if this were not what the old man had noticed when he came to the plays. Perhaps this was why he had refused to come with me. On the train back to Tokyo I thought about it all for a long time.

Half a year has passed since my trip to Shikoku. Yesterday I received the Oyumi puppet I asked the old man to make. Unable to forget the puppet I had seen at my friend's house the spring before, I had asked Kyūkichi to make me one like it. Perhaps it was just my imagination, but I felt that the puppet I now held in my arms was much, much better than the one I had seen earlier. To borrow the old man's words, the puppets might have been exactly the same in form, "without a splinter of difference," and yet they were different. The difference lay, I knew, in the heart of the old puppet maker.

I dressed the puppet in a kimono and searched about for an antique comb to fix in her hair. While I busied myself I was overcome by a strange feeling. By doing what I was doing, that is, by dressing the puppet and looking for a comb for her hair, was I not offering proof, if but slight, that the puppet would not perish? I was certain that the old man, too, had known this all along.

NOTES

1. Uno Chiyo, "Bunraku to watashi," *Uno Chiyo zenshū,* vol. 10 (Tokyo: Chūō Kōronsha, 1977), 175.
2. "Hisa" is an alternate reading of the character read "Kyū" in "Kyūkichi." Uno has indicated that the name of the puppet maker in her story is to be read "Kyūkichi," not "Hisakichi" (interview with Uno, 21 June 1984).
3. "Bunraku to watashi," 176.
4. Interviews with Uno, November 1987.
5. *Keisei Awa no Naruto* (The Tragedy of Awa), a *jōruri* play written in 1768 by Chikamatsu Hanji and others.
6. 1858.
7. *The Household-Precept Letter Writer,* a collection of model letters, is believed to have been written by the Buddhist priest Gen'e (1279–1350).
8. En'ya Hangan, the lord whose involuntary *seppuku* is avenged by the loyal *rōnin* in *Chūshingura.*
9. Ōboshi Yuranosuke, leader of the *rōnin.*
10. A famous carpenter and sculptor of the late sixteenth and early seventeenth centuries, he is credited with making the "sleeping cat" of the Tōshōgū Shrine in Nikkō and the "nightingale" floors of the Nijō Castle in Kyoto.
11. Another *Chūshingura* character, Bannai is a loyal henchman of the villain Kō no Moronao.
12. A legendary artisan said to have directed the construction of the Imperial Palace when the capital was moved to Kyoto in 784. In one of the *Konjaku monogatari* tales, he engages the famous artist Kudara Kawanari (782–853) in a duel of skills. Hidari Jingorō is described above in n. 10.
13. A Tengu is a mythical creature thought to live in the trees deep in the forest. Masks depicting this creature are generally red and have long, grotesque noses. "Tengu" is also used to refer to someone who brags, exaggerates, and lies.
14. Kumagai Naozane (1141–1208), the Genji warrior who beheaded Taira Atsumori (1169–84) at the battle of Ichinotani and, overcome with remorse, became a monk.
15. A character in *Yoshitsune senbon-zakura* (Yoshitsune and the Thousand Cherry Trees).
16. Masatsura (1326–48) was the son of Kusunoki Masashige (1294–1336), the famed warrior in Emperor Go-Daigo's forces whose heroics are portrayed in *Taiheiki* and in various plays.
17. The famous *gidayū-bushi* chanter Toyotake Yamashiro no Shōjō (1878–1967). Originally named Kanasugi Yatarō, he succeeded to the professional name of Toyotake Kōtsubodayū in 1909. Prince Chichibu granted him the court title of Yamashiro no Shōjō in 1947.
18. Kyūkichi is referring to the "*eejanaika*" outbreak of 1867. Rumors began to circulate that sacred amulets from Ise Shrine were falling from the skies over Nagoya, prompting a rash of near-hysterical celebrations that swept through the Kansai. The common people, long suppressed by the government and baffled by the

many changes taking place, interpreted the amulet rumors as a sign that good times were ahead. They dressed in gaudy costumes and took to the streets, bursting into the houses of the wealthy and feasting on whatever they could find, all the while exclaiming *"Eejanaika!"* ("Why not? Anything goes.").

19. The god of good fortune.
20. The Toba-Fushimi Battle, first of several conflicts accompanying the Meiji Restoration. Shogunate troops stationed at Osaka Castle marched toward Kyoto to rout the Satsuma and Chōshū forces but were intercepted on 27 January 1868 at Toba-Fushimi and defeated.

"Birdhouses" by Nogami Yaeko

TRANSLATED BY JULIET WINTERS CARPENTER

TRANSLATOR'S INTRODUCTION

During an active writing career that spanned eight decades, Nogami Yaeko (1885–1985) made a unique and important contribution to modern Japanese literature. In addition to several prize-winning historical novels, she wrote shorter prose fiction and essays, numerous plays (drawing on sources as diverse as Ibsen and the Nō), travel sketches, children's stories, and translations including *Heidi*, *Bulfinch's Mythology*, and works by Jane Austen and Charles Lamb. Her intellect and curiosity were wide-ranging, her common sense and positive outlook unwavering, her dedication to her craft untiring.

She was born Kotegawa Yae, the eldest child of a wealthy sake brewer in Usuki-machi, Ōita Prefecture. From childhood she received a thorough grounding in such works of Japanese classical literature as *Man'yōshū*, *Kokinshū*, and *The Tale of Genji*, as well as in the Chinese classics. After graduating from higher elementary school, she began the study of English, and in 1900, at the age of fifteen, she went to Tokyo to live with her father's younger brother (an economist with a Ph.D. in American literature from the University of Michigan). He arranged for her to attend Meiji Girls' School, a Christian-oriented, progressive school where the famous Christian leader Uchimura Kanzō (1861–1930) taught. Upon graduating in 1906, she married Nogami Toyoichirō, a student in the English department of Tokyo University and a pupil of the great writer Natsume Sōseki (1867–1916). Through her husband she, too, was able to receive guidance from Sōseki; together they joined the "Thursday Club," meeting at Sōseki's house every week.

On Sōseki's enthusiastic recommendation, her first story, "Enishi" (Ties), appeared in *Hototogisu* in 1907, followed by a second story a

223

few months later, again highly praised by Sōseki. In 1911 she joined *Seitō* (Bluestocking), the magazine founded by Hiratsuka Raichō (1886–1971), a prominent feminist. Gradually Nogami gained confidence and developed her own style, continuing to publish in influential magazines and constantly experimenting in new directions, even as she bore and raised three sons. Besides *Machiko* (1928–30), a novel exploring questions of marriage and women's social responsibility, two long historical novels won her enduring fame: *Meiro* (The Labyrinth, 1948–56), dealing again with morality and social activism, and *Hideyoshi to Rikyū* (1962–63), a masterful exploration of circumstances leading to the forced suicide of tea master Sen no Rikyū at the command of the warlord Toyotomi Hideyoshi. Nogami won respect for her commanding intellect, her sensitivity to contemporary social problems, and her ability to draw on Eastern and Western literary traditions alike, as well as for her supple prose.

"Birdhouses" ("Subako") appeared serially in the *Asahi Shinbun* in the fall of 1970, when Nogami was eighty-five. It is set in a mountain village near Karuizawa, on the boundary between Nagano and Gunma prefectures, southeast of Mount Asama. The village was founded by members of Hōsei University, where Nogami's husband was a professor, and became a popular summer resort, as she describes. Nogami loved the mountains, and it became her custom to live there six months of the year, writing and enjoying a solitary communion with her surroundings.

As she meditates on the theme of harmony with nature, Nogami subtly develops and expands on the metaphor of "birdhouses": she begins by likening the simple cottages in the mountain retreat where she lives to birdhouses, and herself and the summer visitors to birds; she then expands the comparison, finding that human behavior hardly differs from bird behavior, and that in fact "the essential face of life is a great and solemn universal." Further contemplation leads her to a conclusion less flattering to humanity: "the entire human race seems in danger of being ridiculed by wasps and jays for its utter incompetence." Thoughts of aging bring the realization that her own body is a sort of birdhouse, her soul the bird, quite happy in its mountain surroundings, "far more at home among the silent trees of the forest . . . than amid the milling throng on Tokyo streets." She concludes by revealing that in her semieremitism, she is haunted by urgent global questions affecting us all: the danger of nuclear holocaust and our responsibility to preserve our planet, the cradle—no, nest—of life. The last "birdhouse" is Earth itself. The essay thus closes on an ironic note: after writing movingly of a life in harmony with nature, she contemplates the disharmony among people—the "stupidity"—that may destroy our natural environment forever.

The close observation of nature and attention to minute seasonal changes in "Birdhouses," tied to discursive reflections on the nature and meaning of human life, are qualities with a long and distinguished tradition in Japanese writing. Among prose works, one thinks first of *Hōjōki* (An Account of My Hut, 1212), a poetic essay written by the literary recluse Kamo no Chōmei (1155–1216) when he was nearly seventy. Chōmei's essay, considered a chief exemplar of the genre known as *zuihitsu* (following the brush), or discursive essay, is built around the theme of life's evanescence. Life is compared in the famous opening lines with "the flow of the river" and "bubbles that float in the pools, now vanishing, now forming."[1] After cataloguing life's vicissitudes and hardships, Chōmei devotes the latter half of the essay to a description of his hermit's life—a life of religious meditation, aesthetic pursuits, and solitary toil, in which, he says, "my greatest joy is a quiet nap, my only desire for this life to see the beauties of the seasons." The simple tranquility of his solitary existence, broken only by the hooting of owls, provides deep satisfaction. Chōmei's essay also ends on a note of irony: in obedience to Buddhist teaching, he has retired to his mountain hut to transcend life's turmoil and pain, by withdrawing from all desire—and thus the deep attachment he has formed for the hut may thwart his very purpose in going there.

Other classical works could be cited with which Nogami's essay also has affinities. One is *Ora ga haru* (The Year of My Life, 1819), the poetic diary of Kobayashi Issa (1763–1827). Using a mixture of poetry and prose, Issa describes his life in a poor mountain village; included are many descriptions of nature, such as the valiant struggles of a chestnut tree to remain alive despite the destructive weight of snow each winter—a struggle that all living things, Issa and we included, carry on, each in our own way.

And yet, despite such links with Japanese literary tradition, and scattered allusions to Nō drama and ancient Greek mythology, Nogami's work seems modern in tone. It is not only the mention of computers, television, and atomic bombs that makes her modern. One is struck by her lack of sentimentality; by her wry humor and self-deprecation; and by her obvious awareness of the oneness of the world, and of our mutual responsibility to it and to each other. Today in Japan the vague term *kokusaika,* "internationalization," is ubiquitous. Nogami Yaeko, throughout her near century of life, demonstrated a truly international perspective, one rooted in her own tradition but not bound by it.

She closes by imagining the violent destruction of our planet, and then, as if worn out by the prospect, wends her way back home to take a nap. One can only hope that the jays did cooperate—and that the earth will indeed long stay "round and blue," as she wished.

The translation is based on the essay as it appears in *Nogami Yaeko zenshū*, vol. 23 (Tokyo: Iwanami Shoten, 1982), 189–201.

BIRDHOUSES

In May, the village on the plateau is still empty. In the three long vertical cracks on the face of Mount Asama, the last vestiges of snow—known as the "three long onions"—disappear after having lingered there, frozen, for so long. The meadows are palest green, thinly covered over with grass, and scattered larch shoots sticking out from the trunks like whiskers on the Nō mask of Okina, the Old Man, are still a fresh and tender shade of green. Before long the young pear trees will be in bloom. Massed with blossoms from the lowest branches to the crown, even to the tip of every frail twig, they look as if they are still laden with winter's heavy snows. Even on windless days, petals drift through the air like great snowflakes, spilled by passing birds.

Already the birds, wakened fully to the spring, are busy with their songs of courtship. Day after day goes by and I see no human figure, and hear no human speech—the only voices anywhere are those of the birds. Night and day, they never leave off their chattering. In Tokyo—lower in elevation than here by a good three hundred feet—one hears birds like the nightingale, the cuckoo, the bush warbler, the olive-backed pipit, and the black paradise flycatcher only on tape, in televised documentaries; here, they are like so many naughty little boys, raising a ruckus wherever they go. Sometimes I even scold: "Can't you be still for one minute?"

How many years ago would it be, I wonder. A little nightingale flew in through the open terrace doors. He might have come to check me out, thinking, perhaps, "She looks like one of us, all right, but why does she stay quiet all the time and never sing? What kind of bird *is* she?" He stuck out his tail like the bow of a boat, perched for an instant on the corner of a long table in the hall, and then flew off, out the opposite window. Doubtless he went back and reported on the existence of a highly peculiar member of the family.

In fact, the houses in this village on the plateau do bear a great resemblance to birdhouses. This summer village began as a collection of mountain huts set up in lieu of tents by people from the university. The later additions are not as rough as their pioneering predecessors, and they boast a more modern design, but they remain a far cry from the luxury of neighboring Karuizawa. Scattered amid the larch forests, oak groves, and dense undergrowth on gentle slopes, they look like nothing so much as sporadic clusters of birdhouses, taking up scarcely more space than the real thing.

In May these "birdhouses" are all still empty. But when June is gone and July is perhaps ten days along, some of them fill with moving shapes and sounds, and out of doors one hears voices in conversation. Ah—a burst of surprised recognition—people! This is the advance contingent of the migratory flock. As summer vacation wears on, gradually little families begin to appear: braces of parent birds with their chicks. Every birdhouse is full. The occupants wake with the morning light and retire at dusk, managing somehow, if less easily than in Tokyo, to fill their bellies with what lies at hand. In place of birdtalk they chatter loudly back and forth with "words," and laugh boisterously like so many kingfishers. They are in no wise different from fowl.

But they do not stay for long; by September the village is empty again. Like those birds who leave Japan each fall to wing their way to tundras far in the north, these visitors too take off eventually for homes in other parts.

Fall comes early to the mountains. Day by day as the chill sets in, the blue crystalline sky deepens in hue, until the sharp, metallic point of Mount Asama seems about to pierce it through. Then one morning suddenly all is white with frost, and it is time for the leaves to change. The autumn leaves last an extraordinarily long time. Heralded by the many-colored grasses along the paths and on the hillsides, the foliage changes color gradually, often—depending on the variety of tree—turning from color to color as time goes by. The oak leaf, for example, surpassed in numbers here only by the larch, begins by turning vivid yellow; this gives way to light red, followed in turn by glowing vermilion, deep purple, and finally light brown. Nor are such wondrous transformations limited to the oak. Some trees that are evergreen at lower elevations put on magnificent displays of autumn foliage here. And so the foliage is more varied and richer here than in places known only for the gaudy scarlet of their maples. Mount Asama alone stands stern guard over the deep purple of its valleys, but throughout the surrounding hills, even where the trees are scarcely worth chopping down for kindling, there is a kaleidoscope of colors: the hillsides are a succession of palettes crowded with every imaginable pigment, squeezed from numberless tubes.

The feast of colors goes on and on, until one day it is over and the leaves fall in a sudden rush. The mountain wind is not so accommodating as to sweep down just enough for a cozy fire. As autumn deepens, the wind grows ever more stubborn and willful, until the night when for whatever reason it decides to go on a rampage; by morning every tree and branch in the forests and woodlands has been stripped bare, as if by highwaymen. The one exception is the larch: at the very top, narrow needles shorter than matchsticks rise perpendicularly, clinging to the branches like tufts of blond hair. This is autumn's last flicker of brightness, and before long this too fades into a scorched coffee color. Then all is winter.

The village on the plateau, surrounded by chill forests of bare-branched trees, is now completely deserted. Birds fall silent, their youth spent, their few songs hushed. Human voices have long since vanished, along with human shapes, and do not return. What now makes its presence felt is the mountain stream at the foot of the cliff; free of its former screen of overhanging leaves, it calls out openly. As I concentrate, it almost sounds as if small children of *kappa,* river elves, were shrieking together beneath the water. Yet the clamor does not disturb the general tranquility; rather it deepens and lends rhythm to the quietness of the vast spaces.

Though as a rule even in the mountains I live the slothful life of a mole, at this season I slip outdoors with surprising frequency. Mornings and evenings are as cold as midwinter in Tokyo, but in gentle afternoon sunshine I am comfortable in just a light jacket over ordinary clothes, and set off for wherever my feet may take me. Village houses do have locks on their doors, but there are no walled gates or even hedges to separate neighbor from neighbor. These were not considered necessary, given the origin of the village; some of the newer houses do have them, but they don't amount to much. A break in a low earthen wall at the edge of the road is enough to mark the entrance, and for gateposts two sticks of oak from a nearby tree do very well. Those at my own dwelling rotted away years ago.

And so it is that I may trespass on my neighbors' property and cut across their yards as much as I like. Each house is an old friend; I feel quite at home marching in and throwing myself down on the grass, or taking a breather in a terrace lawn chair. As I am lolling about, sometimes I take it into my head to turn toward the house and call out, "Anybody home?" It almost seems that in reply a window will be thrown open and a gaily welcoming voice cry out, "Well, hello there!" But the window stays shut, and there is no reply. The people have all gone away; the birdhouses are all empty. The tiny red rubber shoes lying fallen on the terrace steps, belonging to a small tot who learned to walk this summer; the garbage pit near the back door filled with empty cans; the gas cylinder drained of its contents, standing neglected yet imperturbable in its roundness—all betray the loneliness of the abandoned nest.

At last I continue my walk. Of course I come across no one. Only the river-elf children tag noisily along, keeping their distance, and now and then a gray thrush bursts into spiraling song, unmistakable from the first notes. The gray thrush is one bird that sings more in the fall than in the early summer. That elaborate, exquisite song, while certainly the result of its unique singing apparatus, may also require the tutelage and supervision of a parent bird—no less than the arts of flying and searching for food. As I stroll idly along, letting my feet carry me where they will, whimsical thoughts like these fill my mind until gradually my speculations take a still queerer turn. Really, I wonder, how much difference is there between birds and humans, anyway? That thought may have lain vaguely behind my repeated observations of similarities between these scattered mountain cabins and birdhouses.

In fact, life in these human birdhouses is not in the least different from that in true aviaries. In either case, the occupants eat and sleep and chatter; love between parent and child, romantic attraction between male and female, even ways of demonstrating affection are much the same. Nor is there any essential difference between human behavior and bird behavior even after the humans quit the mountains and go back to the city. The similarity extends not only to birds, but equally to squirrels that come darting playfully into the garden, and ants wearing down paths here and there on foot trails through the forest. Even bears living in the mountains across the stream dote on their children, wild beasts though they are, and use their sharp claws to tear up grasses around their caves in order to make a smooth turf for the cubs to roll and play on. Whichever way one looks, the essential face of life is a great and solemn universal, so much the same in every living creature that theories of metempsychosis and transmigration of souls have the appeal of something homely and familiar.

But I am simplifying far too much. Perhaps I have been influenced by the rustic, uncomplicated thought processes of mountain folk: a charcoal maker or a logger places far greater faith in a trail of volcanic smoke over Mount Asama than in a TV weather forecast as an indicator of tomorrow's chances for rain. I know perfectly well that things that seem the same never are, and even things that seem quite similar often have nothing in common. Besides, given the task of investigating the similarities and differences not only of humans and birds, but of beasts, insects, and all the infinite forms of life, even the cleverest computer would be toppled instantly from its almighty status and cursed instead as useless. It is a terrible and a shameful thing not to recognize one's limitations. Therefore I have no intention of pursuing the matter deeply. Just to complete my train of thought, however, I will offer one further observation—fully aware that it is on a scientific par with weather predictions based on smoke over Mount Asama. One major difference between birds and humans lies, it seems to me, in their attitudes toward their residences. The following incident deeply impressed me with this difference.

One year when I came here from Tokyo as usual in the early summer, I learned from the cleaning staff that birds had nested on top of the shutter box outside the hall. After the nest was taken down I had a look at it. It was woven of twigs, and roughly as big as a good-sized casserole. Around the slightly raised perimeter, stout twigs had been used, the thickness of the twigs decreasing toward the bottom to form a rounded, hollow construction rather like a flat, light gray cage. It was so cleverly constructed that it might have been a piece of folk art. The bottom was spread with leaves, and there were also traces of a brownish moss used as filler: unmistakable signs of the parent birds' determination to provide a soft and comfortable bed for the babies who would some day hatch there. I had the housekeeper put it back where it had been, remembering the swallows in my childhood who would come back every spring to their old nest under the eaves of our house in the country. Surely the owners of this nest would do the same, I thought, and began to look forward to their return. I was a little disappointed, however, when I heard people say that, judging from the nest's construction, it belonged to a jay. I don't really have strong preferences about birds, but if pressed I would have to say I am not all that fond of jays. The combination of grape-colored bodies with white and indigo wings is pleasing enough, and the perky cap of black and white stripes they wear jauntily on their small heads gives them the air of being smart young matrons of the forest—but for that very reason, their rasping voice is all the more disturbing. My surprise at the splendid handiwork of that stylish young matron, however, invested even the memory of her rasping voice with such charm that I could hardly wait to welcome her back.

I waited, but the jay never came back. Soon summer vacation began, and a friend from the village who was knowledgeable about birds came and examined the shutter box of my cabin. My friend confirmed that it was indeed a jay's nest, and explained that although jays are master nest-builders, they use each nest only once. With few exceptions, this is in fact the common practice of all birds, I learned. I was reminded of the time when digger wasps built a hive under the eaves of the home of friends. Terrified because the wasps would fly right into their rooms and buzz around, the people sought help in having the hive removed, but were told not to worry. "Wasps never make an unprovoked attack, so just leave them alone this summer; next summer they'll go off and make a new hive somewhere else, and never bother you again." Sure enough, the problem disappeared after that summer.

Le Corbusier said, "A house is a machine for living in." For wasps, a house is more than a house; it is society and nation as well. For that very reason they work diligently to create it, but when it has served its purpose they abandon it after a single year and move on to a new one. How unlike the ways of humans! Though a house may be nothing but a machine where people live together during their stay on earth, in time it develops kinks, and gradually may fall into such disrepair that it threatens imminent collapse. In consternation, people jabber and argue about what should be done, differences of opinion sometimes turning into a battle. And yet it is rare for a single panel or pillar to be replaced; basic, large-scale repairs are even rarer, however badly needed. And so, unable to part with their homes, people make frantic efforts to patch up old hovels; swarming within the walls, saddled with possessions, they scramble to pay residence taxes and inheritance taxes until the entire human race seems in danger of being ridiculed by wasps and jays for its utter incompetence.

In any case, how very long ago it seems that I first spent the summer here. Back then there were no buses or cars. The sole means of transportation was the train from Karuizawa to Kusatsu, but that was little better than a toy: every time it derailed we passengers would all troop off, heave it up, and hoist it back on the tracks. The railroad company was so pleased about our new village that it gave us each a free pass. The funny thing was that although we faithfully turned in our passes for new ones every year, the contents never varied. On my own pass, my age, printed next to my name, remained "44" year in and year out. We used to joke that while not perhaps a guarantee of immortality, this did seem like insurance against growing old. But in a few years they stopped issuing the passes. So the operators of that little plateau railroad were not the equal of Zeus, after all.

And it seems that aging is indeed the certain fate of our mutable race. I have become a proper crone, my age now just double what it was then. While the other members of that first, pioneering group— and of other groups of friends—keep dying off year by year, I alone cling stubbornly to my original birdhouse. What would the jay think of that? I'll wager she would be scandalized by the shallowness and peculiarity of my human ways, so inconceivable to her bird mind. Still, I have no intention of giving up my birdhouse just yet. Indeed the older I get, the more precious life here becomes, so that now I settle in not just for the summer months, but for half of every year. To attribute this to the depth of my love for nature, and the purity of my desire to escape the rude world, would sound very fine; what it really amounts to, though, is a kind of progressive vegetativeness, born of a physical debilitation that makes it increasingly difficult to respond in kind to the overflowing, intense energy of the city. For the same reason, I feel far more at home among the silent trees of the forest—far better able to communicate my inmost thoughts with them—than amid the milling throng on Tokyo streets. If I could, I would like to stay with the trees year round. I may be getting old and feeble, but I can still get about quite well, and I am sure I would be able to withstand the rigors of life here around the calendar. My long years of experience have given me reason to be confident.

Even to those who spend years in her bosom, of course, Nature does not reveal her heart of hearts if the intimacy is confined to the summer (or even spring and summer) months. That is the time of the year when she puts on a smiling, "company" face, as if determined to be a charming hostess. With the approach of winter she reveals a different side altogether, embarking on a severe and ruthless tyranny. At night the outdoor temperature frequently plunges as low as minus twenty degrees, centigrade. Indoors, ink freezes—bathwater and tea freeze—and unless the lids are left off, containers burst wide open. In any event, the crucial thing is never, ever to let the fire in the stove go out.

How I treasure the old wood stove, so trustworthy and comforting, that I had made over thirty years ago in the nearby village of Kaji! Though solid and sturdy, it is basically nothing more than a sheet of iron twisted into an oval and fitted with a pipe, and so ungainly that it too seems likely to earn the scorn of that master craftsman, the jay; yet it suits my mountain cabin perfectly. As I toss in whole armfuls of chopped oak firewood, crouching alone in the stillness, shut off from all sounds except the crackle of the roaring fire and the occasional rattle of bare branches in the wind, I fall prey unawares to a strange hallucination. Something of fearsome size is bound fast to snowy Mount Asama, covering its slopes from the crest down. A hulking, naked, bloody man: though Mount Asama be no Caucasus, it is unquestionably *he,* that giant of antiquity.

Only a few months had passed since the bomb fell on Hiroshima. We were wintering here for the first time, because of the war. At first we learned only vaguely of the infernos in Hiroshima and Nagasaki, but as more and more details became clear, the phantom of that eagle-torn giant burned into my mind with the sharp clarity of white snow and crimson blood. The gift of fire, so precious that for stealing it from heaven for mankind's sake the giant was visited with everlasting punishment—could he have but known that it would lead to the atomic bombs of our day, would he still have turned it over so readily into human hands? Even as I wondered, I couldn't help but think yes. However foolish mankind may be, not even Prometheus could have suspected us capable of such recklessness.

Much though I would like to stay in my mountain retreat twelve months of the year, I have no desire to repeat the experiences of that wartime winter when we took refuge here. Nor must such terrible happenings ever be allowed to recur. But trouble of one sort and another brews regularly in Middle Eastern deserts and Southeast Asian jungles, and every day the media bring us word of what new events are hatching. We know all too well what havoc a single match can wreak. It is appalling to contemplate, but if for some reason a fire smoldering in a corner of the world map should spread suddenly to engulf the whole—if, in plain language, World War Three were to break out—where on earth could one possibly flee to find refuge? The only way to escape the shower of bombs and the radiation of long-range missiles would be to remove to some planet hundreds of millions of miles away. Even if such a thing became possible, and we somehow contrived to land there safely, looking back on the planet Earth we left behind would we find it still "round and blue," in the words of the Soviet cosmonaut? Charred by bombs and shattered by missiles, it might be reduced to a mere lump of coal. And if, mixed in with our fellow absconders, there should be one who had shared with us these summer vacations, he might be reminded of the sight of the village here as seen from the top of Mount Asama, and realize that the strange creatures formerly inhabiting that distant birdhouse called Earth (to his eyes now a tiny bit of flotage drifting perilously through the vast emptiness of space, far, far smaller than any mountain cabin) were none other than we humans ourselves. And then, realizing afresh the enormous stupidity of what we had done to each other, he would be filled with bitter anguish.

On an Indian summer afternoon, as I stroll through the grasses thinking these desultory thoughts, I hear a chorus in back of me— "It's so, it's so, it's so, it's so." The voices of the river-elf children. "You understand it all far better than we do," I think. "But good-bye for today." At the edge of the forest they take leave of me, heading off for the stream at the foot of the cliff, while I go back to my old nest amid the trees. Time for my afternoon nap. The jays have quit their noisy screeching, so I can sleep undisturbed. May they not be so inconsiderate as to wake me up.

NOTE

1. Translation by Donald Keene, in his *Anthology of Japanese Literature* (Rutland, VT, and Tokyo: Tuttle, 1982), 197–212.

"On Poetry" by Yosano Akiko, with a Selection of Her Poems

Translated by Laurel Rasplica Rodd

TRANSLATOR'S INTRODUCTION

In February 1931, Kōdansha published *Gaitō ni okuru* (Sent to the Public), the fourteenth of fifteen collections of essays by Yosano Akiko (1878–1942), a woman celebrated today almost exclusively as a poet. In fact, as Akiko's fame as a poet grew in the late Meiji era, she was bombarded with requests from publishers for articles on a variety of topics, and she was well known in the teens, twenties, and thirties for the torrent of essays on social, political, economic, and educational issues that flowed from her pen into the pages of the journals and newspapers of her day. These essays were collected in fifteen volumes published between 1911 and 1934 and make up six of the twenty volumes of Akiko's collected works published by Kōdansha in the eighties.[1]

Akiko was typically apologetic in her introduction to *Gaitō ni okuru*, explaining that she wrote her essays not with her audience in mind, but to please herself, and stressing, as she did in her writings about her poetry, the creative impulses that brought them into existence.[2] The need to earn a living was a given in Akiko's life; as the mother of eleven children, and with a husband who was also a poet (and not as successful a writer as she), Akiko was driven to publish. Fortunately, she also felt herself inspired, and so was lucky enough to be able to combine necessity with desire. In addition, she came to view her prose as a kind of substitute for the volunteerism and activism for which her work left little time:

> I realized my own lack of influence early on, and so I have often stood on the sidelines as a spectator, making no effort to participate in what was going on in the world. For example, although there have been demands for women's liberation and women's suffrage since the Meiji period, I

have not directly participated in what is called the women's movement. But I have hardly been an aloof onlooker. . . . I have continued to be deeply concerned, especially about problems of politics, economics, and education for girls, though I have not actively joined in movements because I know I lack confidence and talent for that kind of thing.

In my essays, as my readers have recognized, I sometimes make assertions and even entreaties, but I am not urging my own position. I am not so audacious as to seek the role of leader or preacher. In short, these essays are monologues resulting from an overflow of concern about events in the world.

So then, why put them in writing? I have no other aim than to jot down my thoughts as a kind of diary. I use my writings as a kind of mirror to reflect my thoughts about different problems. . . . This is no more than the sorry record of one woman.

Then there's no need to publish it, you say. That, too, I know all too well. Nevertheless, I have recently been struggling in circumstances that dictate that if I do not offer even such jottings to the public, I cannot support my family. My dozen or so prior volumes of essays were all published at the request of others. This is the first that I have submitted to the publishers of my own volition. . . .[3]

I just want to add that not one of all these books I have published was written for money. I wrote them because I wanted to write. I have never written anything I did not want to write, even if I had a request from a newspaper or magazine. Never have I written on a topic assigned by someone else. I have written when I was inspired in order to satisfy my own creative impulses, just as when I write my *waka* and *shi*.[4] Consequently, I look back in good conscience, seeing no place where I twisted or falsified my own self. Still I can't help but be embarrassed at going so far as to send such things—of my own accord—out into the world [*gaitō ni okuru*].

As is true of all Akiko's collections of essays, *Gaitō ni okuru* brings together pieces originally published elsewhere. In this instance, almost all the essays had appeared first in the *Yokohama bōeki shinpō*. Among them are travel notes written during the short trips Akiko loved to take, pieces on women's lives and women's writing, exhortations to self-improvement and social activism, articles on control of agricultural production and social policy, open letters to her eleven

children, and essays on such literary topics as the attitude of the author, the reader's response, criticism and its validity, and the "true"
and the "false" in *tanka*.

The essay "Shi ni tsuite" (On Poetry) first appeared in the *Yokohama bōeki shinpō* in two parts on 1 and 2 December 1929. In it Akiko
focuses on poetry in forms other than *tanka* and haiku and discusses
her disappointment with the majority of contemporary poems. She
analyzes the reasons for this disappointment and finds that they tend
to cluster around problems of expression: whereas real poetry should
show signs of careful crafting, making every word count, much contemporary poetry is flabby and thus powerless to affect the reader.
Akiko bemoans the lack of concern for the sculptural and musical
qualities of poetry and the acceptance of verbose prose as poetry that
seem to her to be endemic among her contemporaries. Akiko speaks
in this essay not as a poet but from the point of view of a reader of
poetry. She did not append any examples of her own poetry to her
essay and did not set herself up as a model. Still, the reader cannot
help but wonder whether she was able to apply her admonitions to her
own writing. Best known as a *tanka* poet, Akiko believed that the
creative impulse that welled up in the writer would select its own
form: inspirations that were suited to *tanka* would take form in *tanka*,
while inspirations suited to longer poetic forms or prose expression
would take those shapes. Most of her inspirations took form as *tanka*
(seven volumes of the Kōdansha collected works), but she did publish
enough *shi* to fill two of the twenty Kōdansha volumes. These poems
were first published in such magazines and newspapers as *Myōjō*,
*Yoshiashigusa, Tokihagi, Jogaku sekai, Subaru, Shinchō, Mita bungaku,
Waseda bungaku, Yomiuri shinbun, Tōkyō niroku shinbun*, and *Tōkyō ni-
chinichi shinbun*, and many were incorporated into her volumes of
tanka. It was not until 1929 that Jitsugyō-no-Nihonsha published a
volume devoted to Akiko's *shi*. Translations of several of Akiko's *shi*
have been appended to the essay "On Poetry" below.

The translation is based on the text in *Teihon Yosano Akiko zenshū*,
vol. 20 (Tokyo: Kōdansha, 1979–81), 18–23.

ON POETRY

Today I'd like to write a little about *shi*, a type of poetry I enjoy
reading and sometimes write. My interest is always piqued by the new
poems that appear in newspapers and magazines. Frankly, though, I
wonder why so few of these compositions please me.

Poems are both verbal music and verbal sculpture. Each poem must be a perfect work of art. A perfect poem must contain nothing that prevents it from being a work of art, nothing extraneous. Just as sake must be pure sake, without the addition of oil or vinegar or salt or impurities, a poem must exclude prosaic thoughts and feelings. Writings that incorporate prosy expressions of logic, opinion, description, explanation, or conversation must be considered something other than poetry. Not only do many of today's *shi* incorporate such elements, some are made up of nothing else.

This is the source of my dissatisfaction. Thinking perhaps I was lacking in critical ability and was misjudging these poems, in recent years I have questioned many of my friends and teachers—people who are not bad judges of literature, some having an interest in contemporary fiction and others admiring Western fiction and poetry, some being avid readers of classical Japanese *waka* and haiku and classical Chinese poetry, and some even being fans of my *waka*. When I asked these people their frank opinion of contemporary Japanese *shi*, they unanimously agreed that it is uninteresting and suggested that rather than read such proselike poetry, one might better read fiction, or *tanka* and haiku, or French poetry in the original.

These are my feelings exactly! But while I felt relieved that there was no major difference between my critical judgment and that of friends and teachers whom I respect, I came to feel increasingly uneasy about the majority of contemporary *shi*. Has *shi* in our country had no opportunity to enter into the "domain of true poetry" where it might satisfy us?

I suspect that many people besides my friends and teachers feel the same kind of regret or scorn for contemporary *shi*. Is it good for poetry to be so remote from the contemporary reader?

Akutagawa Ryūnosuke wrote: "The artist must aspire above all to perfection. If not, service to Art becomes meaningless. If one seeks only deep humanistic sensibility, one can find it in a mere sermon; to serve Art we must seek to give our product artistry. We have no other choice than to aspire to perfection." This is the kind of poem I seek, but I think that what most of today's poets are giving us are not works of art. I can find no *shi* polished like sculpture or music. The only exceptions are the lustrous poems of two or three poets like Kinoshita Mokutarō, Takamura Kōtarō, and Kitahara Hakushū.

Akutagawa also wrote:

Tanka written by the "life" school have been appearing in *tanka* magazines. It is rude of me to say so but . . . I do feel that if they are going to commemorate such commonplace feelings, they would do better to choose a form more suited to narration or description and should not feel constrained to play around with thirty-one syllables. I cannot bring myself to feel any of these poems are worthy of admiration. . . . I believe that *waka* and haiku, apart from the question of workmanship, must seek to grasp the wordless workings of the heart. Only when these are captured will feelings of appreciation well up in the reader. If poets continue to wander about the precincts of prose as in the poems of the "life" school, I cannot see how the reader can be satisfied.

Doesn't this scathing criticism apply directly to contemporary *shi* as well?

How can we possibly say that a poem is perfect verbal music if it is "like prose written in partial lines" (the criticism formerly made of French free verse), or is so ridiculously long that you forget your response to the beginning before you get to the end, or has lines so long that they cannot be read in a single breath? Are not the message and charm of a poem found in the use of a limited number of well-tempered words to express a candid response that could not be conveyed even in a thousand words of prose?

Verlaine sang that "music is all" (*De la musique avant toute chose*) in poetry. Any writing called a poem, whether free verse or *tanka* or haiku, must have a new and perfected rhythm. Words with rhythm are poetry. To divide art into content and form is the superficial approach of those who have not had the experience of creating art. Such comments as "the content is poetic but the form is not" represent facile criticism by those who do not know poetry; they are as ridiculous as saying "this flower is a rose but in form it is not a rose." If there is no rose form, where can the flower be? There is no poetry in lines of words that lack the music of poetry.

I am not calling all of contemporary *shi* unpoetic. Frequently I sense an exciting poetic rhythm in a line or even in several lines. But these are, in fact, only poetic fragments, and the hard-won poetic feelings are negated by the prosy cacophony that precedes and follows. It must certainly be a great annoyance to the poet for the reader to pick out a few poetic lines from a poem that should be appreciated as a whole. I do undertake such selective reading, but many people have become so estranged from poetry that they have given up reading it altogether.

While free verse is an invention of the late nineteenth century in Europe, in fact flawless examples of *shi*—the *chōka* found in the early histories of Japan and the old verse of Han and Wei China—were actually written very early in the East. How then can the poets of our country today, unable to create contemporary free-verse poems, remain satisfied with this abysmal state of affairs? I don't know what aspects of French free verse served as their model, but each of those French poems is a new composition with a new rhythm. No longer are French poems "like prose written on partial lines." Though they may seem strange and deviate from conventional standards in the same way as paintings by modern French painters do, they are united by a different "music of words." Workmanship aside, these poems clearly have an independent existence in a different world from prose— namely, the domain of "poetry"—unlike the *shi* of our country, which people insist are poems but which merely parade a prosy cacophony. It is not just the prosody, but the reverberations between words, the consonance between lines, and the overall melodic harmony that constitute the free verse of France.

In general, a true poem will be interesting no matter how many times you read it. This is demonstrated by the excellent *tanka* and haiku of old. I think there are few contemporary poems that one wants to read twice and then three times, few that affect the reader strongly and deeply and have eternal appeal. I am not alone in feeling this way; my friends and respected teachers confirm my impressions.

Why has today's *shi* been arrested at this prosy stage? The problem may be the character of the poets, but another factor has been suggested by my husband: the unfortunate influence of verbose and prosy translations of European poetry. Perhaps this trend was begun by those who could not read European poetry in the original and so began to write poems based on prose translations.

Because the scripts of translated plays performed at the Tsukiji Little Theater are direct translations, they are roundabout and clumsy as Japanese dialogue. In the same way, translated poems are shockingly verbose compared with the originals.

In China there is a saying, "Five words, Great Wall." This means that even a short, five-word line can have the grandeur of the Great Wall. A poem must suggest profound feelings using concise phrases, avoiding verbosity, being chary of words. The great haiku and *tanka* poets of the past understood this. I would like *shi* poets to reflect on this most important point as well.

Japanese *shi* have no set meter and do not use rhyme, and so our poetry is the "freest." I believe that writing free verse is a task that requires even more temperance and careful choice of words than writing haiku and *tanka*, if one is to write new poems that do not abuse freedom but are polished and taut and unified, with no excess in any word or line. This is a task that cannot be achieved with a half-hearted effort. But aren't *shi* of today heading in the opposite direction from that I desire?

SOME *SHI* BY YOSANO AKIKO[5]

Moonflower

> Although it is a swift-fading flower,
>   the moonflower
> calls to mind the meadows of home,
> reminds me of my mother,
> reminds me of the days of first love,
>   held between my fingertips,
>   moonflower.

First Person

> If only I could write purely in the first person,
> I, a woman in a lonely little corner,
> If only I could write purely in the first person,
> I . . . I . . .

Women

> "Don't forget your whip," said
> Zarathustra.
> "Women are oxen, oxen."
> As a postscript I would add,
> "Release them into the meadows."

The Spring in the Trees

> Sadness of night settles on the spring in the trees:
> Shivering silence of young leaves, white breath of
>   evening mist.
>
> Sadness of night settles on the spring in the trees:
> When the gentle breeze sighs regrets, bodies steeped in
>   blossom fragrance writhe.
>
> Sadness of night settles on the spring in the trees:
> Wearing a golden hair ornament, the moon princess
>   wandered with swimming eyes.
>
> Sadness of night settles on the spring in the trees:
> Flute, flute, flute, flute, we too play the sad flute.

Poppies

> As the poppies fall to pieces,
> The shoulders of the rollicking wind
> Are rent and bathed in blood.
>
> As the poppies fall to pieces,
> The fields turn to fiery channels
> Where the setting sun flows toward the sea.
>
> As the poppies, and my love, too,
> As they fall, as they fall to pieces,
> Yes, they dazzle as they fall.

On a Postcard from Paris

> My third day in Paris
> I took a huge red peony
> And stuck it in my hat,
> Wondering aloud
> What would be the end of all this.

In Praise of May

> May is a charming month, month of flowers,
> Month of buds, month of fragrance, month of color,
> Month of poplars, chestnuts, plane trees,
> Azaleas, peonies, wisteria, caesalpinia,
> Lilacs, tulips, poppies,
> Month fragile with
> Women's gauzy garments, month of love,
> Month of the horse-racing festival
> When men of the capital wear hollyhocks
> In curved court hats and arrows on their backs,
> Month when the maidens of the Paris streets
> Select an exquisite and gracious queen
> To celebrate the flower festival,
> And—if I may be so bold—
> Month when I myself traveled through Siberia, traveled
>   through Germany,
> Yearning for my love, and
> Arrived in far-off Paris,

Month when we celebrate the birth last year
Of our fourth son Auguste;
Together with the swords and banners of the iris,
Through the narrow window of my study
The bright sky and the hemp palms
Recall the islands of Malaya in this
Month of gentle breezes, blue month,
Month of platinum clouds,
Month of honeybees, month of butterflies,
Ants and moths, and canaries, too,
Clinging to their eggs—month of births;
Appetites whetted by the world around us, this is
Month of the senses, month of the flesh,
Month of Vouvray wine, of perfume,
Of dance, of music, of song, month when
With me in their midst ten thousand things
Embrace tightly, entangle,
Moan, kiss, sweat,
Month of the sun, of the blue sea,
Of forests, of parks, of fountains,
Finally arrived—May in a straw hat
Sipping lemonade
From a fragile glass—come to
Spill over me such a sweet dizziness.

An Instant

As I stroke my small daughter's hair,
    memories of home float through my mind.
My mother, my dead sister, my aunt,
    this and that, incoherent ramblings—
    and for an instant golden raindrops fall on me.

Sleeping Alone

In my husband's absence, sleeping alone,
What should I wear to bed?
The modest night garments of Japanese women
Are so shabby—the beggar's look,
The rough sketch of "Death,"
Frightens my children.

I will choose instead
A gown madder-dyed the color
Of crepe dawn,
Soft as midnight flowers
Wet in the gently falling mist.
Each time I wear it I think
How happy I was to be born a woman.

Each time I tie this long gown
With its fraying collar
And trailing hem,
I feel I am subduing
My hopelessly yearning,
Youthfully impatient soul.

I love this long gown,
A chimera illuminated
By a white taper,
So bewitching I catch my breath
As it sways in my lonely bedchamber
In this alluring light.

Going round once more to see
My children's sleeping faces
I turn out the lights,
And in my cold February bed
I wrap my hem about my shins
And modestly tuck up my knees.
When I loosen my nightgown,
Even now they return—
Those girlish feelings
When I first loved you—

Is my wandering husband, too,
Drowsing in his room in Paris,
Dreaming of me now,
Dreaming of me, a bird of paradise?

Travel Sorrow

I did not know. Till yesterday
I thought my sorrow my own,
But now it's overflowed to you.

Are your smiling days
On Paris streets made bleak
By sympathy with my woe?

Your heart dances,
But my fierce flame is quenched.
The time to cry my grief has come.

The music I hear is steeped in brine.
The roses I see are ghostly pale.
The wine I drink has turned to vinegar.

Today my heart endlessly
Strikes out for the eastern skies
That arch above my children.

Delivery Room Dawn

Dawn outside the glass
Like a pale cocoon . . .
Something crawls on my delivery-room walls
Silently pulling a beacon of branching coral
In a faint straight line.
Seeing it, I rejoice—
The butterfly of the feeble
Early winter day emerges.

Here a woman—
A woman who eight times evaded death—
A pale woman and
My daughter Ellen—tight-budded bush camellia, born of
my fifth birthing—and
A single jar of roses and
The light peach-colored day's butterfly
Bashful as first love—
All in the quiet, bracing dawn.

Dear, precious day! Now
Like one wounded in battle
I lie devitalized and drained.
But like the sunworshippers
I extend my hands to yours,
Oh sun, oh queen of dawn.

Oh sun, you too are afflicted by night and by winter.
In a million years how many times
Have you endured death's pangs to find reborn
That all-powerful heavenly flame?
In your trace will I follow
Though only eight times resurrected,
Though merely eight times, with screams, and with blood,
Have I crossed the valley of death.

NOTES

1. Kimata Osamu et al., eds., *Teihon Yosano Akiko zenshū*, 20 vols. (Tokyo: Kōdansha, 1979–81) (hereafter *TYAZ*).
2. Akiko sought to broaden her own range of experience and to refine her personality, in accordance with her belief that the most accomplished, "perfected" person would prove the most accomplished poet. She wrote, "I am a human being. To the extent of my ability, my desire is to live an abundant, full life, active in whatever directions I can take. Interested and enthusiastic, I participate in everything— scholarship, politics, economy, labor." She advised everyone to develop "the habit of writing down your feelings about everything in a notebook. It doesn't matter what form the notes take as long as you get your thoughts down as clearly as possible. . . . They will be unlike the writing of your predecessors. They will incorporate your new ideas and have the fresh flavor of your own True Feelings, and they will be magnificent original literature" ["Uta no tsukuriyō," *TYAZ* 13: 58].
3. Although the Yosanos were never well-to-do, they were comparatively comfortable by the early thirties, when Akiko wrote these words. During the first decade of their marriage, they were continuously in debt, struggling to support not only their growing family but also the journal *Myōjō* and its activities. Akiko and her husband Hiroshi (Tekkan) earned their tenuous living by offering lectures on the classics, correcting poetry, teaching, and writing. To supplement their income, Akiko sold "hundred-poem screens" (*hyakushu byōbu*) on which she inscribed her poems in her own handwriting. Hiroshi published little after 1910, but Akiko's frantic writing pace made up for this. After the couple's participation in the founding of the Bunkagakuin (Cultural Academy) in the early twenties, both taught there and enjoyed a regular income for the first time. In 1927 they were finally able, with the generous assistance of disciples, to purchase land in the Tokyo suburb of Ogikubo and construct a house to their own design. Hiroshi's prickly personality, however, led to his resignation from the Bunkagakuin in 1930 and precipitated another financial crisis.
4. By "*shi*" Akiko means poetry other than that written in such strict poetic forms as *waka* (*tanka*) and haiku. She includes both free verse and longer poetic forms that may have meter but do not have fixed length.
5. For the original poems, see the following pages of *TYAZ*: "Moonflower," 9: 206; "First Person," 9: 289–90; "Women," 9: 292; "The Spring in the Trees," 10: 98– 99; "Poppies," 10: 84–85; "On a Postcard from Paris," 10: 190; "In Praise of May," 10: 66–67; "An Instant," 9: 231; "Sleeping Alone," 10: 180–83; "Travel Sorrow," 10: 242–44; "Delivery Room Dawn," 9: 93–95.

Two Poems by Tanikawa Shuntarō

TRANSLATED BY WILLIAM CURRIE, S.J.

TRANSLATOR'S INTRODUCTION

Until April of 1971, Tanikawa Shuntarō (b. 1931) was to me simply a name attached to four attractive lyrics in *The Penguin Book of Japanese Verse*. His poems came at the end of the volume because he was the youngest of the poets in the anthology.

Then one spring Sunday afternoon the name became a face at a cocktail party held by Professor Seidensticker in his Ann Arbor apartment to welcome three visiting poets from Japan. The poets, Tamura Ryūichi, Tanikawa Shuntarō, and Katagiri Yuzuru, were on a poetry-reading tour of United States campuses, and the University of Michigan had been included in their itinerary.

Professor Seidensticker's guests that day were numerous, including most of the faculty and graduate students involved in Japanese studies at the university. His hospitality was lavish, and he took care to see that all of his graduate students had an opportunity to meet and talk with the three guests of honor.

The first impression I received was that the three had little in common except for the fact that they were Japanese poets. Tamura Ryūichi seemed to be a sort of elder statesmen of the Japanese poetry world, making suddenly profound observations about everyday things, showing traces of humor tempered by disillusionment and a sense of tragedy. Katagiri Yuzuru was young and bushy-bearded, animatedly discussing the American involvement in Vietnam, to which he was violently opposed.

Tanikawa Shuntarō struck me as someone who possessed a rare combination of gifts: wisdom and perpetual youth. Unaccustomed to speaking with famous poets of any nationality, I found his unpretentiousness, friendliness, self-deprecating wit, and warmth not only refreshing, but nothing short of amazing. He showed a curiosity about everything American and seemed constantly to be absorbing

impressions from everything and everyone around him. He was extremely knowledgeable about contemporary American poetry and
shared insights into the work of recent Japanese writers. The afternoon passed too quickly, and I left Professor Seidensticker's party
determined to discover more of the poetry of Tanikawa Shuntarō.

The following few days provided me with that opportunity. A
poetry reading was held the next day, with each of the poets reading
his own work in Japanese, followed by a reading of the English translation by Professor Seidensticker or Professor Donald Hall. All three
poets were skillful interpreters of their own poetry, but of the three
Tanikawa Shuntarō seemed most at home reading his poetry before
an audience. The listeners, mostly undergraduates, responded enthusiastically to the dramatic changes in mood, tone, and rhythm.

The three poets made themselves most accessible during their
stay on campus. They took the time to visit my class (a middle-aged
graduate student in those days, I was a teaching assistant giving a
survey of modern Japanese literature in translation) and talk to my
students about poetry. The poets' distinct personalities and their dif-
fering views on poetry came through clearly, but I discovered that

Arigatō

> kamisama ga daichi to mizu to taiyō o kureta
> daichi to mizu to taiyō ga ringo no ki o kureta
> ringo no ki ga makka na ringo no mi o kureta
> sono ringo o anata ga watakushi ni kureta
> yawarakai futatsu no tenohira ni tsutsunde
> marude sekai no hajimari no yō na
> asa no hikari to issho ni
>
> nani hitotsu kotoba wa naku to mo
> anata wa watakushi ni kyō o kureta
> ushinawareru koto no nai toki o kureta
> ringo o minoraseta hitobito no hohoemi to uta o kureta
> moshi ka suru to kanashimi mo
> watakushitachi no ue ni hirogaru aozora ni hisomu
> ano atedo nai mono ni sakaratte
>
> sōshite anata wa jibun de mo kizukazu ni
> anata no tamashii no ichiban oishii tokoro o
> watakushi ni kureta

they had something in common after all: a love of life and a passion to express in striking images their insights into the human condition.

When the bell rang for the end of class, my students had not had enough, and the poets, to my surprise, seemed to want to continue, too. We hastily arranged an informal gathering at my apartment that evening, where poets and students could continue sharing reflections on poetry and life. The evening was a great success, attended, appropriately, by Professor Seidensticker, who contributed his typical pithy comments on a variety of subjects.

In spring of 1972 I returned to Tokyo, where I have lived ever since. Over the years Tanikawa Shuntarō has become a good friend who on several occasions has given poetry readings for my literature classes at Sophia University, always enthusiastically received. Since our friendship had its start thanks to Professor Seidensticker, this is one more element of the huge debt of gratitude I owe to my *Daisensei*. It is appropriate that one of the Tanikawa poems I have translated here is entitled "Thanks."

It, and the other poem presented here, are being published for the first time.

Thanks

> God gave earth, water, and sun
> earth, water, and sun gave an apple tree
> the apple tree gave a bright red apple
> that apple you gave to me
> enclosed in your two gentle palms
> together with the morning light
> just like the beginning of the world
>
> Without a single word
> you gave me today
> you gave a time that will not be lost
> you gave the smiles and songs of the people who grew
>   the apple
> perhaps their sadness, too
> in the face of that endless thing
> concealed in the blue sky spread out above us
>
> And then you, without noticing it yourself,
> gave me
> the most delicious part of your soul

Kokage

kokage ni ikou monotachi no karada wa
minato ni tomaru fune no yō ni kutsuroide iru
da ga kokage ni ikou monotachi no tamashii wa
yasuragi no uchi ni ononoite iru
aozora no akarusa ni
kage o kakushita kokoro wa mushibamare
yozora no fukasa ni
hikari o motomeru kokoro wa obieru

daichi o haha to shi kigi o chichi to shite
ki no naka ni mi o hisome kokage ni nogarete mo
hanasareta koto mo kakishirusareta koto mo nai
   kotoba wa
kūchū ni michiafure
sono yobikake ni kotaeyō to shite
kemonotachi wa naki kotoritachi wa utau
hitobito no inori no kotoba mo mata
sorera no koe ni magirete ten ni noboru

kokage ni ikou monotachi no tamashii wa
yasuragi no uchi ni ononoite iru

The Shade of a Tree

> The bodies of those resting in the shade of a tree
> are relaxed like a ship at anchor in a harbor
> but the souls of those resting in the shade of a tree
> tremble in the midst of repose
> Hearts that hide their shadows are eaten away
> by the brightness of the blue sky
> Hearts that seek the light are intimidated
> by the depth of the night sky
>
> Even if one could hide inside a tree and escape in
>   shadows
> with earth for mother and trees for father
> words never spoken and never written down
> are brimming over in the air
> Wishing to respond to this call
> beasts cry out, little birds sing
> and mixed with their voices
> the words of people's prayers also
> climb to heaven
>
> The souls of those resting in the shade of a tree
> tremble in the midst of repose

Bibliography of
Edward Seidensticker

COMPILED AND EDITED BY AILEEN GATTEN
AND FRANK JOSEPH SHULMAN

NOTE: Edward Seidensticker is a prolific writer whose publications regularly appear in Japanese and other languages. Since a complete bibliography is beyond the scope of this book, we have limited the following list to works published in English. Even with such a large limitation, this bibliography cannot claim to be comprehensive. Unintentional omissions are perhaps inevitable in a bibliography of this range and size. Moreover, a lack of bibliographical data has made it necessary to omit most book reviews, occasional newspaper articles, and prefaces to works written or translated by others.

Two sections of this bibliography, "Book-Length Translations" and "Short Translations," are arranged alphabetically by author; the other sections are ordered chronologically by initial date of publication. Volume and issue numbers in periodical entries are separated by a period: e.g., 137.24 stands for volume 137, number 24; 6.234 stands for volume 6, number 234. All Japanese names are entered in Japanese order, that is, family name followed by given name.

BOOKS

Japan. Editors of *Life,* co-authors. Life World Library. New York: Time, Inc., 1961. 160pp. Revised British edition: Sunday Times World Library. London: Sunday Times, 1962. 159pp.

Kafū the Scribbler. UNESCO Collection of Representative Works: Japanese Series. Stanford: Stanford University Press, 1965. vi, 360pp. Paperback edition: Stanford: Stanford University Press, 1968; Michigan Classics in Japanese Studies, no. 3: Ann Arbor: Center for Japanese Studies, University of Michigan, 1990.

Genji Days. Tokyo and New York: Kodansha International, 1977. 225pp.

Guides to Japanese Culture. Murakami Hyōe, co-editor. Tokyo: Japan Culture Institute, 1977. x, 209pp.

Nichi-Bei kōgo jiten = Modern Colloquialisms: Japanese-English. Matsumoto Michihiro, co-compiler. Tokyo: Asahi Shuppansha, 1977. 626pp. Revised edition published under the title *Saishin Nichi-Bei kōgo jiten = Modern Colloquialisms Revised: Japanese-English.* Tokyo: Asahi Shuppansha, 1982. xv, 1191pp.

This Country, Japan. Tokyo and New York: Kodansha International, 1979. x, 332pp. Paperback edition: Tokyo and New York: Kodansha International, 1984.

Low City, High City: Tokyo from Edo to the Earthquake. New York: Alfred A. Knopf; London: Allen Lane, 1983; Rutland, VT, and Tokyo: Tuttle, 1984; Harmondsworth, Middlesex: Penguin, 1985; San Francisco: D. S. Ellis, 1985. ix, 302pp.

Tokyo Rising: The City Since the Great Earthquake. New York: Alfred A. Knopf, 1990. ix, 362pp.

BOOK-LENGTH TRANSLATIONS

Fujiwara Michitsuna no Haha [The Mother of Fujiwara Michitsuna]. *The Kagerō Nikki: Journal of a 10th Century Noblewoman.* Transactions of the Asiatic Society of Japan, 3rd series, vol. 4. Tokyo: Asiatic Society of Japan, 1955. 258pp. Revised as *The Gossamer Years: The Diary of a Noblewoman of Heian Japan.* UNESCO Collection of Representative Works: Japanese Series. Rutland, VT, and Tokyo: Tuttle, 1964. 201pp.

Inoue Yasushi. Trans. with James T. Araki. *Lou-lan [Rōran] and Other Stories.* UNESCO Collection of Representative Works: Japanese Series. Modern Japanese Authors, vol. 2. Tokyo and New York: Kodansha International, 1979. 160pp.

Kawabata Yasunari. *Snow Country [Yukiguni].* UNESCO Series of Contemporary Works: Japanese Series. New York: Alfred A. Knopf, 1956, 175pp.; London: Secker and Warburg, 1957, 188pp.; Rutland, VT, and Tokyo: Tuttle, 1957; New York: Berkley, 1960, 1964, 142pp.; New York: The Limited Editions Club, 1990, viii, 130pp. [Limited edition, revised introduction and translation].

———. *Thousand Cranes [Senbazuru].* New York: Alfred A. Knopf, 1958, 147pp.; London: Secker and Warburg, 1959; Rutland, VT, and Tokyo: Tuttle, 1960; New York: Berkley, 1965, 144pp.; New York: Putnam Perigee, 1981.

————. *Snow Country, and Thousand Cranes.* The Nobel Prize Edition of Two Novels. New York: Alfred A. Knopf, 1969. x, 175; vi, 147pp. [2 vols. in 1; Borzoi Book.] Harmondsworth, Middlesex: Penguin Books, 1971. 206pp.

————. *House of the Sleeping Beauties [Nemureru bijo] and Other Stories.* Tokyo and Palo Alto, CA: Kodansha International, 1969. 149pp. London: Quadriga Press, 1969; New York: Ballantine Books, 1970; London: Sphere, 1971.

————. *Japan the Beautiful and Myself [Utsukushii Nihon no watakushi].* [The Japanese text and English translation of the 1968 Nobel Prize acceptance speech.] Tokyo and Palo Alto, CA: Kodansha International, 1969. 74pp.

————. *The Sound of the Mountain [Yama no oto].* UNESCO Collection of Representative Works: Japanese Series. New York: Alfred A. Knopf, 1970; London: Peter Owen, 1970; Rutland, VT, and Tokyo: Tuttle, 1971; London: Secker and Warburg, 1971; Harmondsworth, Middlesex: Penguin Books, 1974; New York: Putnam Perigee, 1981. 276pp.

————. *The Master of Go [Meijin].* New York: Alfred A. Knopf, 1972 [Borzoi Book]; London: Secker and Warburg, 1973; Rutland, VT, and Tokyo: Tuttle, 1973, viii, 187pp.; New York: Berkley, 1974; Harmondsworth, Middlesex: Penguin Books, 1976; New York: Putnam Perigee, 1981. 144pp.

Komiya Toyotaka, ed. Trans. with Donald Keene. *Japanese Music and Drama in the Meiji Era.* Centenary Cultural Council Series: Japanese Culture in the Meiji Era, vol. 3. Tokyo: Ōbunsha, 1956. xiii, 535pp.

Mishima Yukio. *The Decay of the Angel [Tennin gosui].* Vol. 4 of the tetralogy, *The Sea of Fertility [Hōjō no umi].* New York: Alfred A. Knopf, 1974 [Borzoi Book]; Rutland, VT, and Tokyo: Tuttle, 1974; London: Secker and Warburg, 1975; New York: Pocket Books, 1975. 236pp.

Murasaki Shikibu. *The Tale of Genji [Genji monogatari].* New York: Alfred A. Knopf, 1976; London: Secker and Warburg, 1976; Rutland, VT, and Tokyo: Tuttle, 1978; Harmondsworth, Middlesex: Penguin Books, 1981. xix, 1090pp.

————. *The Tale of Genji.* New York: Vintage Books, 1985, xvi, 238pp.; 1990, 360pp. [Abridged editions].

————. *The Tale of Genji: The Uji Chapters.* Franklin Center, PA: Franklin Library, 1983. xviii, 307pp. [Limited edition].

Nagai Kafū. *A Strange Tale from East of the River [Bokutō kitan], and Other Stories.* Rutland, VT, and Tokyo: Tuttle, 1972. 172pp.

Tanizaki Jun'ichirō. *Some Prefer Nettles* [*Tade kuu mushi*]. New York: Alfred A. Knopf, 1955 [Borzoi Book]; London: Secker and Warburg, 1956; Rutland, VT, and Tokyo: Tuttle, 1956, xvii, 202pp.; New York: Berkley, 1960, 1965; Harmondsworth, Middlesex: Penguin Books, 1970; New York; Putnam Perigee, 1981.

———. *The Makioka Sisters* [*Sasameyuki*]. New York: Alfred A. Knopf, 1957, 530pp. [Borzoi Book]; Rutland, VT, and Tokyo: Tuttle, 1958; London: Secker and Warburg, 1958; New York: Grosset and Dunlap, 1966; New York: Berkley, 1975; London: Pan Books in association with Secker and Warburg, 1983.

———. Trans. with Thomas J. Harper. *In Praise of Shadows* [*In'ei raisan*]. New Haven, CT: Leete's Island Books, 1977. 48pp.

Trans. with John Bester and Ivan Morris. *Modern Japanese Short Stories.* Tokyo: Japan Publications Trading Co., 1961. 286pp. Rev. ed., 1970, 227pp.

Trans. with Ivan Morris, George Saitō, and Geoffrey Sargent. *Modern Japanese Stories.* Ivan Morris, ed. London: Eyre and Spottiswoode, 1961. 527pp.

ARTICLES AND ESSAYS

"Japanese Views on Peace." *Far Eastern Survey* 20.12 (13 June 1951): 119–24.

"Japanese Fisheries Reform: A Case Study." *Far Eastern Survey* 20.19 (24 October 1951): 185–88.

"Modern Japanese Literature: Two Views of the Novel; The Conservative Tradition." *Atlantic Monthly* 195.1 (January 1955): 168–69.

"Thoughts on Anti-American Sentiment in Japan." *Japan Quarterly* 3.2 (April–June 1956): 176–83.

"On the Diaries of Nagai Kafū and Certain of His Novels." *Transactions of the International Conference of Orientalists in Japan* 2 (1957): 48–49.

"Words and the P.E.N." *Japan Quarterly* 4.4 (October–December 1957): 461–64.

"The World's Cities: Tokyo." *Encounter* 9.5 (November 1957): 23–32. Reprinted under the title "Tokyo" in *This Country, Japan*, 203–17. (See Books, above.)

"Japan's Most-Read Novelist." [On Natsume Sōseki.] *New Republic* 137.24 (2 December 1957): 19–20.

"On Trying to Translate Japanese." *Encounter* 11.2 (August 1958): 12–20. Reprinted [slightly revised] in John Biguenet and Rainer

Schulte, eds., *The Craft of Translation* (Chicago: University of Chicago Press, 1989), 142–53.

"The View from Okinawa." *Japan Quarterly* 6.1 (January–March 1959): 36–42.

"Recent and Contemporary Japanese Literature." *Oriental Economist* 27.579 (January 1959): 34–35.

"Origami—Japanese Paper Folding." *Oriental Economist* 27.584 (June 1959): 372–73.

"Marxism, Baseball and Suicide." *Reporter* 20.8 (16 April 1959): 29–31.

"Tell Me All About Japan." *Japan Quarterly* 7.2 (April–June 1960): 228–30.

"The Sun Also Sets." [Literary letter.] *Commonweal* 72.11 (10 June 1960): 283–84.

"Through Foreign Eyes: Redskins in Japan." [On American literature in Japan.] *Kenyon Review* 22.3 (Summer 1960): 374–91. Reprinted under the title "Redskins in Japan" in *This Country, Japan*, 188–202. (See Books, above.)

"Ideographs Delight." [On Chinese characters in Japanese.] *Encounter* 15.1 (July 1960): 67–69.

"The Intellectuals & the Crisis." *Oriental Economist* 28.598 (August 1960): 445–47.

"Japanese and the Quick Change." *Today's Japan* 5.1 (January–February 1960): 99–103. Reprinted in Maurice Schneps and Alvin D. Coox, eds., *The Japanese Image* (Tokyo and Philadelphia: Orient/West, Inc., 1965), 76–81.

"Non-Gentle Men of Japan." [On the May–June 1960 demonstrations in Tokyo.] *Commonweal* 72.17 (19 August 1960): 419–21.

"An Eastern Weimar Republic?" *New Leader* 43.34 (5 September 1960): 7–9.

"Thoughts on International Misunderstanding." *Today's Japan; Orient/West* 5.10 (October 1960): 21–24.

"On Retranslation." *Japan Quarterly* 7.4 (October–December 1960): 487–90.

"Okinawa: A Province with a Difference." *Today's Japan; Orient/West* 5.12 (December 1960): 41–44.

"The Shikoku Pace." *This Is Japan* 8 (1961): 224–27.

"The Year Just Past: A Literary Letter from Japan." *New York Times Book Review* (15 January 1961): 18.

"May in Japan." *New Leader* 44.23 (5 June 1961): 7.

"Japan's Life without Father." *Commonweal* 74.14 (30 June 1961): 346–48.

"Literary Letter from Japan." *New York Times Book Review* (10 September 1961): 57.

"Train Ride with a Visitor." *New Leader* 44.33 (18 September 1961): 13–14.

"Japan: An Expatriate's Love Affair." *Holiday* 30.4 (October 1961): 36, 38–41.

"Japan." *Holiday* 30.4 (October 1961): 36.

"The Touchy Traders of Japan." [On U.S.-Japanese trade.] *Commonweal* 75.6 (3 November 1961): 150–52.

"A Life of Quiet Squalor." *New Leader* 44.37 (13 November 1961): 16–17.

"Japan: Umbrella and Admonitions." *New Leader* 44.38 (27 November 1961): 11–12.

"Pause for Drinking." *This Is Japan* 9 (1962): 275.

"Japan: Divisions in Socialism." In Leopold Labedz, ed., *Revisionism: Essays in the History of Marxism Ideas* (New York: Praeger; London: Allen and Unwin, 1962), 363–73.

"On Miner on Translating Japanese Poetry." *Orient/West* 7.1 (January 1962): 17–20.

"How Japan Remembers Pearl Harbor." *New Leader* 45.1 (8 January 1962): 22–23.

"The Kennedy Image—One Year Later: In Tokyo." *New Leader* 45.2 (22 January 1962): 10–12.

"When Mugwort Last in the Dooryard Bloomed." *Japan Quarterly* 9.1 (January–March 1962): 89–92.

"Japan's 'Strange' Party." *New Leader* 45.5 (5 March 1962): 12–13.

"Socialists in Japan." *Commonweal* 75.24 (9 March 1962): 610–11.

"Petty Asian Differences." *New Leader* 45.12 (11 June 1962): 10–11.

"Comfortable Marxists of Japan." [On the Socialist Party of Japan.] *Spectator* 207.6992 (29 June 1962): 846–47.

"Tradition, Change, and Baseball." *Japan Quarterly* 9.4 (October–December 1962): 475–77.

"Probing the Japanese Body Politic." *New Leader* 45.22 (29 October 1962): 28–30.

Articles contributed to *The Concise Encyclopaedia of Modern World Literature*, Geoffrey Grigson, ed. (London: Hutchinson & Co., Ltd., 1963, revised 1970), including:

"Japanese Literature," 21–22 (12–14).

"Dazai Osamu," 125–26 (103–4).

"Kawabata Yasunari," 246–47 (193–94).

"Nagai Kafū," 316 (257–58).

"Natsume Sōseki," 317–18 (259–60).

"Ōoka Shōhei," 322–23 (266–67).

"Tanizaki Jun'ichirō," 438–39 (347–49).

"Strangely Shaped Novels: A Scattering of Examples." In Joseph Roggendorf, ed., *Studies in Japanese Culture: Tradition and Experiment* (Tokyo: Sophia University, 1963), 209–24.

"Free versus Literal Translations." *Orient/West* 8.2 (March–April 1963): 19–26. Reprinted in Maurice Schneps and Alvin D. Coox, eds., *The Japanese Image* (Tokyo and Philadelphia: Orient/West, Inc., 1965), 317–26.

"The Goldwater View." [On the teaching of Japanese.] *Journal-Newsletter of the Association of Teachers of Japanese* 1.2 (April 1963): 5–8.

"Who's Americanized?" *Show* 3.5 (May 1963): 84–85.

"Reasons for Travel." *Atlantic Monthly* 212.1 (July 1963): 122, 124–25.

"Japan's Flaming Conservatives." *New Leader* 46.15 (22 July 1963): 12–14.

"The Unshapen Ones." [On contemporary Japanese novels.] *Japan Quarterly* 11.1 (January–March 1964): 64–69.

"Japan's Fallible Pope." *New Leader* 47.3 (3 February 1964): 27–29.

"The Reader, General and Otherwise." [Paper read at a panel entitled "Problems of Translation from Japanese."] *Journal-Newsletter of the Association of Teachers of Japanese* 2.1–2 (May 1964): 21–27.

"Kafū and Tanizaki." *Japan Quarterly* 12.4 (October–December 1965): 491–94.

"Change and Tradition in Japanese Literature." *This Is Japan* 13 (1966): 72–75.

"The Image" [of U.S.-Japanese relations]. In Herbert Passin, ed., *The United States and Japan* (Englewood Cliffs, NJ: Prentice-Hall, 1966), 5–28. 2nd ed., Washington, DC: Columbia Books, 1975.

"The 'Pure' and the 'In-Between' in Modern Japanese Theories of the Novel." *Harvard Journal of Asiatic Studies* 26 (1966): 174–86. Reprinted in *This Country, Japan*, 98–111. (See Books, above.)

"The Xenophiliac Xenophobes." *Japan Quarterly* 13.4 (October–December 1966): 490–92.

"Tanizaki Jun-ichirō, 1886–1965." *Monumenta Nipponica* 21.3–4 (1966): 249–65.

"The Japanese Novel and Disengagement." *Journal of Contemporary History* 2.2 (April 1967): 177–94. Reprinted in *This Country, Japan*, 83–97. (See Books, above.)

"A Time for Me." *Japan Quarterly* 14.4 (October–December 1967): 494–97.

"A Decade or So for Genji." *Delos* 2 (1968): 126–31; and *This Is Japan* 15 (1968): 65–67.

"Travellers from Japan." *Japan Quarterly* 15.4 (October–December 1968): 489–94.

"Kawabata." *Hudson Review* 22.1 (Spring 1969): 6, 8, 10.

"Kawabata, Hemingway, and James." *This Is Japan* 17 (1970): 65–66.

"The Japanese Love of the Moon." *Queen* (7–20 January 1970): 22.

"The Pulverisers." [On the Japanese student revolt.] *Encounter* 34.6 (June 1970): 81–87.

"Kobayashi Hideo." In Donald H. Shively, ed., *Tradition and Modernization in Japanese Culture* (Princeton, NJ: Princeton University Press, 1971), 419–61.

"On Kawabata Yasunari." *Bulletin of the Asiatic Society of Japan* 2 [Special Issue] (February 1970): 3–20. Reprinted in *This Country, Japan*, 112–28. (See Books, above.)

"The Remarkable Homogeneity of a Writer's Spiritual Archipelago." [On Kawabata Yasunari.] *Orientations* 2.1 (January 1971): 20.

"Mishima Yukio: Life, Works and Death." *Pacific Community* 2.3 (April 1971): 477–89.

Review article of *Madly Singing in the Mountains: An Appreciation and Anthology of Arthur Waley*, Ivan Morris, ed. *Journal of Asian Studies* 30.3 (May 1971): 638–42. Reprinted in *This Country, Japan*, 57–63. (See Books, above.)

"Mishima Yukio." *Hudson Review* 24.2 (Summer 1971): 272–82. Reprinted in *This Country, Japan*, 129–38. (See Books, above.)

"Mishima's *The Sea of Fertility*." *Transactions of the International Conference of Orientalists in Japan* 18 (1973): 26–27.

"On Being Faithful to Murasaki Shikibu." In Nihon Bunka Kenkyū Kokusai Kaigi Gijiroku Henshū Iinkai, ed., Nihon Bunka Kenkyū Kokusai Kaigi *Gijiroku* 1 = International Conference on Japanese Studies *Report* (Tokyo: Japan P.E.N. Club, 1973), 328–32. Reprinted in *This Country, Japan*, 64–70. (See Books, above.)

"Tribute to a Friend." [In memory of Hirabayashi Taiko.] *Solidarity* 8.2 (August 1973): 9–10.

"The Japanese Intellectual Establishment." *Asian Affairs: An American Review* 1.2 (November–December 1973): 68–79.

Articles contributed to the *Dictionary of Oriental Literature*, Jaroslav Prusek, gen. ed. *Volume 1: East Asia*, Zbigniew Slupski, ed. (London: George Allen & Unwin, Ltd., 1974), including:

"Kawabata Yasunari," 76–78.

"monogatari," 120–21.

"Murasaki Shikibu," 122–24.

"Nagai Kafū," 125–26.

A Hundred Things Japanese. Japan Culture Institute, ed. (Tokyo: Japan Culture Institute, 1975). Essays on "Fugu" (50–51), "Satsuma-imo" (56–57), and "Do" (196–97).

"The Great Amateurs." [On W. G. Aston, C. Eliot, E. M. Satow, and G. B. Sansom.] *Transactions of the Asiatic Society of Japan* 3d series, vol. 12 (1975): 39–50.

"Japan after Vietnam." *Commentary* 60.3 (September 1975): 55–60.

"Intellectuals, Japanese-Style." *Commentary* 60.5 (November 1975): 57–61.

"The Decline of an Establishment." *Asian Affairs: An American Review* 4.4 (March–April 1977): 209–20.

"Eminent Women Writers of the Court: Murasaki Shikibu and Sei Shônagon." In Murakami Hyōe and Thomas J. Harper, eds., *Great Historical Figures of Japan* (Tokyo: Japan Culture Institute, 1978), 60–71.

"The Japanese and Nature, with Special Reference to *The Tale of Genji.*" In *This Country, Japan,* 1–23. (See Books, above.)

"The Conservatism of the Japanese." In *This Country, Japan,* 24–56. (See Books, above.)

"On Translating an Exotic Language." In *This Country, Japan,* 71–82. (See Books, above.)

"*Sea of Fertility.*" In *This Country, Japan,* 139–48. (See Books, above.)

A Hundred More Things Japanese. Murakami Hyōe and Donald Richie, eds. (Tokyo: Japan Culture Institute, 1980). Essays on "Taifū" (30–31) and "Onsen" (108–9).

"Chiefly on Translating the *Genji.*" *Journal of Japanese Studies* 6.1 (Winter 1980): 15–47.

Review article of *Japan as Number One: Lessons for Americans,* by Ezra F. Vogel. *Journal of Japanese Studies* 6.2 (Summer 1980): 416–24.

"A Splendor of Scholarship." [Review essay of *A Tale of Flowering Fortunes: Annals of Japanese Aristocratic Life in the Heian Period,* trans. William H. and Helen Craig McCullough.] *Monumenta Nipponica* 36.2 (Summer 1981): 195–200.

"The Free Ways of Arthur Waley." *Times Literary Supplement,* no. 4100 (30 October 1981): 1279–80.

"*The Tale of Genji*: Here and There." *Yearbook of Comparative and General Literature* 31 (1982): 47–53.

"Rough Business in 'Ukifune' and Elsewhere." In Andrew Pekarik, ed., *Ukifune: Love in The Tale of Genji* (New York: Columbia University Press, 1982), 1–19.

"Trollope and Murasaki: Impressions of an Orientalist." *Nineteenth-Century Fiction* 37.3 (December 1982): 464–71.

Articles contributed to the *Kodansha Encyclopedia of Japan* (Tokyo and New York: Kodansha International, 1983. 9 vols.), including:
"Kagerō nikki," 4: 104.
"Kawabata Yasunari," 4: 175–77.
"Murasaki Shikibu," 5: 267–69.
"Tale of Genji," 7: 328–31.

"The Death of Kobayashi Hideo—The End of an Era." *Japan Quarterly* 30.3 (July–September 1983): 270–73.

"Japan." *New York Times Book Review* 88 (11 December 1983): 14, 33.

"Free, Unfettered but Timid." *Far Eastern Economic Review* 124.23 (7 June 1984): 21–22. Excerpted under the title "Japan's Timid Media." *World Press Review* 31.8 (August 1984): 60–61.

"Tale and Novel: The Power of the *Genji monogatari.*" *Transactions of the International Conference of Orientalists in Japan* 30 (1985): 179–82.

"Driving Forces of the Spirit to Succeed." *Far Eastern Economic Review* 128.22 (6 June 1985): 51–54.

"Hard Times, Good Times." *Reader's Journal* 1.1 (Summer 1985): 13.

"Idols Created from the Ranks of the Mediocre." *Far Eastern Economic Review* 129.35 (5 September 1985): 47–49.

"How They Have Looked to Us." [American views of Shōwa Japan.] *Daedalus* 119.3 (Summer 1990): 279–98.

SHORT TRANSLATIONS

The following title abbreviations are used below:

APA   *Asian PEN Anthology,* ed. F. Sionil José (New York: Taplinger, 1966), xix, 358pp.

CJL   *Contemporary Japanese Literature: An Anthology of Fiction, Film, and Other Writing Since 1945,* ed. Howard Hibbett (New York: Alfred A. Knopf, 1977), xiv, 468pp.

DM   Mishima Yukio, *Death in Midsummer and Other Stories* (New York: New Directions, 1966), 131pp.; (London: Secker and Warburg, 1967), 224pp.

HSB   *House of the Sleeping Beauties and Other Stories* (see Book-Length Translations, above).

JQ   *Japan Quarterly* (October–December 1954–). Tokyo: Asahi Shinbun.

KS   *Kafū the Scribbler* (see Books, above).

LOS   *Lou-lan and Other Stories* (see Book-Length Translations, above).

MJL   *Modern Japanese Literature: An Anthology,* comp. and ed. Donald Keene (New York: Grove Press, 1956), 440pp.; (Rutland, VT, and Tokyo: Tuttle, 1957).

MJS   *Modern Japanese Stories,* ed. Ivan Morris. UNESCO Collection of Representative Works: Japanese Series. (London: Eyre and Spottiswoode, 1961), 527pp.; (Rutland, VT, and Tokyo: Tuttle, 1962), 512pp.

MJSS   *Modern Japanese Short Stories* (see Book-Length Translations, above).

ST   *A Strange Tale from East of the River, and Other Stories* (see Book-Length Translations, above).

Dazai Osamu. "Cherries" ["Ōtō"]. *Encounter* 1.1 (October 1953): 26–28.

_____. "Of Women" ["Mesu ni tsuite"]. *Encounter* 1.1 (October 1953): 23–26; *Atlantic Monthly* 195.1 (January 1955): 145–47.

_____. "Osan." *JQ* 5.4 (October–December 1958): 478–87; *MJSS* (1961), 38–51; (1970), 31–41.

Eguchi Kan. "The Surplus Bride" ["Hanayome to uma ippiki"]. *Atlantic Monthly* 195.1 (January 1955): 160–64.

Fujiwara Michitsuna no Haha. [The Mother of Fujiwara Michitsuna.] "Kagerō Nikki" [excerpts]. In Donald Keene, comp. and ed., *Anthology of Japanese Literature from the Earliest Era to the Mid-Nineteenth Century* (New York: Grove Press, 1955), 97–105.

Funabashi Seiichi. "Thistledown" ["Gamō"]. *JQ* 8.4 (October–December 1961): 431–59.

Higuchi Ichiyō. "Growing Up" ["Takekurabe"]. *MJL,* 70–110.

Hirabayashi Taiko. "The Black Age" ["Kuroi nenrei"]. *JQ* 10.4 (October–December 1963): 479–93; *Comment* 20 (1963): 39–51; *Solidarity* 3.3 (March 1968): 11–19.

_____. "I Mean to Live" ["Watashi wa ikiru"]. *JQ* 10.4 (October–December 1963): 469–79; *APA,* 144–54; *Solidarity* 8.2 (August 1973): 2–8.

Ibuse Masuji. "No Consultations Today" ["Honjitsu kyūshin"]. *JQ* 8.1 (January–March 1961): 50–79; *No Consultations Today* [Japanese text and English translation], Modern Japanese Authors, vol. 3 (Tokyo: Hara Shobō, 1964), 7–123.

Inoue Yasushi. "The Azaleas of Hira" ["Hira no shakunage"]. *JQ* 2.3 (July–September 1955): 322–47; *MJSS* (1961), 141–77; *Lou-lan* [Japanese text and English translation], Modern Japanese Authors, vol. 2 (Tokyo: Hara Shobō, 1964), 125–229; *MJSS* (1970), 112–40; reprinted under the title "The Rhododendrons" in *LOS*, 105–38.

――――. "Lou-lan" ["Rōran"]. *JQ* 6.4 (October–December 1959): 460–89; *Lou-lan* [Japanese text and English translation], Modern Japanese Authors, vol. 2 (Tokyo: Hara Shobō, 1964), 8–123; *LOS*, 7–45.

――――. "Princess Yung-t'ai's Necklace" ("Eitai Kōshu no kubikazari"). *LOS*, 65–83.

Izumi Kyōka. "A Tale of Three Who Were Blind" ["Sannin no mekura no hanashi"]. *MJL*, 242–53.

Kawabata Yasunari. "The Izu Dancer" ["Izu no odoriko"]. *Atlantic Monthly* 195.1 (January 1955): 108–14; *The Izu Dancer* [Japanese text and English translation], Modern Japanese Authors, vol. 1 (Tokyo: Hara Shobō, 1964), 7–67; *The Izu Dancer and Other Stories* (Rutland, VT, and Tokyo: Tuttle, 1974), 9–29.

――――. "The Mole" ["Hokuro no tegami"]. *JQ* 2.1 (January–March 1955): 86–93; *MJL*, 366–74; *MJSS* (1961), 190–200; (1970), 151–59; *The Izu Dancer* [Japanese text and English translation], Modern Japanese Authors, vol. 1 (Tokyo: Hara Shobō, 1964), 133–61.

――――. "The Sound of the Mountain" ["Yama no oto," excerpts]. *JQ* 11.3 (July–September 1964): 309–30, and 11.4 (October–December 1964): 446–67.

――――. "One Arm" ["Kataude"]. *JQ* 14.1 (January–March 1967): 60–71; *HSB*, 103–24.

――――. "Japan, the Beautiful, and Myself" ["Utsukushii Nihon no watakushi"]. [Nobel lecture.] *Jiji eigo kenkyū* 24.3 (1969): 19–27; *Social Education* 33.7 (November 1969): 827–29, 890.

――――. "Of Birds and Beasts" ["Kinjū"]. *HSB*, 135–58.

――――. "House of the Sleeping Beauties" ["Nemureru bijo"]. *HSB*, 13–99.

――――. "The Cereus" ["Gekka bijin"]. *CJL*, 308–9.

――――. "The Jay" ["Kakesu"]. *CJL*, 300–3.

――――. "The Plum" ["Kōbai"]. *CJL*, 299–300.

――――. "Summer and Winter" ["Natsu to fuyu"]. *CJL*, 303–6.

――――. "The Bamboo Leaves" ["Sasabune"]. *CJL*, 306–7.

――――. "The Camellia" ["Sazanka"]. *CJL*, 295–99.

――――. "The Pomegranate" ["Zakuro"]. *CJL*, 293–95.

Kawaguchi Matsutarō. "A Bell in Fukagawa" ["Fukagawa no suzu"]. *JQ* 6.2 (April–June 1959): 211–27; *MJSS* (1961), 15–37; (1970), 12–30.

Kōda Aya. "The Black Skirt" ["Kuroi suso"]. *JQ* 3.2 (April–June 1956): 196–212. Reprinted under the title "The Black Kimono" in *MJSS* (1961), 118–40; (1970), 94–111.

Mishima Yukio. "Death in Midsummer" ["Manatsu no shi"] [abridged translation]. *JQ* 4.3 (July–September 1956): 315–40; *MJSS* (1961), 201–35; (1970), 160–87; *DM*, 1–29.

———. "Three Million Yen" ["Hyakuman'en senbei"]. *JQ* 9.2 (April–June 1962): 190–200; *DM*, 30–42; *APA*, 58–67.

———. "Thermos Bottles" ["Mahōbin"]. *JQ* 9.2 (April–June 1962): 201–14; *DM*, 43–58.

Murō Saisei. "Brother and Sister" ["Ani imōto"]. *MJS*, 137–54 [Eyre and Spottiswoode edition]; 144–61 [Tuttle edition].

Nagai Kafū. "A Strange Tale from East of the River" ["Bokutō kitan"], *JQ* 5.2 (April–June 1958), 195–222; *KS*, 278–328; *ST*, 106–56.

———. "Hydrangea" ["Ajisai"]. *MJS*, 65–77 [Eyre and Spottiswoode edition]; 65–80 [Tuttle edition].

———. "Quiet Rain" ["Ame shōshō"]. *JQ* 11.1 (January–March 1964): 46–63; *KS*, 253–77; *ST*, 81–105.

———. "The Peony Garden" ["Botan no kyaku"]. *KS*, 219–25; *ST*, 47–53.

———. "The Scavengers" ["Katsushika miyage"]. *KS*, 339–44; *ST*, 167–72.

———. "Coming Down with a Cold" ["Kazagokochi"]. *KS*, 226–36; *ST*, 54–64.

———. "The Decoration" ["Kunshō"]. *KS*, 329–35; *ST*, 157–63.

———. "The Dancing Girl" ["Odoriko"] [chapter 10]. *KS*, 336–38; *ST*, 164–66.

———. "Tidings from Ōkubo" ["Ōkubodayori"] [excerpts]. *KS*, 237–43; *ST*, 65–71.

———. "The River Sumida" ["Sumidagawa"]. *KS*, 181–218; *ST*, 9–46.

———. "Rivalry" [from chapter 12 of *Ude kurabe*]. *KS*, 244–52; *ST*, 72–80.

Nagai Tatsuo. "Brief Encounter" ["Aibiki"]. *JQ* 7.2 (April–June 1960): 200–211; *APA*, 19–29; *CJL*, 390–99.

———. "One" ["Ikko"]. *JQ* 7.2 (April–June 1960): 211–17.

———. "Morning Mist" ["Asagiri"]. *MJS*, 288–305 [Eyre and Spottiswoode edition]; 302–19 [Tuttle edition].

Niwa Fumio. "A Touch of Shyness" ["Shūchi"]. *JQ* 2.1 (January–March 1955): 76–85; *The Hateful Age* [Japanese text and English translation], Modern Japanese Authors, vol. 11 (Tokyo: Hara Shobō, 1965), 103–37.

Okamoto Kanoko. "Scarlet Flower" ["Hana wa tsuyoshi"]. *JQ* 10.3 (July–September 1963): 331–48.

Onuma Tan. "Daphne" ["Chinchōge"]. *Kenyon Review* [New Series] 1.4 (Fall 1979): 109–20.

Ozaki Kazuo. "The Thin Rooster" ["Yaseta ondori"]. *JQ* 2.2 (April–June 1955): 184–201; *MJSS* (1961), 263–86; (1970), 209–27.

Satō Haruo. "The Tale of the Bridal Fan" ["Jokaisen kitan"]. *JQ* 9.3 (July–September 1962): 309–36.

Satomi Ton. "The Camellia" ["Tsubaki"]. *MJS*, 133–36 [Eyre and Spottiswoode edition]; 138–43 [Tuttle edition].

Sawano Hisao. "The River at Night" ["Yoru no kawa"]. *JQ* 4.3 (July–September 1957): 339–57.

Shiga Naoya. "At Kinosaki" [partial translation of *Kinosaki nite*]. *MJL*, 272–77.

Shimazaki Tōson. "The Broken Commandment" [chapter 7 of *Hakai*]. *MJL*, 134–41.

Shōno Junzō. "A Shoal of Brine Shrimp" ["Koebi no mure"]. *Kenyon Review* [New Series] 3.1 (Winter 1981): 74–82.

Takeda Taijun. "The Misshapen Ones" ["Igyō no mono"]. *JQ* 4.4 (October–December 1957): 472–99; *MJSS* (1961), 52–89; (1970), 42–71.

_____. "To Build a Bridge" ["Hashi o kizuku"]. *CJL*, 239–46.

Tanizaki Jun'ichirō. "'In Praise of Shadows': A Prose Elegy by Tanizaki" [excerpts from "In'ei raisan"]. *JQ* 1.1 (October–December 1954): 46–52; *Atlantic Monthly* 195.1 (January 1955): 141–44.

_____. "Some Prefer Nettles" [excerpt from *Tade kuu mushi*]. *Mademoiselle* 40.6 (April 1955): 128–29, 176–86; *Treasury of World Literature*, Dagobert David Runes, ed. (New York: Philosophical Library, 1956; reprinted, Paterson, NJ: Littlefield, Adams, 1961), 1288–91.

_____. "The Firefly Hunt" [excerpt from book 3 of *Sasameyuki*]. *MJL*, 383–86.

_____. "The Mother of Captain Shigemoto" [excerpts from chapters 9 and 10 of *Shōshō Shigemoto no haha*]. *MJL*, 387–97.

Uno Kōji. "Children for Hire" ["Ko o kashi ya"]. *JQ* 10.2 (April–June 1963): 200–31.

Yamakawa Masao. "The Talisman" ["Omamori"]. *Life* 57.11 (11 September 1964): 94, 97.

Yasuoka Shōtarō. "The Glass Slipper" ["Garasu no kutsu"]. *JQ* 8.2 (April–June 1961): 195–206.

_____. "The Pawnbroker's Wife" ["Shichiya no nyōbō"]. *JQ* 8.2 (April–June 1961): 188–95; *New Writing in Japan*, Mishima Yukio and Geoffrey Bownas, eds. (Harmondsworth, Middlesex: Penguin Books, 1972), 123–32.

Yokomitsu Riichi. "Machine" ["Kikai"]. *MJS*, 207–28 [Eyre and Spottiswoode edition]; 223–44 [Tuttle edition]; *Time, and Others* [Japanese text and English translation], Modern Japanese Authors, vol. 10 (Tokyo: Hara Shobō, 1965), 105–75; *The World of Japanese Fiction*, Hakutani Yoshinobu and Arthur O. Lewis, eds. (New York: E. P. Dutton, 1973), 211–31.

FICTION

"The Business at Hand," *Kenyon Review* 23.3 (Summer 1961): 510–20 (revised version). Original version in *This Country, Japan,* 218–28 (see Books, above).

NEWSPAPER COLUMN

"This Country," English *Yomiuri* (Tokyo), 1958–62 [articles appeared either weekly or fortnightly], 1989–present [at irregular intervals]. Selections from former group reprinted in *This Country, Japan,* 230–332 (see Books, above).

Contributors

PAUL ANDERER is Professor of Japanese and Chairman of the Department of East Asian Languages and Cultures at Columbia University. He studied with Edward Seidensticker at the University of Michigan, and was his colleague at Columbia from 1980 until Professor Seidensticker's retirement in 1985. His publications include *Other Worlds: Arishima Takeo and the Bounds of Modern Japanese Fiction* and a forthcoming book on the early writings of Kobayashi Hideo.

ROBERT BORGEN, who studied with Edward Seidensticker from 1967 to 1971 as a graduate student at the University of Michigan, has fond memories of seminars on Natsume Sōseki's *Sanshirō* as well as on *Genji* and *Heike*. He is Associate Professor of Japanese at the University of California at Davis, and directs the Program in Chinese and Japanese. The author of *Sugawara no Michizane and the Early Heian Court,* Borgen is currently completing a translation of Jōjin's *San Tendai Godai san ki.*

JULIET WINTERS CARPENTER majored in Japanese language and literature at the University of Michigan, from which she received her A.B. in 1969. After studying and working as a magazine translator in Tokyo for three years, she returned to Michigan as a graduate student in 1972, attending Edward Seidensticker's *Genji* seminars for three consecutive years. She has lived in Nara, Japan, with her family since 1975. She is currently Associate Professor of English at Dōshisha Women's College in Kyoto. Her published translations include *Secret Rendezvous* and *The Ark Sakura* by Abe Kōbō, *Masks* by Enchi Fumiko, and *Salad Anniversary* by Tawara Machi.

ANTHONY HOOD CHAMBERS went to Stanford in 1965, after his graduation from Pomona College, to study with Edward Seidensticker and the late Robert H. Brower. In 1968, having completed his M.A. at

Stanford, he followed Professors Seidensticker and Brower to the University of Michigan, where he participated in Professor Seidensticker's *Genji* seminar. He wrote a dissertation on Tanizaki Jun'ichirō under Professor Seidensticker's supervision and received his doctorate in 1974. His translations include Tanizaki's *The Secret History of the Lord of Musashi, Arrowroot,* and *Naomi.* Since 1975 he has taught at Wesleyan University, where he is Professor of Asian Languages and Literatures.

REBECCA L. COPELAND was born in Fukuoka, Japan and reared in North Carolina. She studied at Columbia University from 1978 to 1986, during which time she wrote her dissertation, "Uno Chiyo: The Woman and the Writer," under the direction of Edward Seidensticker. She has the distinction of being his final dissertation advisee. She is Assistant Professor of Japanese at Washington University in St. Louis. Her publications include *The Sound of the Wind: The Life and Works of Uno Chiyo* and articles on modern Japanese writers. Currently she is translating additional works by Uno Chiyo and is preparing a study of prewar women writers.

EDWIN A. CRANSTON first met Edward Seidensticker in 1962 as a graduate student at Stanford University. Professor Seidensticker directed his M.A. translation, from *Utsuho monogatari,* and his doctoral dissertation, a study and translation of *Izumi Shikibu nikki.* Cranston's publications include *The Izumi Shikibu Diary: A Romance of the Heian Court.* He is completing work on *A Waka Anthology, Volume One: The Gem-Glistening Cup.* Since 1965 he has taught at Harvard University, where he is Professor of Japanese Literature.

WILLIAM CURRIE has lived in Japan since 1960, except for the years from 1968 to 1972 when he studied under Edward Seidensticker at the University of Michigan. He received his Ph.D. from Michigan in 1973. A Jesuit priest, he has taught at Sophia University in Tokyo since 1972. He currently serves as Dean of the Faculty of Comparative Culture, where Professor Seidensticker taught in the 1960s.

AILEEN GATTEN studied with Edward Seidensticker at the University of Michigan from 1969 until 1977, when she received her Ph.D. with a dissertation on *Genji monogatari.* The principal translator of the first three volumes of Konishi Jin'ichi's *History of Japanese Literature* and the author of several articles on *Genji* and other works of Heian fiction, Gatten is Research Associate at the Center for Japanese Studies at the University of Michigan. She wishes to thank the Japan Foundation for research support, and Konishi Jin'ichi and Marian Ury for commenting on "Death and Salvation in *Genji Monogatari.*"

THOMAS BLENMAN HARE is Associate Professor of Japanese at Stanford University. He studied *Genji monogatari* with Edward Seidensticker in the 1976–77 academic year at the University of Michigan and had the benefit of his erudition and the pleasure of his company during the 1981–82 academic year while Professor Seidensticker was a visiting professor at Stanford. Hare is the author of *Zeami's Style: The Noh Plays of Zeami Motokiyo*.

T. J. HARPER is Lecturer in Japanese at the University of Leiden, The Netherlands. He studied under Edward Seidensticker at Stanford University and the University of Michigan from 1962 to 1967.

LAUREL RASPLICA RODD, who studied with Edward Seidensticker as a graduate student at the University of Michigan from 1970 to 1977, is Associate Professor of Japanese at Arizona State University. Her publications include *Nichiren: Selected Writings* and *Kokinshū: A Collection of Poems Ancient and Modern*. She wishes to thank the Women's Studies Program of Arizona State University for summer research funding, the Northeast Asian Area Council of the Association for Asian Studies for travel assistance, and Mrs. Mori Fujiko for interviews, advice, and friendship.

HARUO SHIRANE, Associate Professor of Japanese at Columbia University, studied with Edward Seidensticker at the University of Michigan from 1976 to 1977, moved with him to Columbia University in 1977, and finished his Ph.D. dissertation, on *Genji monogatari,* in 1982 under Professor Seidensticker's direction. Shirane is the author of *The Bridge of Dreams: A Poetics of The Tale of Genji*.

FRANK JOSEPH SHULMAN, an independent professional bibliographer for Western-language reference works on Asia, pursued his doctoral studies in Japanese history and library science at the University of Michigan during the years when Edward Seidensticker taught there. Shulman is the author or coauthor of several book-length bibliographies and scholarly guides, including *The Allied Occupation of Japan, 1945–1952, Doctoral Dissertations on Japan and on Korea, 1969–1979*, and *Japan* (vol. 103 of the "World Bibliographical Series," Clio Press). He is also the compiler/editor of the Association for Asian Studies' annual bibliographical journal, *Doctoral Dissertations on Asia*, and Curator of the East Asia Collection at the University of Maryland (College Park) Libraries.

CARL F. TAEUSCH II began his studies under Edward Seidensticker in 1968 at the University of Michigan where, upon acceptance of his dissertation, "Ozaki Kōyō and His Approach to the Modern Novel," in 1977, he received his Ph.D. He taught Japanese language and literature at the University of Rochester from 1973 to 1977, when he entered Columbia University School of Law. In 1984 he joined Merck, a pharmaceutical company, as counsel for Japan operations and worked with the company's subsidiary in Tokyo until May 1988. He is currently based in New Jersey, where he continues to have international legal responsibilities with Merck. Taeusch is grateful to William F. Sibley, the late Robert H. Brower, and, of course, Edward Seidensticker, for their patience and critical guidance during his academic years, and for their continuing friendship thereafter.

Index

Abe Kamekichi, 191
ageku (closing verse), 91
"Agemaki" (Trefoil Knots), 7, 11
aisatsu (greetings), 89–111; death
references in, 108–9; definition,
89, 90; as dialogue, 89, 98; direct
expression, 95, 96, 103; examples,
90–93; indirect expression, 93–
96, 103; key word in, 95, 97, 99,
100; prose as, 104–9; seasonal
imagery in, 91–92, 98, 102; spiritual, 102–3, 109–11; to the land,
101–4, 112n.13; as visual art,
106–7, 108; writing process, 96–
101, 106–7
Akashi empress (fictional character),
9
Akegarasu hana no nureginu, 118
Akegarasu nochi no masayume, 119
Akegarasu yume no awayuki. See
"Raven at First Light, The"
Akutagawa Ryūnosuke, 238
allegory, 51, 94
allusive variation, 68, 72, 73
Amida and Amidist movement, 19,
20, 22–23, 26nn.18, 20, 27n.30
Amidakyō, 20
Amitābha, 77
amulet rumors, 221–22n.18
ancients. *See* spiritual greetings
animal imagery, 47, 53, 55, 92,
125n.10

anthologies, 46, 60, 64, 70
Anxiety of Influence, The (Bloom), 111
Aoi (fictional character), 13, 14
apostrophic mode, 89
arhat, 87n.18
Ariès, Philippe, 24n.2
"Arigato" (Tanikawa), 248
associative words, 103
Atemiya (fictional character), 18–19
Atsumiyama poem, 100
autobiography, 64
Awa no Naruto, 188

Baidaoyou statue, 82
Ballad music, 115–25; origins, 116–
17
Bashō, 89, 91, 92, 93, 96–97, 98,
99, 101, 106, 107–9; *see also
aisatsu*
Benkichi, 211
Biography of Great Master Chishō, The,
79
"Birdhouses" (Nogami), 223–34; nature images in, 224–25; text, 226–
34; translation notes, 223–26
Bloom, Harold, 111
bodhisattva, 50, 65, 77, 81
borrowed language, 68–74; effects
of, 71–72; studies of, 86–87n.8;
types of, 69–70
box puppeteers, 190
Braeme, Charlotte Monica, 146–47